ENERGY AS A FACTOR IN SOVIET FOREIGN POLICY

Energy as a factor in Soviet foreign policy

JEREMY RUSSELL

Published for
THE ROYAL INSTITUTE OF INTERNATIONAL AFFAIRS
by

SAXON HOUSE | LEXINGTON BOOKS

Published by

SAXON HOUSE, D. C. Heath Ltd.
Westmead, Farnborough, Hants., England.

Jointly with

LEXINGTON BOOKS, D. C. Heath & Co.
Lexington, Mass. USA

ISBN 0 347 01137 3

Printed in Great Britain by Butler and Tanner, Frome and London

Contents

Tables

(Tables 4.2, 5.1, 7.1, 7.2, 7.3 and 7.4 are based on Iain F. Elliot's *The Soviet Energy Balance,* Praeger, New York 1974)

Foreword

This volume brings together two important strands from the network of Chatham House research. The Institute has a long and distinguished tradition of research into Soviet and East European affairs. That strand in the book's lineage needs no further explanation. More recently, however, in common with so many other centres of research, we have become preoccupied also by the problems engendered in the fields of foreign policy and international affairs at large as a result of changes in the pattern of relationships between producers and consumers of natural resources. That preoccupation represents the second parent of this book.

In the immediate aftermath of the 1973/74 'oil crisis', many of us who had previously been concerned about the potential impact of resource issues on international relations found that our efforts to understand what new agonies or ecstasies might lie in the future needed to be not so much intensified as extended laterally. At Chatham House, we were already involved, before October 1973, in two substantial research projects in the field. One, which sought to analyze the broader international implications of changes in the ownership, supply, cost and consumption of natural resources, has since culminated in publication.* The other, which is examining the relations between oil companies and the governments of oil-importing countries in the developed world, continues. To these, we added, in early 1974, a third research project on the attempts to achieve effective Atlantic co-operation on energy matters.

As these projects developed, it became apparent that one of the features which they had in common was that those concerned were forced to write the same 'unknowns' into many of their economic or political equations. Some of the 'unknowns' were clearly fated to remain within that category. Others, however, might yield to more determined investigation. One of the most obtrusive 'unknowns' in that latter group reflected our inability to find any thorough and persuasive analysis of the course which the Soviet Union was likely to follow in exploiting its reserves of oil and gas — not only in technical or economic terms but also politically. Hence there has emerged the present book.

We were aware from the beginning that there existed a considerable

---

* P. Connelly and R. Perlman, *The politics of scarcity* (London, 1975).

body of knowledge about the Soviet oil and gas industries and about the physical and administrative environments within which they operated. We were also, of course, aware of many scholars with great experience in the analysis of Soviet external policy. With only rare, if distinguished, exceptions, however, those who were expert in Soviet energy matters were much less familiar with general Soviet foreign policy, and *vice versa.*

After a good deal of consideration and debate, it was decided, therefore, that we should find someone to carry the main burden of research who had an excellent knowledge of the Soviet oil and gas industries, coupled with a general sensitivity to foreign policy issues, but that we should also bring together a small group of experts in the broader field of Soviet political and economic policy to assist and support that person throughout the project.

In the event, we were extremely fortunate on both counts. Jeremy Russell, who played the leading role in the research and who has written this book, brought to both tasks a most impressive familiarity with the economic and technical aspects of Soviet oil and gas development. His knowledge is founded upon some fifteen years of specialization in Soviet and East European affairs within the Shell Group, where he has been, since 1969, the Area Manager for the USSR and Mongolia and the Manager for Regional Economics and Planning in the East European Division. Without the grasp of the subject which that experience has given him, our research project would hardly have been possible. Nor, however, would it have been possible without the powerful support of the consultant group which we had also originally envisaged. That group, as whose chairman I served, met during the year of research to discuss with Jeremy Russell the design and progress of his investigation and the various drafts from which he has now distilled the text of his book. Its members, from government as well as the private sector, gave generously of their time and unselfishly of their knowledge and skill. Their role, individually and collectively, was literally an essential one. Some of those concerned, in view of their positions, would not, however, have been free to play that role had their involvement not been covered by the Chatham House rules of confidentiality and personal anonymity. At the same time, it could only mislead readers to name some of the members of the group without naming all of them. In the circumstances, it has seemed best to extend anonymity to all. The fact remains that, without them and without the care which they severally devoted to scrutinizing and commenting upon the final drafts of the book, the final outcome of our work would have lacked some important part of that quality which it has, I believe, attained.

IAN SMART

Acknowledgements

A particular debt of gratitude is owed to Jonathan Stern, the Research Assistant to the study project at Chatham House which gave rise to this book, for his invaluable contribution in preparing and tabulating all the statistical material it contains. I owe a separate debt to Hermia Oliver for the patience and diligence with which she has edited the text on behalf of Chatham House.

Others to whom the book owes parts of whatever merit it may have are too numerous to mention in a short space. I must nevertheless record my sincere, if collective, gratitude to all those experts — from governments, universities and companies, in Europe, the United States and elsewhere — with whom I have had an opportunity to discuss my work during the year in which the book was prepared. Amongst them, I am especially grateful to the members of the small consultative group which convened at Chatham House during that year under the chairmanship of the Institute's Director of Studies, Ian Smart, to discuss and advise me upon particular aspects of my research. The detailed comments, constructive criticism and wise guidance of individual members of that group have been of inestimable value throughout. Needless to say, the sole responsibility for any errors, omissions or eccentricities which survive lies with the author.

J.R.

Abbreviations

Ek. gaz.	*Ekonomicheskaya gazeta* (USSR)
Ek. neft. prom.	*Ekonomika neftyanoi promyshlennosti*
Ek. prom.	*Ekonomika promyshlennosti*
Gaz. prom.	*Gazovaya promyshlennost*
Nar. khoz.	*Narodnoe khozyaistvo*
Neft. khoz.	*Neftyanoe khozyaistvo*
Sots. ind.	*Sotsialisticheskaya industria*
Vnesh. torg.	*Vneshnaya torgovlya* (USSR)

Explanatory notes

Values and conversion factors

Billion = 1,000 million.
Tons = metric tons (or tonnes).
1 ton of crude oil = 8·0—6·6 barrels (depending on specific gravity).
$1 = 0,7565 rubles for Soviet trade in 1974—75 (i.e. the average for 12 months' official exchange rate from June 1975).

Soviet energy statistics are normally recorded in terms of tons of standard fuel equivalent (SFE), standard fuel being defined as that containing 7,000 kl per kg. The conversions used by Soviet statisticians for basic fuels are as follows (equivalents in standard fuel):

Crude oil	1 ton = 1·430 tons
Natural gas	1,000 cu. metres = 1·190 tons
Coal	1 ton = 0·718 tons
Peat (for 1960 & 1965)	1 ton = 0·400 tons
(from 1970)	1 ton = 0·325 tons
Oil shale	1 ton = 0·325 tons
Firewood	1 ton = 0·249 tons
Electric power	1 kWh = 345 grammes

In regard to conversion factors for coal, some Western commentators, notably Strishkov, Markon, and Murphy (in a paper entitled 'Soviet Coal through 1980', *Mining Congress Journal*, Oct 1974, pp. 40—52) maintain that the figure given above is far too high since it applies not to 'clean' coal but to 'run of the mine' coal, which has a much lower calorific value. East European conversion factors for coal are determined by the countries themselves; the calculations in this book are based on a calorific value for

1 ton of brown coal of 0·2—0·4 tons of standard fuel, and for 1 ton of hard coal, 0·6—0·8 tons of standard fuel.

Terminology

'Apparent consumption' refers simply to a gross inland availability figure, i.e. production plus imports minus exports, and takes no account of movements in stocks or losses at any stage of delivery to consumers.

'Oblast' is equivalent to a province, which is a smaller unit than a 'krai', which in turn is smaller than an ASSR (Autonomous Soviet Socialist Republic).

Industry groups 'A' and 'B'. These Soviet classifications of industrial production refer to end use of goods; thus goods which are used for a further production process are classified as group 'A', while those which pass directly to consumers are group 'B'. It will become apparent that some commodities therefore enter both categories, i.e. electric power, the bulk of which is used by industry for the further manufacture of goods, is in group 'A', whereas that part which is fed directly to consumers comes under group 'B'.

Soviet statistical sources

It is necessary to exercise extreme caution when dealing with Soviet growth statistics in value terms (as distinct from physical units). Experts using Soviet statistics differ considerably in their own estimates of gross industrial production and national income, but are unanimous in rejecting the official index of these figures. The problem is that all indices are aggregations which lack accuracy because so much depends on price weights and treatment of new products. Moreover, all Soviet statistics are subject to revision (both upwards and downwards, sometimes amounting to several per cent) a number of times in the year following their initial appearance, only finally coming to rest in the statistical yearbook where they may yet again be revised without explanation. Another problem in compiling Soviet statistics is the constant revision and amendment which takes place from year to year of statistics relating not only to recent years but also those relating to events in the distant past. The practice followed in this book is to take all figures from the most recent statistical sources available; this is especially relevant in the tables containing statistics for a series of years which are drawn from *Narodnoe khozyaistvo*.

Plan figures

Soviet targets are set at the beginning of the plan period and then, usually, subsequently revised (sometimes several times) so that the final annual

xvi

plan may appear closer to the output achievable (especially where targets have been under-fulfilled). I have therefore noted 'original' plans in a separate column from 'revised' or 'annual' plans, the latter referring to figures cited for the year either in January (annual) or at some later date in the year.

The ministerial structure of the energy industries

The energy industries of the Soviet Union are administered by All-Union ministries. The ministry for the oil industry is the Ministry of the Oil Extraction Industry, which is responsible for all phases of oilfield proving, development, and production, and for the treatment of oil and its transportation from the border of the oilfield to the State wholesaling organization, Glavneftesbyt, which then transfers the crude oil to the refineries. The refineries come under the Ministry of the Oil Refining and Petrochemicals Industry, which buys its oil from Glavneftesbyt at fixed prices which include transportation costs, and re-sells products to Glavneftesbyt at a price including refining costs and a standard mark-up. The import of oil products and the export of crude oil and oil products is handled by an organization within the Ministry of Foreign Trade called Sojuznefteexport.

The Ministry of the Gas Industry handles a similar range of responsibilities as the oil extraction ministry, and a detailed breakdown of these activities is shown in Appendix B. There is a recently formed trading organization in the Ministry of Foreign Trade called Sojuzgazexport, which handles the import and export of natural gas. There is a Ministry of the Coal Industry, and a Ministry of Power Electrification is concerned with the construction of thermal and nuclear power stations and with the distribution of manufactured and hydro-electricity. More recently formed is the Ministry for the Construction of Enterprises for the Oil and Gas Industries, which is concerned not only with the construction of pipelines but also of compressor stations and living accommodation, etc. The Ministry of Geology is responsible for locating new potential oil and gas and other raw material deposits and for providing sufficient data to enable the appropriate Industry Ministry to evaluate it at least into the D1 or C2 categories of reserves.

While many of the above ministries are central All-Union ministries, there are Republican sub-ministries in the individual republics. Control, however, is increasingly at the Centre and, for example, the central ministries control directly the activities of a large number of research establishments.

For details of the managerial apparatus of the Soviet energy industries see Appendix C.

Tables

Throughout blank stands for not available, — indicates zero, and neg. indicates negligible.

The 1976-80 plan

The guidelines for the 1976–80 five-year plan were published as this book was going to print, and the targets for 1980 energy production confirmed the predictions made elsewhere in the book. For example, oil production is targeted at 620–640m tons, coal at 800m tons, and gas at 400–430 billion cu. metres. The targets for oil and coal are perhaps somewhat modest, but the whole tone of this five-year plan is rather modest and it may well be that the oil and coal industries will be able to fulfil these plans or even exceed them. It is likely that efforts to improve energy savings will be stepped up, but the overall rate of energy consumption is unlikely to fall below an annual rate of about 5 per cent. Similarly, the rate of oil consumption seems unlikely to drop below 7 per cent.

The other noticeable feature of the new five-year plan is the emphasis upon the contribution to be made by the East European Comecon countries in the development of Soviet energy industries and the creation of an even more closely integrated supply network in Comecon.

1 Introduction and historical background

What role, if any, have energy matters played in Soviet foreign policy considerations thus far and what role are they likely to play in the future?

Soviet, as opposed to Russian, foreign policy has been in existence for less than sixty years, and partly because of the ruthless application of its guiding Marxist–Leninist ideology to domestic issues, partly because of the enormous natural wealth of the land which now makes up the Soviet 'empire', the Soviet Union has become a superpower whose activities have been increasingly felt throughout the world, particularly since the end of World War II. In the earliest years following its creation, the foreign policy of the Soviet State was aimed primarily at ensuring survival in an extremely hostile environment which threatened it on all sides. That it did survive until the outbreak of World War II, and was indeed able to play a major part in determining the outcome of that war was, however, probably due rather less to the success of Soviet foreign policy than to the lack of coherence in the policies of those countries which, from the earliest days, perceived the emergence of the Soviet Union as a future threat to their own well-being. The very fact that the newly formed Soviet regime found itself threatened and opposed by so much of the rest of the world has undoubtedly played a major part in the subsequent evolution of Soviet foreign policy, and its continuing objectives have been both to prevent the build-up of decisively superior military coalitions against itself, and to attempt to create on its southern and western flanks a protective glacis of neutral or friendly nations which would act as a diplomatic and geographical buffer against the threat of an armed invasion. Apart from these purely defensive objectives, which might have been adopted by any regime faced with the task of uniting and governing the substantial part of the northern hemisphere which comprises the Soviet Union, there have always been ideological objectives aimed at spreading the influence of Marxism–Leninism throughout the world, a necessary corollary to which must be the weakening and eventual destruction of the capitalist system upon which the economy of the non-communist world has hitherto depended.

The success of Soviet foreign policy in the postwar period in ensuring the continued survival of the Soviet State is undeniable, and the point has

1

surely been reached where the Soviet Union can no longer rationally consider itself to be under threat of armed invasion from any country or even group of countries in the world. Indeed, so great has its own military power now become, particularly in the conventional fields, that it is the turn of the rest of the world to feel threatened by possible Soviet armed aggression. The Comecon[1] countries of Eastern Europe — the GDR, Poland, Czechoslovakia, Hungary, Romania, and Bulgaria — form an undeniable though reluctant and occasionally fractious bastion against a perceived threat from Western Europe and this bastion is augmented by countries like Finland, Austria, and Yugoslavia which, for political and economic reasons, may be regarded by the Soviet Union as either neutral or partly on its side.

Attempts to form a bastion on the southern flank have been less successful; Turkey and Greece are still members of NATO, and Iran has recently become militarily powerful and pursues a policy of anti-communism, particularly in regard to any manifestations of communist activity in the region of the Persian Gulf. The Soviet Union nevertheless maintains good relations with that country and it must feel itself very far from being threatened by any of its southern neighbours. In the Far East, too, the Soviet Union is clearly facing no military threat; indeed, its most powerful neighbour, Japan, has strong economic incentives for pursuing a policy of mutual co-operation with the Soviet Union, restrained only by its desire to remain on good terms with China as well. For it is at present from the south-east that the modern Soviet State probably believes itself to be most seriously threatened, by the People's Republic of China, with which the Soviet Union has a 4,000 mile border, lengthy stretches of it disputed by the Chinese.

The ideological objectives of the Soviet State, involving the extension of Soviet-style communism on a global basis, are a long way from being realized even though the capitalist system itself is undergoing a severe testing. However, the alternative to a global economy based on capitalism is extremely unlikely to be one based on communist economic principles, as the latter have shown themselves less than adequate for the efficient running of even the Soviet economy itself, and there are many forces in the world, apart from European and American-style capitalism, which are inherently opposed to any extension of Soviet-style communism in all its forms beyond the Soviet borders. Such forces include the growing wave of nationalism sweeping the countries of Black Africa, the Arab world, and Latin America; the world force of Islam; the growing power of the People's Republic of China. Every step backwards taken by the forces of capitalism is thus not necessarily a step forward for Soviet communism.

2

The ability of the Soviet State to pursue its foreign ideological objectives must increasingly depend upon its ability both to maintain or increase its military might and, at the same time, to increase its economic strength and raise the standard of living of the Soviet people to a level at least as high as that enjoyed by the citizens of those industrialized capitalist countries which the Soviet Union finds among its ideological opponents. If the Soviet leadership is unable to cope with military and economic expenditure on what it considers to be a scale adequate for the pursuit of its objectives, it may be faced with the choice of cutting down on one or the other or of modifying those objectives. It could, for example, decide to redouble its efforts to boost domestic economic development, while possibly reducing its current level of expenditure on developing its military strength, or it might increase efforts to undermine further the economic well-being of its capitalist enemies while maintaining or stepping up the current rate of growth of its military capability. This would leave the mounting domestic economic problems unsolved and would do nothing to raise the standard of living of Soviet people, although it might result in a narrowing of the gap between the latter and the standard of living in the advanced Western nations. The second course of action could, however, lead the Soviet Union further into involvement in those areas of international affairs, such as the global energy situation, than it conceivably wishes, in view of possible repercussions affecting its own future interests. If, for example, the Soviet Union were to decide that one of the most harmful ways of striking at the industrialized countries of the capitalist world would be to bring about a severe and lasting disruption of their energy supplies, particularly of oil imported from the Middle East, it would have to take very carefully into account its own energy situation, and that of its Comecon allies in Eastern Europe, not just for the present but also for the longer-term future. Furthermore, such a course of action, assuming that it did not lead to a nuclear confrontation with the United States, would certainly bring about an instant termination of that West–East flow of high technology, equipment, know-how and hard currency credit which the Soviet Union undoubtedly needs. The Soviet leadership in recent years has apparently thought it worth the effort to attempt to obtain as much Western help of this nature as is possible, the acquisition of which is facilitated by a policy of détente with the West.

Does the Soviet Union have an energy problem? Is it, or are its Comecon allies, also affected by the energy crisis affecting almost all other countries, and to what extent? Does the Soviet Union have large reserves of energy, and if it does, can it develop these by itself or will it require Western help? Could the Soviet Union ever become a major exporter of energy to the rest of the world? or will it, too, ultimately become a substantial importer of Middle Eastern oil, like so many of its ideological opponents? If the Soviet Union does have energy problems, either now or in the future, are they such as to encourage the Soviet leadership to attempt to influence the course of world events in one direction or another? What could be the constraints upon the Soviet Union in such an event, and what course of action might the rest of the world contemplate by way of a response? These are some of the questions which will be looked at in this book. It will not be possible to give exact answers to any of them in view of the essentially 'Western' criteria which must, of necessity, be employed in their analysis (in the absence of any clear-cut official Soviet commentary on the subject). An attempt will be made, however, to provide the reader with up-to-date data about the Soviet and East European energy situations and to examine sufficient of the possible implications to enable him to clarify his own thoughts on the matter and to correct some of the misconceptions in which the Western literature on the subject seems to abound.

It might be of value to the reader, at this stage, to outline, briefly some of the main Western viewpoints as revealed in various recent publications.

The Soviet energy position – some Western views

There is at the time of writing, a marked scarcity of forward-looking Soviet material, and the situation is not expected to improve until the five-year plan for 1976–80 is published. There have, however, been increasing contacts between Soviet foreign trade and energy industry officials and representatives of Western governments and private industry, and energy matters have featured prominently in discussions. Nevertheless, there is a considerable difference of opinion amongst Western observers about the actual state of affairs in Soviet energy industries. This is largely due to the scant number of facts which are forthcoming from the Russian side and to subjective interpretations of these facts stemming from previously held convictions, wishful thinking, heightened expectations, and even ideologically motivated sour grapes. Often too little attention is paid to the differences between what the Soviet side actually does and what it says, and to the possible motives behind some of the statements from Soviet officials or the circumstances under which they are made. The waters are further muddied by statements in the public media tending to sensationalize 'good' or 'bad' aspects of the Soviet energy situations which might be expected to have repercussions upon the West. Not least among

4

the offenders in this context have been the Soviet propaganda organs which, in the past, tended to exaggerate Soviet prospects and achievements in the energy field while virtually ignoring the failures or shortcomings. In recent years, however, the whole tone of Soviet pronouncements in the energy field has become much more realistic and the true extent of actual achievements and problems is a little easier to identify.

The spectrum of Western opinion ranges between the pessimistic view, that the Russians and their allies will 'soon' be 'forced' to import large quantities of oil – maybe several hundred million tons annually – from the OPEC countries unless there is massive Western assistance in the development of Soviet energy resources;[2] to the optimistic view, that Russia will be able to make available 'hundreds of millions' of tons of oil for export to the West, particularly if there is massive Western involvement in resource development. Between these two extremes are views which see the Russians stabilizing their supplies of energy to their East European allies at the current level, or even reducing them, to enable Russia to export more to the West to earn hard currency, or which see the Soviet Union and its allies withdrawing entirely from the international energy scene to look after their own interests and to guarantee self-sufficiency in all energy matters. One view attributes to a Soviet master plan all the adverse developments of recent years which have affected the international energy industry – a plan which aims at eventual Soviet control of the 'Black Crescent' (see p. 198) stretching from the West of Africa up through the Middle East and into the Volga–Urals and Siberian regions of the Soviet Union. According to this view, the Soviet Union would obtain control over some two-thirds of the world's total hydrocarbon reserves, thus giving it a stranglehold on the energy supply lifeline of nearly all the Western industrialized countries. Another view would see the Soviet Union finding it too expensive to develop further the huge but disadvantageously located Siberian industry resources and turning instead to develop off-shore energy supplies, e.g. in the Middle East, by whatever means available to it.

Since the Kremlin leadership has been devoting the greater part of its foreign policy effort to reaching some position of détente with the other superpower, the United States, and since both the US government and private industry have been heavily involved over the past two to three years in the major schemes for energy co-operation with the Soviet Union, it is illuminating to examine what may be taken as a typical American view of the Soviet energy position, as set down in a publication entitled *US–Soviet Commercial Relations: The Interplay of Economics, Technology Transfer, and Diplomacy,* prepared for the Subcommittee on National

5

Security Policy and Scientific Developments of the Committee on Foreign Affairs of the United States Senate, dated 10 June 1973.[3] The importance which the Soviet leaders attach to technological improvements as a means of modernizing the Soviet civilian economy and raising the efficiency of economic planning and management, as evidenced in the 1971—75 five-year plan, has been noted, and equated with a need for technological assistance from abroad and a reordering of priorities leading to increased commercial relations with the United States. The Soviet leaders are seen as increasingly concerned that Soviet technology is lagging considerably behind that in the industrial West. Soviet ability to stimulate economic growth through technological change will depend largely on the expansion of energy from hydrocarbon sources. Since most of the hydro-carbon reserves are situated in Siberia and will be extremely costly to exploit, the Soviet leadership may have to choose between major economic growth and costly defence programmes. If they choose the former they will have to make substantial changes in business relationships with the rest of the world, and this will lead to major changes in domestic economic management etc., and there will have to be a shift in resource allocation policy from military to civilian investment and consumption. Unless military spending is curtailed, increased requirements for moderni-zation and consumer improvement must lead to over-commitment in the 1971—75 five-year plan period. A further dilemma is seen as the difficulty or, maybe, impossibility of shifting resources from the military to the civilian programme, in view of the long completion times required for both sophisticated military and civilian projects. The military forces are, furthermore, seen as the only source of suitable labour on a scale large enough to cope with the enormous schemes envisaged for Siberian energy resource development. The United States is viewed as the preferred Soviet Western partner for the provision of technology and finance etc., and the report concludes that Soviet obligations to the United States can be expected to grow at a rapid rate and that the Soviet Union will meet these obligations by increased exports of raw materials, particularly energy, metals and industrial goods, and by gold sales, etc.

A great many highly competent experts have lent the full weight of their experience to the formulation of the above views, but it is difficult to avoid the impression that the alternatives facing the Soviet government are depicted in far too clear-cut a manner. Too little account appears to have been taken of a fundamental Soviet reluctance to allow the formu-lation of some of its most basic policies to be so dependent upon outside influences. The Soviet leaders and their people take a great and justifiable pride in their achievements, and would find it extremely difficult to swallow

6

any suggestion that they were being 'obliged' to go cap in hand to the capitalists to enable them to meet their own essentially communist goals. Again, perhaps too much attention has been paid to the apparent difficulties facing the Soviet energy industries. It is perfectly arguable that, judged by contemporary Western criteria, the Soviet way of running an energy industry should be doomed to failure. But insufficient credit has probably been given to the very substantial achievements of the Soviet energy industries during the last twenty years, 'in spite of' the communist system of management.

Typical of a rather different assessment of the Soviet Union's energy position is that held by Japanese experts, and as Japan has been discussing energy projects with the Soviet Union since 1966, it should be well placed to evaluate the extent to which the USSR does have an energy problem, and what its policy for solving any such problem might be over the next decade. A careful exposition of the Japanese view was given in an article in the *Chemical Economy and Engineering Review* of November 1973, entitled 'Soviet Economy and Energy Supply and Demand', by Kazu Ogawa, chief researcher, Japan Association for Trade with the Soviet Union and socialist countries of Europe. He identifies one of the characteristics of the Soviet energy economy as a trend towards self-sufficiency, reflecting the fact that the country is endowed with huge reserves of energy resources. Recognition is given to the difficulties which the Soviet Union is facing in terms of development costs, technology, and infrastructure, and the considerable financial burden which these impose upon the country. The Soviet Union is seen as being ready to supply its energy resources to Western countries in exchange for their financial and technological assistance, and its ability to do so is rated highly. The Soviet Union will continue to meet its obligations to its allies in Eastern Europe even if this were to mean diverting oil produced in the Middle East to the other Comecon members.

Soviet production of crude oil and natural gas is expected to expand rapidly during the remainder of the 1970s, while that of coal is only expected to grow slowly, and as a result, the share of both crude and natural gas in total energy output will continue to expand to a point where crude will account for an estimated 45·7 per cent in 1980 while the share of natural gas should reach 22·9 per cent. The share of coal will shrink to 25 per cent in 1980. Since the energy consumption growth rate is expected to decline through the rest of the decade, the Soviet Union is therefore seen as capable of expanding its export of energy resources. Ogawa draws attention to the longer-term problems facing the Soviet oil industry and the need for another major oilfield of the same order of magnitude as Samotlor in western Siberia to be developed after 1977.

It must be pointed out that Ogawa's article was published in the middle of 1973, before the international oil crisis broke and before the 1973 plan-fulfilment results for the Soviet Union were available. It already begins to look as if the basis for the 1975 and 1980 production estimates for both oil and coal have changed considerably, and whereas the oil figures now seem substantially too high, the coal figures seem likely to be much too low. The author's conclusions seem to have been based upon information supplied by Soviet sources, who would have had a considerable vested interest in encouraging the Japanese to involve themselves in the development of Soviet eastern energy resources.

There is no doubt that Japanese authorities generally became convinced that there were sufficient oil reserves in the Tyumen region in western Siberia at least to justify a large-scale pipeline-to-Nakhodka scheme. (This is considered in detail in Chapter 12.) However, there are a great many political and other overtones which tend to blur the economic consider-ations, and it is likely that the recent apparent lack of progress in the Soviet—Japanese negotiations on a possible major Tyumen scheme has in part been occasioned by the review which the Soviet Union is undertaking of its total energy policies, coupled with the upheavals in the international energy and financial situations sparked off towards the end of 1973.[4]

There is no shortage of European views about the Soviet energy position, but there is far from being a definitive view, or indeed, any published official government view from any of the larger European nations which have, over the past five years or more, been negotiating with various branches of the Soviet energy industry about the possibility of exports, etc. The NATO Directorate of Economic Affairs held a round table conference early in 1974 on the general subject of the 'exploitation of Siberia's natural resources'[5] and the published papers by experts from the UK, West Germany, the Netherlands, Italy, and France (as well as from the United States) give a comprehensive picture as perceived at the end of 1973. Siberia is identified as the key area in the future develop-ment of Soviet energy resources with the implications that whatever happens to Siberia will determine the extent to which the Soviet Union will be able to play a part in global energy affairs over the next few decades. The Soviet Union is seen as possibly the only country in the world to enjoy all possible energy options, enabling it to display greater flexibility in its overall development planning and its export strategy.

A crucial choice facing the Soviet leaders is between maintaining the current level of Soviet oil exports outside Comecon, allowing the East European countries to obtain substantial external oil supplies, or giving priority to Russia's East European partners and sacrificing much needed convertible currency with which it would be able to buy more Western technology and equipment. It is pointed out that the built-in resistance to change in the Soviet system will make it difficult for the central authorities to modify their short and medium-term plans to avail themselves of the new opportunities arising as a result of the fourfold increase in world oil prices. On the other hand, the Soviet Union can probably afford to wait and see how the longer-term price structure of crude oil and other energy products will develop before deciding where their main efforts should be directed.

The conference was of the opinion that a rather strained situation might develop in the Soviet energy field towards the end of the 1970s, and that the Soviet leaders would, in the case of reduced export capabilities, favour their Comecon partners for the sake of maintaining some cohesion within the bloc. After 1980 the flexibility of the Soviet position would become increasingly dependent upon the development of additional Siberian resources, and the problems facing the Soviet planners in this connection were recognized as being extremely daunting. It was considered most unlikely that the Soviet Union would make its energy resources available to the West except under fully commercial conditions liable to prove extremely unpalatable to Western partners. The Soviet Union is considered to have the means and the technological know-how to develop its oil and natural gas resources without Western help, although such a policy would probably result in a slower average growth rate of production. Particularly in the case of natural gas, it would probably be in the Soviet interest to import increasing quantities of pipeline and equipment from the West, provided payment for these could be made in terms of exports of natural gas. Regarding the development of oil resources, the Soviet Union might well adopt a policy of conservation of reserves, at least until it was satisfied that it actually possessed the proven and exploitable vast volumes in eastern and Arctic Siberia which geologists have predicted. The conference concluded that Siberia is a potential major exporter of various fossil fuels in the long term and that its development, so absolutely necessary for the Soviet Union, must therefore, in the final analysis, be also desirable for the West. However, only marginal supplies of energy could be expected to be available from the Soviet Union in the medium term.

All the participants in the above conference were from non-governmental organizations such as universities, international and national energy companies, and the world of journalism. The views expressed about the Soviet and East European energy situation are considerably more charitable than those representing the typical American view, although they are not quite as optimistic as earlier Japanese views. They do not consider that the Soviet Union will be in any way 'forced' to resort to the West for assistance in the development of its energy resources, but neither do they suggest that the Soviet Union will have considerably increased supplies of energy available for export to the West. They do, however, see rather wide ranges for potential exports and imports.

Global energy matters, the economic situation in the major industrialized countries of the capitalist world, and East—West relations generally were in a very turbulent state throughout 1975, and there were, moreover, no data available on the 1976—80 five-year plans of the Soviet Union and its allies at the time that this book was being completed. It can be expected to do no more, therefore, than attempt to illuminate a few frames of a rapidly moving film, and one which is very far from being only in black and white. It is hoped, however, that the resulting picture is in reasonably sharp focus, and that it will assist its audience to perceive in true perspective what the main action is, who the main actors are, and something about the plot so far and how it may develop.

Before giving more detailed consideration to Soviet and East European source material on their energy industries it is useful to take a brief look at the relevant historical developments.

Historical background

Since the earliest days of the creation of the Soviet State the development of a powerful industrialized economy and the widespread provision of adequate supplies of energy have been the fundamental elements of Soviet policy; in Lenin's well-known phrase, 'Communism equals Soviet power plus the electrification of the whole country'. As with virtually every other sector of Soviet industry the development of the energy sectors was undertaken without recourse to external assistance, and it has only been during the last ten years that the situation has begun to change. After World War II, the East European countries which belong to the Comecon organization — Bulgaria, Czechoslovakia, the GDR, Hungary, Poland, and Romania — were isolated, on Soviet insistence, from economic interdependence with the rest of Europe, particularly in the energy field. Severe reparations for war damages were exacted by the Soviet Union from these countries and the development of their economies since 1945 was in large measure directed towards paying off these reparations by exports of heavy industrial and agricultural products. The directions of

10

their economic development were initially aligned with that of the Soviet Union, resulting in a deterioration in some aspects of the standards of living, particularly in Czechoslovakia and Hungary. Emphasis was placed upon a high level of investment and the rapid development of heavy industry and producer goods, at the expense of consumer industries; the cream of East European industrial production was appropriated by the Soviet Union, which guaranteed its allies military protection and the supply of raw materials, including energy.

In the immediate postwar period, in the Soviet Union and the other East European countries, excluding Romania, hard coal and lignite provided almost the sole source of energy, and it was not until the early 1950s that the redevelopment of Soviet oil production, which had languished since 1940, started to gather momentum. Peat, shale, wood and hydro-electric power were extensively used, but it was only in 1957 that natural gas started to play a significant role in the energy field. Romania, in contrast, relied for over 80 per cent of its energy upon hydrocarbons, and exported quantities of oil products to the other East European Comecon countries, including the Soviet Union.

Soviet oil production increased rapidly from 1955 onwards; the export of oil and products also grew rapidly throughout the 1960s to Eastern Europe, and subsequently to the rest of the world, and moves to improve the fuels—energy balances of the Comecon countries through substitution of coal by oil were put in hand. Exploration for and development of domestic hydrocarbon resources received increasing attention during the 1960s, but it was only in the Soviet Union that substantial additional reserves were discovered. Almost 100 per cent of the bloc's oil requirements came to be supplied by the USSR, initially by rail and to a lesser extent by marine transport, but towards the end of the 1960s, with the completion of the first string of the Druzhba pipeline, increasingly by that method. Because of their isolation from the Western economic and financial system, the Comecon countries had no large reserves of hard currency with which to purchase oil from non-Soviet sources; as their energy requirements increased and as coal was replaced by oil, so their indebtedness to the Soviet Union for its supply of oil increased. It was extremely difficult for them to earn the volumes of hard currency which they would require for energy purchases, since what was left of their industrial production after satisfying domestic and Soviet needs was not generally of a quality acceptable to the capitalist countries, although agricultural produce and other raw materials were finding a market. Such hard currency as was earned was needed for importing sophisticated Western technology and equipment which was vitally necessary for improving both

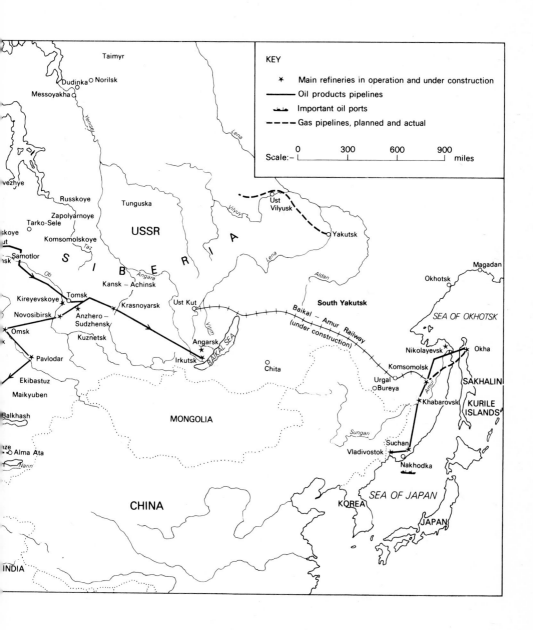

KEY

✳ Main refineries in operation and under construction
━━━ Oil products pipelines
⛴ Important oil ports
╍╍╍ Gas pipelines, planned and actual

Scale:— 0   300   600   900   miles

Taimyr

Dudinka ○ Norilsk
Messoyakha ○

Yenisey

Lena

Ust Vilyusk

Russkoye
Tunguska

Zapolyarnoye
Tarko-Sele ○
...skoye ○
Komsomolskoye

USSR

Vilyuy
Yakutsk

Lena
Aldan

Magadan
Okhotsk

Samotlor
Taz
Ob

S I B E R I A

Angara
Kansk — Achinsk

Kireyevskoye
Tomsk
Krasnoyarsk
Novosibirsk
Anzhero — Sudzhensk
Kuznetsk
Omsk

Pavlodar

Ekibastuz
Maikyuben

Balkhash

Alma Ata
Narin

Ust Kut

South Yakutsk

Baikal — Amur Railway
(under construction)

SEA OF OKHOTSK

Nikolayevsk
Okha

Komsomolsk
SAKHALIN

Angarsk
BAIKAL SEA
Irkutsk
Vilvm

Chita

Urgal
Bureya
Khabarovsk

KURILE ISLANDS

MONGOLIA

Sungan

Amur

Suchan
Vladivostok
Nakhodka

SEA OF JAPAN

CHINA

KOREA

JAPAN

INDIA

13

the overall efficiency of the East European economies and the standards of living, which were fast falling behind those of the industrialized West.

The Soviet Union was, meanwhile, producing substantially more energy than was required to satisfy domestic demand, and was able to export some 10–12 per cent of overall energy production, mainly as oil, of which exports amounted to some 20–25 per cent of production.

In the 1960s, Soviet attempts to dispose of volumes of crude oil surplus to its domestic requirements and to those of its Comecon allies were often associated with sales to developing countries at extremely low prices, at a time when there was a general position of over-supply in the world petroleum industry. This generated antagonism between the Soviet and international oil industries and led to accusations that the Russians were using their oil for disruptive and political purposes. The rapid rate of increase of Soviet exports also led some observers to believe that world markets would be flooded with Soviet oil before very long. There was no question at that time that the Soviet bloc might ever need to import oil from, for example, the Middle East, and there was no reason why the smaller Comecon countries should bother to set up oil trading relations with the oil-producing countries when the Soviet Union had assured them that it would have enough and to spare to cover their requirements for the foreseeable future. The Soviet Union was also supplying almost the total requirements of the non-European Comecon countries – Cuba, Mongolia, and China and also North Korea and North Vietnam.

Towards the end of the 1960s, however, a marked slowing down in the average annual increases of Soviet crude exports was detectable, accompanied not only by diminishing increments to Soviet production rates but also by an increase in East European and Soviet consumption rates. For the first time, the Comecon countries were given to understand that it might be prudent if they were to start looking elsewhere for some of their crude oil requirements, and at about this period Soviet exports to the rest of the world began to be concentrated in hard currency areas, particularly Western Europe. There were indications that the mighty Volga–Ural oil-fields had reached the peak of their production and that future major increases in crude oil production would have to come from western Siberia. In certain circumstances, Soviet economists were suggesting, it might become appropriate for the Soviet Union to import oil from the Middle East for logistical reasons, and in exchange for economic aid, etc., although it would of course remain a net exporter of oil.

Meanwhile, Soviet natural gas production was increasing at a rapid rate and schemes for exporting it from the Ukraine to Eastern Europe and, ultimately, Western Europe were being put in hand; work began on the construction of the 'Brotherhood' (Bratstvo) gas pipeline which would supply Poland, Czechoslovakia, and East Germany. For logistical reasons the Soviet Union had reached agreement with Iran and Afghanistan to import their natural gas into the southern parts of the Soviet Union, for use in areas which were themselves often gas producers but which supplied their gas to the main industrial areas to the north and west of the country.

The Soviet Union and other East European countries were beginning to establish industrial and economic aid programmes in various Middle East countries, notably Iraq, and repayment was to be made in supplies of crude oil over an extended period. By 1970, the Soviet bloc was taking its first small imports of Middle Eastern oil, lifted mainly in Soviet vessels, but supplied to Bulgaria and the GDR. Overall exports of Soviet oil were levelling off around the 100m ton per annum mark, just under half of which was going to the East European countries and most of the rest to the industrialized Western countries.

In recent years, the proportion of Soviet oil exports going to the East European countries has surpassed the 50 per cent mark while supplies to the rest of the world have remained steady. Imports by the Soviet bloc from the Middle East had reached 14m tons by 1973 and would-be Western purchasers of Soviet oil were being told that there would be no additional supplies available for the next few years.

The position of the Soviet bloc regarding energy matters at the end of 1973, before the full impact of the global upheaval had been felt, was one of net energy surplus, but with a sufficient number of areas of uncertainty to raise questions in both Soviet and Western observers' minds about how long this position could be maintained. The quadrupling of world oil prices in the winter of 1973 was on the one hand a severe blow to those East European countries, who were seeking to increase their imports from the OPEC countries but on a barter basis. They would find it virtually impossible to import even 1973 volumes at 1974 prices if they were obliged to pay in hard currency, and failure to obtain sufficient quantities of crude oil would have serious repercussions on their economies in which so much investment had been directed over the last decade to reducing coal consumption and increasing oil and gas consumption. The Soviet Union, on the other hand, benefited enormously in terms of hard currency earnings from the increases in oil prices, although Soviet overall imports from the oil-consuming countries of the industrialized West are now reflecting the increase in energy prices generally. It must be emphasized that inflation is the major factor in price increases of Soviet imports from the West.

The Soviet Union will become a net gas exporter *to the West* by the end of this decade and will begin to earn substantial quantities of hard currency to augment oil and other export earnings. However, the implications are that unless its Comecon allies can come to a long-term agreement with the oil-producing countries to make at least part of their supplies of crude oil available in exchange for barter as opposed to hard currency payment, the Soviet Union will be faced with the choice of reducing its own exports of crude to the West in order to supply the rest of Comecon or of seeing their economies severely affected by an energy shortage. The Soviet Union might, of course, undertake a crash programme of energy production to make additional supplies available for export, but many questions are being asked about its capability of doing this and, indeed, whether it has a resource base which would make such a move possible even if the necessary finance and infrastructural inputs could be made available, perhaps by diversion away from some other sector of the Soviet economy. The country might sell some of its reputedly enormous reserves of gold to finance imports of energy, and it could certainly obtain substantial volumes of credit from the West to finance oil imports, at least in the short term, if it so desired.

There is a great deal of speculation in the West on just how serious the energy problem in the socialist countries is, if indeed there is a problem, and about possible solutions which these countries themselves, or the West might come up with. In the first Part of this book the aim is to attempt to clarify the current energy position of the socialist countries, identifying trends in production and consumption and following these to see what may happen to the situation through to the end of this decade and into the early 1980s. It is unfortunate, from the point of view of timing, that the five-year plans of these countries covering the period from 1976 to 1980 have not yet been published, although it is known that the Soviet planners are undertaking a thorough reappraisal of their energy policies, some pointers to which could be expected in the plans, taking into account the impact of the external energy upheavals. However, there are sufficient data from published Soviet and other East European sources to enable a fairly comprehensive picture of the 1973–74 position for the Soviet Union to be constructed.

The following tables show the Soviet energy picture up to 1974.

Table 1.5 shows in more detail and in terms of basic units how Soviet energy production has developed in relation to planned performance.

Table 1.6 shows the relationship between overall energy consumption and economic growth between 1961 and 1975, while Table 1.7 shows total energy consumption for the three years 1960, 1965, and 1970.

16

Table 1.1

Industrial production 1960–75: key economic indicators
(Expressed as percentages of growth from the preceding year)

	National income (current prices)	Industrial output (total)	Industrial output Group 'A'	Group 'B'	Oil	Gas	Coal	Electric power
1960	7·7	9·5	10·8	7·1	14·1	28·0	1·0	10·0
1961	6·8	9·1	10·3	6·8	12·3	30·2	−1·0	12·1
1962	5·7	9·7	10·8	7·4	12·1	24·6	2·2	12·7
1963	4·0	8·1	9·4	5·1	10·7	22·2	2·8	11·7
1964	9·3	7·3	8·8	3·9	8·5	20·9	4·2	11·3
1965	6·9	8·7	8·9	8·3	8·6	17·6	4·3	10·4
1966	8·1	8·7	9·2	7·4	9·1	12·0	1·4	7·5
1967	8·6	10·0	10·1	9·9	8·7	10·1	1·6	7·9
1968	8·3	8·3	8·3	8·5	7·3	7·4	−	8·7
1969	4·8	7·1	7·0	7·3	6·2	7·1	2·3	7·9
1970	9·0	8·5	8·3	8·9	7·5	9·3	2·7	7·5
1971	5·6	7·7	7·7	7·7	6·8	7·3	2·7	8·0
1972	4·0	6·5	6·8	5·7	6·2	4·2	2·2	7·1
1973	6·8	7·3	8·2	5·9	7·1	6·7	1·9	6·7
1974	5·0	8·0	8·3	7·2	6·9	10·3	2·4	6·6
1975(plan)	6·5	6·7	7·0	6·0	6·7	9·4	2·3	6·2

Sources: Nar. khoz.; Ek. gaz., 5 (1973); R.A. Clarke, *Soviet economic facts 1917–70* (1972), pp. 6–9.

Table 1.2

Production of major fuels 1960—75

Year	Oil incl. gas condensate (million tons)	Natural and assoc. gas (billion cu.metres)	Coal (million tons)	Electric power (billion kWh)
1960	147·9	45·3	509·6	292·3
1961	166·1	59·0	506·4	327·6
1962	186·2	73·5	517·4	369·3
1963	206·1	89·8	531·7	412·4
1964	223·6	108·6	554·0	458·9
1965	242·9	127·7	577·7	506·7
1966	265·1	143·0	585·6	544·6
1967	288·1	157·4	595·2	587·7
1968	309·2	169·1	594·2	638·7
1969	328·4	181·1	607·8	689·1
1970	353·0	197·9	624·1	740·9
1971	377·1	212·4	640·9	800·4
1972	400·4	221·4	655·2	857·4
1973	429·0	236·3	667·6	914·7
1974	458·8	260·6	684·0	975·0
1975*	489·4	285·2	700·0	1,035·0

*Revised plan figure.
Sources: Nar. khoz.; Ek. gaz.

Table 1.3

Energy production 1960, 1965, and 1970
(Million tons standard fuel)

	Oil	%	Gas	%	Coal	%	Peat	%	Shale	%	Firewood	%	Hydro-electric	%	Total	Ave. ann. % increase for 5-year period
1960	211·4	29·4	54·74	7·6	373·1	52·0	20·4	2·8	4·8	0·7	28·7	4·0	23·9	3·3	716·6	
1965	346·4	34·9	149·8	15·1	412·5	40·8	17·0	1·7	7·4	0·7	33·5	3·3	33·8	3·4	1,000·4	7·0
1970	502·5	39·3	233·5	18·5	432·7	34·4	17·7	1·4	8·8	0·7	26·6	2·1	45·8	3·6	1,267·6	4·9

Sources: *Nar. khoz.*; K. Ogawa, in *Chemical Economy and Engineering Review*, Nov. 1973.

Table 1.4

Fuel and power production 1960–70, planned and actual

	Oil (incl. condensates) (million tons)			Natural and assoc. gas (billion cu. metres)			Coal (million tons)			Electric power (billion kWh)		
	Actual	Plan Orig.	Revis.	Actual	Plan Orig.	Revis.	Actual	Plan Orig.	Revis.	Actual	Plan Orig.	Revis.
1960	147·9	144	144	45·3	60·0	53·0	509·6	536·3	515·0	292·3	291·0	
1961	166·1	161	164	59·0		60·1	506·4	554·6	511·7	327·6		
1962	186·2	181	185	73·5		70·5	517·4	571·5	512·8	369·3		366·0
1963	206·1	200	205	89·8		91·6	531·7	586·4	522·0	412·4	407·9	411·6
1964	223·6	220	222	108·6			554·0	599·8		458·9		
1965	242·9	230–240	242	127·1	150·0	129·4	577·7	612·0		506·7	500–520	510·0
1966	265·1		264	143·0	142·0	148·0	585·6	598·0		544·6	560·5	
1967	288·1		286	157·4	158·3	160·0	595·2		591·0	587·7		598·0
1968	309·2		309	169·1	170·3	171·3	594·0	*		638·7	650·0	
1969	328·2	326·5		181·1	191·1	184·0	607·8	595·0	593·4	689·1	687·0	
1970	352·6	345–355	350	197·9	225–240	198·0	624·1	665–675	618·0	740·9		740·0

Note: The natural gas plans for 1961–64 are difficult to estimate from published data, but one source (Strishkov, Markon, and Murphy, in *Combustion*, Jan. 1972) states that the natural gas plan has not been fulfilled since 1956.

*The 1968 coal plan was not published with other fuel industry plans and there are indications that coal output at this time had fallen far behind original intentions.

Sources: Ek. gaz.; Isvestiya, 16 Dec. 1966; *Plan. khoz.*; R.E. Ebel, *Communist trade in oil and gas* (1970).

Table 1.5

Oil, gas, coal, and electric power production 1970–75, planned and actual

	1970		1971		1972		1973		1974		1975
	Plan	Actual	Plan	Actual	Plan	Actual	Plan	Actual	Plan	Actual	Plan
Crude oil (million tons)	348·8	348·8	371·3	371·8	395	393·8	429·0 (424*)	421·8	461·0 (452*)	452·0	496 (482·8*)
Gas condensate (million tons)		4·2		5·3		6·6		7·2	6·1	6·8	9 (6·6*)
Natural gas (billion cu. metres)	198·0*	197·9	211·0*	212·4	229	221·4	250·0 (238*)	236·3	280·0 (257*)	260·6	300–320 (285*)
Coal (million tons)	618·0	624·1	620·4 (633*)	640·9	634 (650*)	655·2	651·5 (665*)	667·6	670·2 (679*)	684·0	685–695 (700*)
Electricity (billion kWh)	740·0	740·9	790·0	800·4	850	857·4	913·0	914·7	975–985	975·0	1,035–1,065 (1,035*)

*Denotes revised plan.
Sources: *Nar. khoz.*; *Gosudarstvenniye pyatiletnii plan SSSR 1971–5.*

Table 1.6

Energy consumption and economic growth 1961–75
(Average annual growth rates, %)

	1961–65	1966–70	1971–75 (est.)
National income	5·7	7·2	6·8
Gross indus. prod.	8·6	8·5	8·0
Total energy consumption	6·4	4·8	5·2

Source: Ogawa.

Table 1.7

Energy consumption 1960, 1965, and 1970
(Million tons standard fuel)

	Oil	%	Gas	%	Coal	%	Peat	%	Shale	%	Firewood	%	Hydro-electric	%	Total	Av. ann. % increase for 5-year period
1960	170·3	25·6	54·5	8·2	366·5	55·1	16·6	2·5	5·1	0·7	28·1	4·2	23·9	3·6	665	
1965	261·7	28·7	152·2	16·6	404·8	44·4	17·8	1·9	7·7	0·9	32·8	3·6	33·8	3·7	911	6·4
1970	373·7	32·6	237·2	20·7	436·8	38·1	17·8	1·5	8·7	0·8	26·6	2·3	46·0	4·0	1,148	4·8

Source: Ogawa.

Table 1.8

Energy consumption by main sectors 1970
(per cent)

	Primary fuels	Coal	Gas	Fuel oil	Diesel oil	Petrol
Industry	69·0	80·9	83·3	89·6	20·7	15·1
Construction	3·4	1·2	0·8	0·9	9·6	11·9
Agriculture	6·3	2·4	0·4	0·3	38·8	24·8
Transport	8·7	2·9	3·4	7·5	25·4	32·4
Municipal*	8·3	8·2	9·3	0·6	0·5	3·8
Others†	4·3	4·4	2·8	1·1	5·0	12·0
Total	100·0	100·0	100·0	100·0	100·0	100·0

*Domestic requirements such as heating from a central source.
†Unidentified in Soviet sources, presumably private consumption.
Source: Economist Intelligence Unit, *Soviet oil to 1980* (1973).

Tables 1.9 and 1.10 show overall trade in the main energy sectors.

Table 1.9

Exports of energy 1970–74

	1970	1971	1972	1973	1974
Oil (m tons)	95·8	105·1	107·0	118·3	116·2
(Crude)	(66·8)	(74·8)	(76·2)	(85·3)	(80·6)
(Products and synthetic liquid fuel)	(29·0)	(30·3)	(30·8)	(33·0)	(35·6)
Gas (bn cu. metres)	3·3	4·6	5·1	6·8	14·0
Hard coal plus anthracite (m tons)	24·5	24·9	24·4	24·5	26·2
Hard coal/coke (m tons)	4·2	4·4	4·5	4·8	4·6
Electric power (billion kWh)	5·3	7·0	7·5	9·9	10·9

Table 1.10

Imports of energy 1970—74

	1970	1971	1972	1973	1974
Oil* (m tons)	4·6	6·6	9·1	14·7	5·4
(Crude)	(3·5)	(5·1)	(7·8)	(13·2)	(4·4)
(Products and synthetic liquid fuel)	(1·1)	(1·5)	(1·3)	(1·5)	(1·0)
Gas (bn cu. metres)	3·6	8·1	11·0	11·4	11·9
Hard coal (m tons)	7·1	8·4	9·7	10·0	9·7
Hard coal/coke (m tons)	0·7	0·8	0·6	0·7	0·7
Electric power (billion kWh)	—	—	—	—	—

*Most crude oil 'imports' are believed not to enter Soviet territory but are transshipped to other Comecon countries (mainly Bulgaria and the GDR). Soviet export figures therefore represent surplus Soviet production plus re-exports.
Source: Vnesh. torg.

Table 1.11

Energy trade in exports (imports) 1970—74

	1970	1971	1972	1973	1974
Oil (m tons)					
Crude	66·8*	74·8	76·2	85·3	80·6
Products	27·9	28·8	29·5	31·5	34·6
Gas (billion cu. metres)	(0·3)	(3·5)	(5·9)	(4·6)	2·1
Hard coal plus anthracite (m tons)	17·4	16·5	14·7	14·5	16·5
Hard coal/coke (m tons)	3·5	3·6	3·9	4·1	3·9
Electric power (billion kWh)	5·3	7·0	7·5	9·9	10·9

*See note to Table 1.10.

If Table 1.10 is subtracted from Table 1.9 the energy trade of the Soviet Union is obtained (see Table 1.11).

Soviet gas imports come from Iran and Afghanistan, coal imports mainly from Poland (see Tables 5.3 and 5.4), and oil product imports mainly from Romania and Western Europe. The sources of the reported crude oil imports vary from year to year but are mainly Iraq, Libya, and Algeria and, as noted above, do not actually enter Soviet territory but are lifted in Soviet vessels and shipped to the Black Sea for off-loading in Bulgaria or to Rostock for the GDR. The USSR primarily exports coal to East European countries including the GDR, Bulgaria, and Czechoslovakia. High quality coking coal and anthracite are exported to Japan, Italy, France, and Austria; natural gas primarily to Czechoslovakia and Poland, and recently to Bulgaria. Exports of natural gas to the West went initially only to Austria but supplies are now being made to West Germany and Italy.

Table 1.12

Export of fuels and electricity 1950–74
(Million tons)

Type of fuel	1950	1955	1960	1965	1970	1974
Crude oil	0·3	2·9	17·8	43·3	66·8	80·6
Oil products and synth. liquid fuel of which:	0·8	5·1	15·4	21·0	29·0	35·6
Petrol	0·3	1·4	2·8	2·4	3·5	5·5
Diesel fuel	0·1	1·3	5·2	7·4	11·4	15·8
Fuel oil	0·1	1·5	5·8	9·7	11·4	10·8
Lubricating oils	0·1	0·2	0·4	0·3	0·3	0·3
Kerosene and jet fuel	0·2	0·6	1·8	1·5	2·1	2·6
Coal (hard)	1·0	2·9	10·5	18·8	20·0	21·4
Anthracite	0·1	1·4	1·8	3·3	4·3	4·6
Hard coal coke	0·7	1·6	2·6	3·8	4·2	4·6
Gas*	0·1	0·1	0·2	0·4	3·3	14·0
Electricity†	—	—	—	1·5	5·4	10·9

*Billion cu. metres   †Billion kWh.
Source: Vnesh. torg.

Table 1.13

Energy resources as a proportion of total value of exports
1940—74
(Percentages)

Type of fuel	1940	1950	1960	1970	1971	1972	1973	1974
Oil	—	0·4	5·0	7·2	8·5	8·6	8·5	11·2
Oil products	13·2	2·0	6·9	4·3	4·8	4·4	6·7	9·8
Coal (hard and anthracite)	0·1	0·7	3·2	2·4	2·6	2·5	2·0	2·1
Hard coal/coke	—	0·7	1·2	0·8	0·9	0·9	0·7	0·6
Gas	—	—	—	0·4	0·5	0·4	0·6	1·0
Electric power	—	—	—	0·4	0·6	0·6	0·6	0·5
Total	13·3	3·8	16·3	15·5	17·9	17·6	19·1	25·2

Source: Vnesh. torg.

Notes

[1] Council for Mutual Economic Assistance, also known as CMEA.

[2] M. Slocum, 'Soviet energy — an internal assessment', *Technology Review* (MIT), Oct./Nov. 1974.

[3] J.P. Hardt and G.D. Holiday, eds., *US—Soviet commercial relations* (1973).

[4] For a full account of Japanese—Soviet relations in the energy field see below, pp. 00—00.

[5] NATO, Directorate of Economic Affairs, *The exploitation of Siberia's natural resources* (1974).

PART I

The Comecon Domestic
Energy Situation

2 Soviet energy: an overall assessment

The 1975 energy position

The consumption of energy in the Soviet Union in 1975 can only be estimated from the production, import, and export figures and by comparisons with previous consumption trends. A likely picture is shown in Table 2.1.

The trend towards the reduction in coal and the increase in oil and gas is being maintained but the rate of growth of the share of gas appears to be losing its impetus.

Table 2.2 shows estimated Soviet energy production in 1975 and compares this with the targets set in the 1971–75 five-year plan.

It seems likely that total energy production targets will have been under-fulfilled by some 40m tons of standard fuel equivalent (SFE), and despite the above-plan achievements of the coal industry, the shortfalls in the oil and gas industries are sufficiently serious to cause an overall energy production shortfall.

While the percentage share of oil in the fuels–energy balance will apparently only be marginally smaller than anticipated, the share of natural gas will be 1·7 per cent lower and the share of coal 1·9 per cent higher.

The effect of the poor performance must have been to slow down the changeover from coal to gas, and this, in turn, may have been partly responsible for an apparent failure to meet the reduction in the quantities of standard fuel needed to produce 1 kWh of electricity – originally planned as being 340 grams in 1975 but now thought likely to be somewhat higher. It is, however, significant that the 1975 annual plan for natural gas of 'more than 285 billion cu. metres' (see Table 2.5) is some 5 billion cu. metres up on the revised 1975 plan figure which was put out in about 1972, when it became clear that the original target of 300–320m cu. metres (see Table 2.5) would not be achieved. The gas industry demonstrates the stepwise development concept even better than the oil industry, and sudden substantial increases to production can be achieved by bringing onstream some major new pipeline with an annual throughput

Table 2.1

Energy consumption 1975
(million tons of standard fuel)

	Quantity	% share of fuels—energy balance
Oil	529	35·8
Gas	339	22·9
Coal	495	33·5
Other solid fuels	51	3·5
Hydro-electric power	56	3·8
Nuclear power	8	0·5
Total	1,478	100·0

Table 2.2

Energy production 1975

Fuel	Basic units (est.)	Millions of tons of standard fuel		% share of fuels—energy balance	
		Est.	Planned	Est.	Planned
Oil	482 million tons	689·3	709·3	42·0	42·4
Condensate	8 million tons	11·4	13·0		
Gas	290 billion cu. metres	345·1	381·6	20·7	22·4
Coal	700 million tons	502·0	483·8	30·3	28·4
Peat	78·3 million tons	23·8	23·8	1·4	1·4
Shale	32·7 million tons	11·9	11·9	0·7	0·7
Wood	55·5 million tons	15·3	15·3	0·9	0·9
Hydro-electric power	165 billion kWh	56·2	56·2	3·4	3·3
Nuclear power	25 billion kWh	8·5	8·5	0·5	0·5
		1,663·5	1,703·4	100·0	100·0

of 25–30 billion cu. metres. If completion of such a pipeline is delayed from the end of one year until the middle of the next year, this could have a substantial effect upon the production figures for the years in question, and it is quite possible that the 1976 increase on 1975 will demonstrate this principle.

Cumulatively, the under-production in the oil industry from the maximum expectations over the last five years totals some 44m tons of standard fuel, and in the gas industry some 71m tons. Coal, on the other hand, will have contributed some 61m tons of SFE over its expected best performance. The resultant cumulative energy deficit over the five years is thus probably between 45m and 55m tons of standard fuel.

The 1980 energy position

In the absence of any data on the Soviet 1976–80 five-year plan, any attempt to assess the 1980 energy production and consumption position must rely upon judicious extrapolations of past growth rates and upon fairly vague indications by Soviet officials and academics which have appeared in the Soviet press and technical literature over the past ten years or so. In January 1967 *Pravda* reported that the extraction of fuel in the Soviet Union might reach 2·5–2·75 billion tons of standard fuel in 1980,[1] and the generation of electric power 2,120 billion kWh. Since that time, however, there has been a downward revision of expectations and best estimates today are of total fuel production in the region of 2,000–2,200m tons of SFE. Energy consumption in 1980 seems likely to fall within the range of 1,900–2,000m tons of SFE. There could therefore be an energy surplus of between 100m and 300m tons of standard fuel. At the moment, it looks as though the surplus will, in fact, be between 200m and 250m tons of SFE. There follows a more detailed analysis of the 1980 situation.

If the above three major sources of fuel do reach what, on the basis of present data, seem to be fairly conservative targets, they will supply some 2,005m tons of SFE in 1980. If oil shale, peat, and firewood contribute no more than their current estimated quantity of 55m tons of SFE, this would bring the total to 2,060m tons. Soviet sources have mentioned a figure of 75 billion kWh of nuclear electricity production in 1980, equivalent to some 25m tons of standard fuel; and hydro-electricity, if it maintains 6 per cent annual increase rates during the next five years, should be contributing a further 75m tons, giving a total production of 2,160m tons of SFE.

It is far harder to estimate consumption patterns in view of the changes which appear to have taken place during the last five years. If oil consumption maintains its 7 per cent annual rate of increase it could amount to 520m tons by 1980. Gas consumption has been going up by some 8·8 per cent over the last five years, and on the basis of 285 billion cu. metres' consumption in 1975, this would point to a requirement of 435 billion cu. metres in 1980. Apparent coal consumption has been increasing at 1·9 per cent annually, and on a 1975 estimated consumption of 690m tons this would give a 1980 requirement of 758m tons. Consumption of the three major sources would therefore, on these bases, work out at 1,806m tons of SFE, and if the contributions from oil shale, peat, wood, hydro-electricity, and nuclear energy are added, this would give an overall consumption of 1,961m tons of SFE. On the other hand, if a current rate of increase in total energy consumption equivalent to that over the last five years of 5·2 per cent is maintained until 1980, based on a 1975 consumption figure of 1,478m tons, this would result in a 1980 figure of 1,904m tons of SFE.

One implication from the above calculations is that the rate of consumption of natural gas is increasing rather faster now than it may be able to do over the next five years, unless there are significant improvements in production rates. On the other hand, there would seem to be ample room for an increase in the rate of coal consumption if this became necessary as a result of gas production shortfalls.

The implications for the overall fuel production balance are shown in Table 2.3.

If a lower consumption figure of 1,920m tons of standard fuel is taken as most probable, natural gas production of 430 billion cu. metres would

Table 2.3

Estimated energy production 1980
(Million tons of standard fuel)

		%
Oil	915	(42·4)
Gas	516	(23·9)
Coal	574	(26·5)
Other solid fuels	55	(2·5)
Hydro-electric power	75	(3·5)
Nuclear	25	(1·2)
Total	2,160	100·0

be about adequate, since imports of 15 billion set against total exports of 50 billion would leave 395 billion cu. metres for domestic consumption, or 474m tons of standard fuel. With the other solid fuels and hydro-electric and nuclear power adding a further 155m tons, the total without coal would be 1,357m tons, and coal's contribution would thus need to be 547m tons of standard fuel, equivalent to 762m tons of coal, a figure clearly well inside production capabilities. Table 2.4 indicates possible consumption in 1980.

Table 2.4

Estimated energy consumption in 1980
(Million tons of SFE)

		%
Oil	744	(38·7)
Gas	474	(24·7)
Coal	547	(28·5)
Other solid fuels	55	(2·9)
Hydro-electric power	75	(3·9)
Nuclear	25	(1·3)
Total	1,920	100·0

These calculations indicate that while energy production is expected to increase by about 5 per cent per annum between 1976 and 1980, the rate of energy consumption will increase slightly faster at 5·2 per cent per annum. Such a development would imply that the proportion of Soviet energy production available for export would be marginally reduced, although the actual volumes could nevertheless be somewhat higher than in 1975. There would also appear to be developing a considerable quantity of coal, surplus to requirements, as indicated by current trends, although such a surplus could be eliminated if consumption of oil and gas was restrained, and their share in the fuels—energy balance was correspondingly lower. In other words, no overall shortage of energy is foreseen, although the energy mix would not appear to be developing in an optimum direction for maximization of oil and gas exports, at least not unless there is a substantial improvement in natural gas production.

As things stand, the Soviet Union looks like having an oil export capability of at least 120m tons and a net gas export capability of 40 billion cu. metres, taking into account some 15 billion cu. metres of import from Iran and Afghanistan.

To the extent that the Soviet export position for natural gas seems relatively clearly established up to 1980, in view of the contracts already entered into for supplies to both Eastern and Western Europe, and because new export projects would require more than five years to put into operation, interest naturally focuses upon the oil and coal situation. As far as coal is concerned, production could clearly be well in excess of expected domestic demand, and there is therefore scope for a rise in Soviet coal exports. The main difficulties here will stem from considerations of quality and transportation, and while exports to Eastern Europe may rise, it is not likely that exports to the West will, except possibly those of coking coal to Japan.

Increases in oil export availability could be made if the substitution of coal by oil was delayed, and the figure of 120m tons takes no account of imports from the Middle East.

Future problems for the Soviet Union and its allies

It will be seen that the total energy deficit of the East European members of Comecon could, in practice, be wholly made up by the Soviet Union from its own surpluses, and that the Comecon bloc as a whole will still be in a position of energy surplus at the end of the decade. However, an import—export relationship with the rest of the world will be maintained, particularly if exports earn hard currency and imports can be paid for in 'soft' currency, by economic and military assistance, etc. Of the East European countries, it will be shown that only Poland will continue to have substantial exports of energy, in the form of hard coal, to the West (see p. 90), and that no other East European country has an energy resource base large enough ever to enable it to export energy. The ability of the Soviet Union to develop its undoubtedly rich energy resources is therefore one of the key factors in assessing the sort of contribution which the Comecon bloc can make to the global energy situation over the next five years and beyond. For a detailed consideration of this see chapters 3—6. It can be said that the main problem here is not that the Soviet Union is short of energy resources but that it is not able to make a good use of those which it has.

It is difficult to draw conclusions from this brief analysis of some of the obstacles facing the main Soviet energy producing industries, particularly when no indication is yet available of the next Soviet five-year plan, let alone the expected fifteen-year plan covering the period 1976—90. It is probably fair to say that, from the Soviet point of view, things are not as bad as they appear to be to Western observers, although there is clearly a great deal of room for improvement. The situation is probably more serious in the oil industry than in the gas and coal industries, in that the reserve position does seem to be less favourable. It is possible that, for the next five years, increases in production can be maintained at at least current rates, since they will depend upon already proven resources, the development of which is well under way. It is equally quite possible, however, that in the early 1980s the position could deteriorate quite quickly if major new oilfields are not discovered in the very near future. Prospects for the gas industry must be considered as brighter, not only because the performance in the past has been so bad, but also because there are signs that it is, at last, beginning to stand on its own feet, the planners having recognized that they were probably over-optimistic in earlier years. The coal industry is quite clearly capable of substantially increasing its output, although the best way to capitalize on its potential presents the planners with perhaps the most complex set of problems of them all.

Some aspects of energy costs and prices[2]

So far no attempt has been made to go into financial aspects of the Soviet energy industries, e.g. production and transportation costs, etc., and one reason for this is that it would require a separate study in itself, as the situation is extremely complex and constantly under change. Another reason is that the subject has been dealt with at some length by such experts as Professor Campbell[3] of Indiana University in his book *The Economics of Soviet Oil and Gas* (1968), Professor Yuri Probst and Academician N.V. Melnikov (in Soviet publications), and by Professor Dienes in an article entitled 'Geographical problems of allocation in the Soviet fuel supply' which appeared in *Energy Policy,* June 1973.

The present study has been primarily concerned with establishing production and consumption volumes, growth rates, and intra-Comecon supply and demand problems. To the extent that the Comecon bloc, taken as a whole, will continue to import and export volumes of crude oil and natural gas, and export volumes of hard coal, the prices at which it does so do have some relevance. However, since Soviet export prices have, over the years, tended towards the maximum achievable on the world market, the key consideration from the Soviet point of view is the minimum margin of profit which can be obtained after averaging up country-wide production and transportation costs and replacement values or opportunity costs.

Before the 1973 jump in global oil prices, Soviet sales of oil to the West provided over 20 per cent of its total hard currency earnings, while the oil that it was importing from the Middle East (for re-export) was mainly being paid for by past deliveries of economic, technological and military aid. Selling prices ranged from $2·50 to $3 per barrel from Black Sea ports, and it is generally agreed that contracts already entered into before 1973 for supply in 1974, and after, were fulfilled at pre-crisis prices, although there is some reason to think that contracted volumes were not always supplied in total (for ruble/dollar values see p. xv). Since the oil price rises, the Soviet Union has moved swiftly into line with the other oil-producing countries, and there is some indication that quantities of oil acquired by barter from the Middle East were offered in Western Europe in early 1974 at prices in excess of $14 per barrel.

Extraction costs of Soviet crude oil vary from about 4 rubles per ton for Tyumen crude, through 5 rubles per ton for most Volga—Urals crude to as much as 12 rubles per ton in Azerbaidzhan, excluding geological and amortization allowances. Total production costs range from 8·5 rubles per ton in western Siberia, through 10 rubles per ton in the Volga—Urals region, and up to 23 rubles per ton in Azerbaidzhan (see Appendix A). The European areas have seen a gradual rise in oil production costs in recent years due to the continuing use of resources in the old producing areas where output is slowing and the wells have low yields. In the Ukraine, for instance, 50·7 per cent of the wells supply only 0·5 per cent of the total output, while the remaining 99·5 per cent comes from only 49·3 per cent of the wells. At Borislav, one of the oldest areas in the Ukraine, the cost of production is 64·8 rubles per ton. Wells such as these are regarded as totally uneconomic by Soviet economists, who have calculated the maximum economic production cost at 37·91 rubles per ton for normal crude or 43·8 rubles per ton for low-sulphur crudes.[4] These figures are based upon the opportunity—cost principle and are arrived at by taking the average coal production costs for coal produced at above the average wholesale price of crude oil (22 rubles per ton of SFE) and removing allowances for refining, transport, and marketing costs. Thus, oil produced at above this cost would more economically be replaced by marginal coal. In consequence of such unprofitable production, average costs for the actual production of crude oil (i.e. not including geological and amorti-zation costs) in the Ukraine rose from 4·65 rubles per ton in 1969 to 5·25 rubles per ton in 1972.

Crude oil transportation costs clearly vary according to the mode of transport, and, for example, transportation of Tyumen crude by rail costs 4·35 rubles per ton up to 1,000 km distance, rising to 7·85 rubles per ton for distances between 1,000 and 2,000 km, and 11·35 rubles per ton for distances between 2,000 and 3,000 km. By comparison, transport by pipeline of 1·22 metres diameter would cost 0·93, 1·83 and 2·75 rubles per ton respectively, while for a 0·720-metre diameter pipeline the corresponding costs would be 1·52, 3·00, and 4·50 rubles per metric ton. In 1969, pipelines handled some 98·7 per cent of the total crude transported while railways moved a little over 1 per cent; there was also some movement by river. West Siberian crude could therefore be delivered to the Soviet western border at a basic price of 12–14 rubles per ton, and Volga–Urals crude would be delivered to the export port of Novorossiisk at about the same price.

Production costs for natural gas also vary very considerably from area to area. Tyumen gas is reported as costing 2·6 rubles per 1,000 cu. metres, while that from Orenburg costs 3·4 rubles. In 1969 the average figure for Ukrainian gas was 1·93 rubles per 1,000 cu. metres but this had risen to 2·05 rubles in 1973. The average price at which Soviet gas was made available to the pipeline association after treatment, etc. was 6 rubles per 1,000 cu. metres in 1970. One of the most promising major Soviet gas fields is that at Vuktyl, and the planned production cost for this field, in 1975, when it is due to reach full production, is 3 rubles per 1,000 cu. metres. The production cost of Central Asian gas is at least 6·4 rubles per 1,000 cu. metres.

Natural gas transportation costs vary from 2·59 rubles per thousand cu. metres, in a 1·42-metre pipeline for distances up to 1,000 km, to 6·27 rubles per thousand cu. metres in a 1·02-metre diameter pipeline over distances up to 2,000 km. On the basis of these figures Tyumen gas costs just under 12 rubles per thousand cu. metres delivered to Moscow, and 13·6 rubles delivered at Minsk, while Central Asian gas costs 15·8 rubles to move to Moscow. This would give a 'no-profit' price at the western Soviet border of about 16–17 rubles per thousand cu. metres.

Coal production costs vary even more widely than those for crude oil and natural gas, depending on whether the mining is open-cast or pit, and whether it is hard coal or lignite. Hard coal in the Don Basin costs 11·2 rubles per ton of SFE, and brown coal in the Moscow and Dnieper regions costs 14·3 and 12·4 rubles per ton of SFE respectively. Hard coal in the Kuznetzk field costs 10·6 rubles and 4·8 rubles for shaft and strip mining respectively, whereas Kansk–Achinsk brown coal, produced by open-cast mining, only costs 1·7–1·8 rubles per ton of SFE. Hard coal production at Ekibastuz costs 2·1 rubles per ton while at Karaganda, 500 km to the south, it costs 9·8 rubles per ton. All these costs include a 12·5 per cent simple interest charge on investment.

Most coal is transported by electrified railway. Kuznetsk coal costs 2·33 rubles per ton of coal to move over a distance of 1,000 km and 4·48 rubles per ton over a distance of 2,000 km. Brown coal from Kansk–Achinsk costs 3·87 rubles per ton to transport over 1,000 km and 7·47 rubles per ton for distances up to 2,000 km.

It is clear that, even taking into consideration the most expensive oil, gas, and coal deposits, and transported over the great distances to the western Soviet border or to export ports in the south or north or, indeed, east of the country, the f.o.b./f.o.r. delivered costs are well below the $80–90 per ton being charged on the international market for crude oil at present. There would appear to be every incentive for the Soviet Union to increase its export capabilities as quickly as possible, but, as expressed elsewhere in this book, it is not particularly easy for this to occur, at least during the next five years, in view of the lead-time necessary to provide transportation. It is also clear that, whatever may have been the inclinations of Soviet planners in the early part of the 1970s, they must now be increasingly in favour of developing Soviet domestic energy resources, which had hitherto seemed to be economically unattractive, at the fastest possible rate.

Notes

[1] N. Melnikov, in *Pravda*, 16 Jan. 1967, p. 2.

[2] For further information and source material see Appendix A.

[3] For a treatment of prices of Soviet oil and gas as a result of the 1965 economic reforms see the same author's 'Price, rent and decision-making: the economic reform in Soviet oil and gas production', *Jahrbuch der Wirtschaft Osteuropas*, 2 (1971), pp. 291–313.

[4] *Ek. neft. prom.*, Nov. 1972, pp. 37–40.

3　The oil industry

History

The presence of large quantities of oil in Russia had been established by the turn of the century when Russia was the leading exporter, and well before the Soviet regime came to power in 1917. Substantial deposits had been located in the Caspian, North Caucasian, and Urals regions, and by the time of the 1917 Revolution the development of these fields by foreign organizations had got under way. The oil-bearing strata were located fairly near to the surface, within the first 2,000 metres, and exploration and development effort was concentrated in or around the already established areas situated mainly to the south and west of the country. Development continued in the 1920s and 1930s, but poor techniques of exploration and shortages of essential materials, notably imported pipe, and metal for the construction of cracking plants, hampered progress and, as a result, ambitious plans were frequently scaled down. The war caused considerable disruption in the industry; because of the fear of enemy occupation, output at the Groznyy fields in Chechen—Ingush ASSR in south-west Russia was curtailed and much of the equipment despatched to the east. Baku output had to be limited because fighting on the Volga and the North Caucasus prevented the delivery of oil to the Centre. Total oil production fell from over 31m tons in 1940 to 19·4m tons in 1945.

In the 1950s and early 1960s significant new deposits were found east of the Caspian Sea and beyond the Ural Mountains. Geological prospects were so favourable that exploration efforts were stepped up, particularly in Siberia, and were rewarded by the discovery of huge deposits in the Tyumen region of western Siberia. Additional deposits were discovered in the Soviet Far East on Sakhalin Island and in Kazakhstan in Central Asia. Meanwhile, in the middle of the 1960s, the Soviet oil industry became aware that production from the Azerbaidzhan, North Caucasian, and Volga—Urals regions could not be expected to maintain the annual increases recorded over the previous decade and that development of the newer areas should be initiated as a matter of some urgency. The problem facing the developers was, however, that the new highly promising areas were located a great deal further away from the main oil-consuming regions of the Soviet Union and in extremely hostile geographical and climatic conditions. Nevertheless, massive effort to develop the Siberian oil resources was authorized for the second half of the 1960s, and by 1970 it became clear that by far the greater part of future increases in overall Soviet oil production would be coming from the Siberian fields, notably from Samotlor in the Tyumen Oblast. Meanwhile, the predicted levelling off of production rates from the older established oilfields was beginning to materialize and an increasing number of oilfield management problems was being encountered as a result, perhaps, of over-hasty development in the past and failure to invest adequately in secondary recovery measures. It was becoming clear that the main energy consuming centres of the Soviet Union situated to the west of the Ural Mountains and in the European part of the country were becoming an energy deficit area of considerable proportions. Annual production was actually declining in Azerbaidzhan[2] and strenuous efforts were having to be made to maintain the level of production in the Volga—Urals region. More than one-third of all newly created production capacity was required to compensate for reduced output from older fields, and in 1971 it was estimated that over 50 per cent of production increases up to 1975 would be required for this purpose.[3]

Reserves

No official figures are published concerning Soviet oil reserves and Western estimates differ greatly, partly due to the confusion arising out of what categories of reserves are being talked about. The Soviet planners distinguish four categories (for comparison with Western methods see Appendix B).

1   The so-called 'explored' reserves comprising the categories A and B; these correspond more or less to 'proven reserves'.
2   The 'commercial' reserves which consist of categories A + B + C1, the last category representing 'probable reserves'.
3   Category C2, or 'prospective reserves', which are more or less equivalent to 'possible reserves'.
4   'Prognostic reserves' represented by categories D1 and D2, which are variously described as 'predicted' or 'geologic' reserves. These are assumed or suspected to exist in an area and as such represent the ultimate reserves of the area in question.[4]

Of the three most important categories — A, B, and C1 — there would currently appear to be in the region of 100—120 billion barrels or about

14 billion tons. Of this, some 42 billion barrels, or 5·7 billion tons, are estimated as proved, giving a 1974 proven reserves-to-production ratio of approximately 13:1 and a proven + semi proven + probable reserves-to-production ratio of 31:1. Ultimately recoverable reserves have been estimated at not less than 350 billion barrels or 50 billion tons. By far the greater part of these reserves are thought to lie to the east of the Urals, in western and eastern Siberia, and in off-shore regions in the Far East and in the Arctic. Reserves in the old producing areas of Azerbaidzhan and the Volga—Urals region have borne the brunt of production so far and are showing signs of exhaustion.

Production

Over the last fifteen years annual increases in oil production have fallen from the early 1960s level of around 12 per cent to a current rate of between 6 and 7 per cent. However, actual increases in terms of volume have gone up from an average of about 20m tons in the 1960s to over 30m tons annually at the time of writing, and oil industry spokesmen have indicated that it is their intention to raise the annual increases in output to 35m tons in the near future. Table 3.1 shows Soviet crude oil production totals since 1960 and annual rates of increase, and Table 3.2 shows a regional breakdown of the total, in addition to the five-year and annual plan figures. The latter table clearly indicates how the bulk of future increases will have to come from the long-haul areas east of the Urals.

Gas condensate

With the discovery in the 1950s of enormous natural gas deposits there arose the question of what to do with the associated gas liquids, generally known as gas condensate and produced in substantial quantities along with the gas. Gas condensate has to be removed from the gas streams before transportation over long distances or else it will separate out and severely reduce the flow in the gas pipeline. It is a highly valuable source of hydrocarbons suitable for petrochemical manufacture and can also be considered as equivalent to the lightest fractions of a barrel of oil; it can therefore be added to the crude oil streams en route to refineries. Many of the new gas fields were some distance away from oilfields and refineries, and since a convenient outlet for the condensate could not be found, it was usually burnt.[5] In the late 1960s the seriousness of this waste of energy and raw materials was severely criticized and an effort was made to construct the necessary treating plants and connecting pipelines so that the condensate could be utilized. In some cases natural gas production was actually held up through lack of the necessary gas condensate handling facilities.[6] In 1960 production of gas condensate was 0·7m tons; by 1965 this had risen to 1·2m tons; by 1970 production was 4·2m tons, and the 1975 plan figure was 6·6m tons. For statistical purposes it is included in the oil production and consumption figures.

Table 3.1

Crude oil and condensate production 1960–75, planned and actual, annual percentage increases
(Million tons)

	Plan*		Actual	Ann. % increase
	Orig.	Rev.		
1960	144	144	147·9	14·1
1961	161	164	166·1	12·3
1962	181	185	186·2	12·1
1963	200	205	206·1	10·7
1964	220	222	223·6	8·5
1965	230–240	242	242·9	8·6
1966		264	265·1	9·1
1967		286	288·1	8·7
1968		309	309·2	7·3
1969	326·5		328·4	6·2
1970	345–355	350	353·0	7·5
1971			377·1	6·8
1972			400·4	6·2
1973			429·0	7·1
1974			458·8	6·9
1975		489·4		6·7

*Plans for the period 1971–75 were expressed in terms of crude oil only, see Table 2.5.
Source: Derived from Tables 2.2, 2.4 and 2.5.

Table 3.2

Oil production 1970, 1974 and 1975, by region
(Original plan and revised plan)
(Million tons)

	1970	1974	1975 orig. plan	1975 rev. plan
European USSR and Urals of which:	285·1	295	314	
Volga—Urals				
Tatar ASSR	100·4	102	100	106
Bashkir ASSR	40·7	40	40	40
Kuibyshev Oblast	34·9	35	35	35
Perm Oblast	16·1	20	22	22
Orenburg Oblast	7·4	12*	14	12
Volgograd Oblast	6·0			
Saratov Oblast	1·0*			
Udmurt ASSR	0·5	3	6	4
North Caucasus				
Chechen Ingush	20·3	⎫	25	
Stravropol Krai	6·4	⎪		7
Krasnodar Krai	5·3	⎪		
Daghestan ASSR	2·2	⎬ 80*		
Azerbaidzhan	20·2	⎪	19	
Komi ASSR	5·6	8 ⎪	14	18
Belorussia	4·2	⎪	10	
Ukraine	13·9	14 ⎭	15	
East of Urals of which	63·7	157	182	
Western Siberia	31·4	116	125	147
Kazakhstan	13·2	22	30	24
(Mangyshlak)	10·4	21	27	22
Turkmen SSR	14·5	15	22	22
Sakhalin	2·5			
Uzbekistan	1·8	1	1	
Others	0·3		5	
GRAND TOTAL	348·8	452	496	482

*Estimated
Sources: Ek. gaz.

Performance

The oil industry established an enviable record of plan fulfilment during the 1950s and 1960s, and it was not until 1972 that it failed by a narrow margin to meet the annual plan for crude production (see Table 2.4). In 1973 it again failed to meet the original five-year plan target set for that year of 429m tons, and it also failed to meet the revised annual plan for crude oil of 424m tons, achieving only 422m. The 1974 target for crude oil production was originally 461m tons, but this was amended in the annual plan to 452m tons, a target that was just exceeded. The 1975 plan was originally for 496m tons of crude oil and for 9m tons of gas condensate, but it was subsequently amended to a total of 489·4m tons of crude plus condensate and this figure too was just exceeded.

It has been Soviet practice to forecast a range for the production expected to be reached by the final year of a five-year plan, and in the case of crude oil the range for the 1971–75 plan has been constantly stated as 480–500m tons. The 1966–70 five-year plan was for 345–355m tons in the final year, and the crude production was in fact 349m tons, with 3·8m tons of condensate. It looks as if the 1971–75 five-year plan was, cumulatively, under-fulfilled by some 30m tons of crude in comparison with the targets at the upper end of the range. At best it can be said that the oil industry has managed to achieve the lower end of the range, whereas in previous five-year periods it was performing in the upper end of the range, though perhaps it is unreasonable to describe this as a general failure. The individual annual plan targets for the later years of a five-year plan period, as originally set down in the plan, are perhaps less significant than the subsequently amended annual plans (see Table 2.6).

The significance of the shortfall in the oil industry is perhaps less great for the domestic economy than for the opportunities which the Ministry of Foreign Trade may miss as a result of having less oil available for export than hoped for or than could have been foreseen. The amount of oil actually used in the Soviet Union in any one year has to be calculated from the production figures minus the net export figures, and the amount actually consumed by Soviet industry can then be estimated by deducting various percentages of production to cover quantities lost during transportation (generally assumed to be about 3 per cent) and volumes used and lost at refineries in the course of electricity and heat-raising operations (estimated at about 9 per cent).[7] For the purposes of calculating overall availability, however, the key figure is that volume of oil which remains in the Soviet Union after subtracting import and export quantities. In 1970 this figure is put at 262·8m tons and in 1973 325·4m tons, giving

44

an average annual increase for the three years of 7·4 per cent. If this rate was applied to 1974 and 1975, it would suggest an overall usage of the Soviet Union in 1975 of some 375m tons. However, in view of campaigns launched at the end of 1973 to reduce energy wastage generally, it might be reasonable to assume that average annual increases could be reduced to 7 per cent, giving a 1975 usage figure of some 370m tons. The surplus for export availability would in this case be 120m tons, and if the imports—re-exports volume is about the same as it was in 1974 — say, 5m tons — this would indicate that there would be some 125m tons at the Soviet Union's disposal. The European members of Comecon consumed some 85m tons of oil in 1975, of which 17m tons were from domestic production, leaving an import requirement of 68m tons, 57·3m tons of which reportedly came directly from the USSR.[8] Other socialist countries dependent upon supplies of Soviet oil required a further 12m tons, so that Soviet commitments, including 'acquired' deliveries, to its allies and associates may have amounted to nearly 80m tons. The availability for the rest of the world therefore was of the order of 40–45m tons, and the total export picture looks very much what might have been expected by a simple extrapolation of the trend over the past few years. (The crude production target in 1975 was exceeded by 1m tons as a morale raiser for the final year of the five-year plan, but unless there was some switching of exports from 'barter' areas outside the socialist bloc, it does not seem likely on 1975 showing that the Soviet Union was able to capitalize upon the increased world prices of crude oil by significant increases in volumes exported to the dollar area over and above what might have been expected.)

To the extent that the oil industry's performance during the 1971–75 five-year plan period can be said to have been below standard, it must reflect the failure of some of the older areas, such as Azerbaidzhan and north Caucasus, to stem the decline in their oil production,[9] as well as the failure of some of the newer areas, such as Mangyshlak, to achieve intended growth rates, mainly as a result of technical difficulties arising from the physical nature of the crude.[10] Production from western Siberia has, however, exceeded expectations. There were indications that the Soviet oil industry is hoping to achieve an annual increase in production of 35m tons sometime during this decade, and annual increments at present are still being achieved. The planned figure for 1975 was an increase of 30·8m tons, which should be exceeded marginally. The 1974 increase was only 30m tons, and in view of the step-wise rather than the graphically smooth development of the Soviet energy industries, it is not yet possible to say that the oil industry has either reached a plateau of annual production increases, or is in a consolidation period before a

Table 3.3

Crude oil and products exports 1965–74

A   Eastern Europe and OECD countries (million metric tons)

	1965	1970	1973	1974
Eastern Europe				
Bulgaria	3·4	7·0	9·3	10·9
Czechoslovakia	6·4	10·5	14·3	14·8
GDR	5·4	9·3	13·0	14·4
Hungary	2·5	4·8	6·3	6·7
Poland	4·7	8·6	12·3	11·9
Sub-total	22·4	40·2	55·2	58·7
Other socialist countries				
Cuba	4·7	6·0	7·4	7·6
Mongolia	0·2	0·3	0·3	0·3
North Korea	0·4	0·8	0·6	1·0
North Vietnam	0·1	0·4	0·2	0·3
Yugoslavia	1·0	2·7	3·9	3·8
Sub-total	6·4	10·2	12·4	13·0
OECD				
Austria	0·5	1·1	1·3	1·0
Belgium	0·1	1·3	1·7	1·8
Canada				0·2
Denmark	0·4	0·4	0·6	0·7
Finland	4·5	7·8	10·0	9·2
France	1·6	2·5	5·3	1·2
Great Britain	neg.		0·8	0·9
Greece	1·2	0·9	0·8	1·0
Iceland	0·4	0·4	0·5	0·5
Ireland		0·2	0·2	0·1
Italy	7·3	10·2	8·7	6·8
Japan*	3·9	2·7	2·0	·1·2
Netherlands		1·4	3·2	3·0
Norway	0·3	0·6	0·6	0·3
Portugal				0·1
Spain	0·1	0·1	0·5	0·5
Sweden	2·8	4·8	3·2	3·0
Switzerland		0·4	0·7	0·8

Table 3.3 cont.

Turkey	0·1	0·2	neg.	
USA		?		
West Berlin		0·1	0·4	0·5
West Germany	3·1	6·2	5·8	6·3
Sub-total	36·3	41·3	43·9	38·8
Grand total (incl. other countries given in Table B)	62·86	95·06	116·60	114·7

Note: Although figures are taken from *Vnesh. torg.*, the totals do not correspond to the totals given in that source which are as follows:

64·4	95·8	118·3	116·2

*In *Vneshnaya torgovlya* 1974 it is stated that the USSR exported an additional 1m tons to Japan in 1973 and 0·2m tons in 1974. These figures are 'not allowed for in the methodology of Soviet trade statistics' and are not taken into account in the totals.

B   Other countries (thousand metric tons)

	1965	1970	1973	1974
Afghanistan	120	141	165	193
Argentina	403			
Bangladesh			48	173
Brazil	2,354			1,233
Burma	140			
China	38			
Cyprus		135	122	106
Egypt	773	1,639	352	229
Ghana	595	515	614	309
Guinea	52	61	85	82
India	1,421	252	477	1,009
Morocco	417	699	943	647
Nepal	—		18	
Nigeria	—	neg.	neg.	neg.
Senegal	—	0·4	11·5	0·1
Somalia	—	59	75	113
Sri Lanka	599			
Syria	155	47	36	51
Yemen Arab Republic		17		
Sub-total	7,067	3,429	2,948	2,914

Source: Vnesh. torg.

significant step upwards. It is certainly not possible to say on the evidence of the 1971–75 five-year plan targets and achievements that there is any sign of any essentially new factor which is seriously affecting oil industry performance. It would probably be more accurate to say that the ability of the industry to overcome problems of long standing has not noticeably improved.

Problems facing the industry

The main problems facing the oil industry can be summarized as follows:

1   The reserves-to-production ratio is falling, due to the inadequate rate at which major new deposits are being discovered. While the volume of annual output is rising, the higher categories of reserves – A + B + C1 – are not being added to, i.e. proved-up, at a fast enough rate.

2   There is a rapidly increasing energy deficit in the European part of the Soviet Union – the 'Centre' – which accounts for over 80 per cent of Soviet industrial productive capacity and energy consumption. This is due in part to stagnating or declining production in the Volga–Urals, North Caucasus, and Ukrainian oilfields and gives rise to sharply increasing logistical difficulties and costs associated with the greater distance from these main consumption areas of the major new production areas of western Siberia and Central Asia.

3   There are chronic shortages of equipment, steel pipeline, personnel, and infrastructural accessories.[11] There is a consistent record of failure by construction, communication, and machinery producing ministries to maintain supply rates adequate to keep pace with the required development rate in the oil industry.

4   It is increasingly difficult and costly both to maintain existing levels of production in regions which have passed their peak, and to compensate for declining production in some other areas, due to deficiencies in the past planning of capital investment in secondary recovery methods.

A catalogue of all the problems and shortcomings in the industry would run to many pages, but it is useful to examine some of the specific aspects referred to in slightly more detail. In recent years, the preparation of reserves of crude oil has lagged behind the increase in production, and in the major old production areas such as the Volga–Urals region, the North Caucasus, and Baku, exploration for new reserves has become increasingly less successful. It is only in the Tyumen district that the Ministry of Geology has discovered sufficient new reserves to enable the reserves-to-

48

production ratio to be increased, and the all-Union objectives for increases to reserves were not met for the first three years of the 1971–75 five-year plan period.[12] The present-day levels of oil production and future growth can only be maintained by the discovery of major new oilfield regions, equivalent in potential to the Volga–Urals area or to western Siberia. New, even quite large discoveries in existing oil-producing areas can only be expected to compensate for the decline of old deposits or, at best, provide for some small increase in overall production over the next few years.[13] Potentially interesting new areas have been found in the remote and climatically hostile parts of the Soviet Union such as eastern Siberia and the north Caspian depression and various off-shore regions, particularly in the north of the country, upon which great hopes are placed for future growth in output, but which has a highly complicated geological character, with oil and gas layers at depths in excess of 5,000 metres. In these high-potential regions the volume of exploratory drilling carried out so far by the Ministry of Geology has been inadequate, and the rate at which oil deposits can be appraised and developed has, along with the volume of exploration and appraisal drilling, remained at about the same level for the last ten years. Recommendations and directives regarding exploration have been criticized in Soviet technical literature as being too vague, and the choice of exploration areas and objectives for drilling is often ill founded. Geophysical techniques are inadequate, particularly in the geologically more complicated areas of the country, and the accuracy and volume of seismic data is inadequate for the successful outlining of non-structural traps. The accuracy of well logging, and the evaluation of carbonate reservoirs and of shaley and thin bedded sequences are poor, and it is claimed that too little attention is paid to the economic aspects of oil exploration. New equipment for exploration drilling is not being made available fast enough.

More effort could clearly be expended in exploration drilling, given the overall tight situation on manpower and equipment (see Appendix D), if less were needed for production and development drilling, but here again performance is lagging seriously behind requirements for the following reasons.

First, in some parts of the country the number of wells actually in production at any one time is lower than it should be because of a lack of well-servicing crews and the bad organization of their operations. Pressure maintenance techniques are not adequately or efficiently employed, and take excessively long to instal. There are long delays in putting wells on gas lift and in developing the gathering and transport systems for oil and gas condensate. Inadequate support services and poor liaison with specialist scientific institutes has received criticism in the North Caucasus, Lower Volga, Ukraine, Turkmenia, and Uzbekistan. New systems for the automatic monitoring of down-hole operations and pump pressures, etc., which should allow for round-the-clock activity, have only been introduced on a very small scale, and although automation of engineering and technical services has been introduced in some areas, many others are failing to make use of developments in this field. Alcoholism, absenteeism, a high accident rate at drilling sites, bad reservoir management, and lack of treatment plants for the removal of salt and water from the crude oil are other criticisms which are frequently encountered. Inadequate use is made of computers and there are insufficient of these available with the required capacity.[14]

Second, severe criticisms have been made of the failure to construct pipelines of the requisite length and diameter in time to allow the maximum benefit to be obtained from newly prepared production potential. Difficulties in the pipeline field of operations are attributable to lack of steel of the right quality, failure to deliver pipes on time, lack of pipe-rolling equipment and of sufficiently strong pipe-laying equipment, the poor quality and condition of pipes that do arrive at the construction site, delays in lining, insulating, and welding the pipes, shortages of pumps and compressors, and delays in the construction of pumping stations, particularly for main trunk lines.[15]

Third, contributing to all the above difficulties are the shortcomings in the overall infrastructure, particularly in the 'new' areas in western Siberia. These include inadequate roads, which are also very costly, and a lack of other means of transport, as well as a chronic shortage of accommodation due both to bad planning and to a lack of construction materials and equipment. There are also shortages of food and other consumer goods, a lack of recreational activities and generally poor human amenities leading to a high turnover of manpower and a shortage of skilled personnel.[16]

It is very easy for Western oil men to form the impression that the Soviet oil industry is on the verge of catastrophic breakdown which must lead to sharply impaired performance and, inevitably, to reduced production targets. It is probably quite true to say that the Soviet method of running an oil industry could not possibly work under Western conditions. It is, however, also possible that Western methods of running an oil industry could not succeed under Soviet conditions, and the important consideration here is whether or not the problems facing the Soviet oil industry today are different from or more acute than those which were facing it ten years ago. It is rewarding to look back at what was happening in the Soviet oil industry in the middle of the 1960s, which was about the time that genuine criticism of supply shortcomings and technical and administrative problems began freely to be expressed in the Soviet media. Study of both the oil industry literature and of more general economic publications of that time reveals a, perhaps, surprising similarity between the problems facing the oil production enterprises then, and those being highlighted at present. There was already an awareness both of the larger and longer-term problems such as the increasing energy deficit of the 'Centre', and of the decline in productivity of the established oilfields. There was also an awareness of the increasing costs associated with developing the more distant new discoveries; of the failure to increase reserves at a rate sufficient to keep abreast of planned increases in production[17] etc., and of all the day-to-day shortcomings arising from the lack of equipment or of its poor quality, bad oilfield management and planning and serious delays in the construction of distributional and infrastructural requirements.[18] It is a matter for some admiration that, in spite of all these problems, the oil ministry managed to complete the production tasks allotted to it for the rest of the 1960s, and it can only be assumed that the planners in the ministry itself had a truly realistic idea of what could and could not be achieved, taking into consideration all the inefficiencies and shortcomings. The ministry, indeed, has always suggested that it could have done substantially better if it had not been let down by other ministries. Sweeping changes in pricing methods and in general accountability and oil industry management (see Appendix C) were brought about during the period of general economic reform promoted by Mr Kosygin during the later 1960s and early 1970s, and while these undoubtedly did reduce inefficiency in many areas and led to a more rational approach to the planning and operation of oil industry developments, the reiteration of old complaints has continued to this day. In recent years, moreover, there has evolved increasingly open discussion of the problems, and although suggested remedies have proliferated, many of the problems have stubbornly refused to go away. Blame has become progressively and freely apportioned to the specifically offending ministries, research institutes etc., and departments of the oil ministry itself have started to come in for increasing criticism.

One thing which does stand out from a comparison of the 'complaints' of the 1960s with those of today is the extent to which the most senior levels of the oil industry, including deputy ministers and the minister himself, are now pronouncing upon the unsatisfactory state of affairs. Furthermore, the seriousness of the problems and the repercussions on production rates if they are not solved, are nowadays stressed to a greater extent than used to be the practice. There seems also to be a mounting realization of the influence which the change of scale is beginning to have upon the whole development of the oil industry. In the 1960s, when annual increases in production were in the order of 17–20m tons, and maximum distances of pipeline were only a few hundred kilometres, when the decline in production from the oilfields was easily compensated for by the bringing on stream of the first of the major new areas in western Siberia, the infrastructure and supporting ministries were reasonably well able to cope with the targets then set. But today, when annual production increases are around 30m tons, and when new areas are thousands of kilometres away from the main industrial centres, it begins to look as if the limits are at last being reached as to what can be done with the improvisations and ad hoc treatment of the less serious problems, in the absence of a thoroughly laid and tested broad basis from which an attack on the major problems can be launched.

Refining

At the end of 1973 there were some 64 refinery complexes in the Soviet Union with an estimated capacity of primary distillation of 360m tons per annum. An additional 55m tons of capacity was believed to be under construction at a further ten sites and, depending upon the completion rates, refinery capacity by the end of the 1971–75 five-year plan could be around 415m tons. The planned increase in capacity for 1975 over 1971 was originally 50 per cent but this was reduced to 40 per cent in 1972.

Much of the technology in use in the Soviet Union has been developed domestically and in some cases is up to the highest Western standards, although in some refineries it has not yet been introduced, and equipment and operational practices are judged to be five to ten years behind what would be acceptable in, for example, the United States. In recent years the Soviet Union has been purchasing licences and equipment from Western oil industry suppliers for some of the most sophisticated techniques used in the petroleum refining industry, but not on a large scale. Rather more serious problems are encountered in the treatment of crude oil to remove sulphur, water and salt. The utilization of refining capacity is believed to be rather less efficient than in the West and is estimated on average to be between 85 and 90 per cent. The use of manpower in refineries and the percentage of fuel losses and refinery uses of energy are higher than would normally be tolerated under Western conditions (USSR refinery losses are 8–10 per cent compared with 7–8 per cent in the West) and considerable wastage occurs during the transportation and storage of products once they leave the refineries (3–4 per cent).

The production of high octane petrol has only been introduced on a significant scale during the last few years, and the quality of lubricating oils for industrial and automotive end uses is still not up to generally accepted Western standards. There is some doubt whether the rate of construction of new refineries will be able to keep pace with the growing demands for suitable raw materials for the petrochemicals industry and for automotive fuels and lubricants likely to be required as a result of the planned increases in truck and car production, although this is seen partly as a regional distribution and logistical problem and considerable effort is being directed towards finding a solution. The tendency is for the construction of much larger refinery complexes with annual throughputs of 12m tons and over, and primary distillation units of at least 6m tons per annum capacity, whereas there were a great many refineries of only 2–5m tons overall capacity in existence built before what might be termed the current boom in refinery construction got under way in the late 1960s.

Transportation

In the early days Soviet oil was primarily transported by rail and by river barges, but volumes and distances increased so fast that the development of a pipeline network became imperative. The map shows the current pipeline network system in the Soviet Union based on material available at the end of 1973. There is a total of 47·2 thousand km of main crude pipelines and 11·2 thousand km of product pipelines. The share of total crude transportation between railways, pipelines and other methods of transport is shown in Tables 3.4 and 3.5.

Table 3.4

Transportation of oil and products 1940–74
(Million tons)

	1940	1950	1960	1965	1968	1969	1970	1971	1972	1973	1974
Rail	29·5	43·2	151·0	222·2	275·9	284·7	302·8	322·8	340·4	360·5	
Rail*	36·4	52·0	205·4	280·4	333·9	342·8	353·9	380·1	409·4	449·7	
Sea	19·6	15·8	32·5	53·5	70·1	70·5	75·1	79·8	83·1	84·2	
River	9·6	11·8	18·4	25·0	29·2	30·3	33·5	35·2	33·7	33·9	
Pipeline	7·9	15·3	129·9	225·7	301·3	324·0	339·9	352·5	388·5	421·4	457·0

Turnover of oil and oil products transported by rail in billions of ton kilometres.
Source: Ek. gaz.; Elliot, p. 111.

Table 3.5

Construction and throughput of oil and products pipelines 1960–75

Year	Length at end of year (000 km.)	Throughput of oil and products (million tons)	Turnover (billion ton – kilometres)
1960	17·3	129·9	51·2
1961	20·5	144·0	60·0
1962	21·7	165·1	74·5
1963	23·9	185·5	90·9
1964	26·9	213·0	112·1
1965	28·2	225·7	146·7
1966	29·5	247·7	165·0
1967	32·4	273·3	183·4
1968	34·1	301·3	215·9
1969	36·9	324·0	244·6
1970	37·4	339·9	281·7
1971	41·0	352·5	328·5
1972	42·9	388·5	375·9
1973	47·2	421·4	439·4
1974	55·5	457·0	533·0
1975 (plan)	60·0		647·0

Sources: Nar. khoz.; Ek. gaz.; Elliot, p. 112.

The 1980 position

Academician Melnikov, writing in the late 1960s indicated a figure of 607m tons crude production in 1980.[19] Since that time, a Soviet deputy oil minister, amongst others, has indicated that the figure may well be nearer 650m tons, and at any rate lying within a range of 625–645m tons. As the 1971–75 five-year period came to a close, the average annual increase in oil production was running at about 7 per cent, and the yearly increments at just under 31m tons. If a rate of 7 per cent is applied to the planned crude oil production figure for 1975 of 482m tons, a 1980 figure of 676m tons would be expected. If, however, annual increments were maintained at 31m tons during the next five years, this would give a total of 155m tons additional between now and 1980 and a 1980 production figure 637m tons. Even if average annual increases over the next five years were only 6 per cent, this would still give a 1980 production figure of

54

645m tons. Soviet oil officials have indicated that their annual increases in production will in fact reach 35m tons by the end of the decade, and this could again result in a 1980 production figure of between 650 and 660m tons. The main problem, therefore, is to know whether optimism in Soviet circles is likely to be justified or whether the difficulties which have caused the oil industry to turn in rather a modest performance during 1971–75 will have an increasingly adverse effect over the next five years. A crucial factor in this connection is the success or otherwise which the Soviet Union will have in developing the western Siberian oilfields. When production first started in this area it was planned that output in 1975 should be some 120m tons, and that this would double by 1980. In the event, production in 1975 was some 147m tons and 1980 targets have been successively raised from 230–260m tons, through 280–300m tons, and in one case even to 300–330m tons. Some Western observers have attributed this substantial raising of western Siberian targets to Soviet realization that oil production in the older parts of the country will decline even quicker than has been anticipated, and that additional Siberian production will be necessary to make good the deficits in the main consuming areas west of the Ural Mountains. However, as of 1975, there was no evidence of any catastrophic decline in the major older areas, although there is evidence of a stepped-up effort to extend secondary and tertiary methods of oil recovery in these areas, and for this, Western assistance has been actively sought. It should be emphasized at this point that none of the 1980 crude production plans are in any way connected with large-scale Western assistance and it is perhaps rather significant that in spite of the extremely difficult conditions facing the oil workers in western Siberia, the massive effort which has been invested in getting the oil out does appear to be paying off. Whether or not it will continue to do so during the next five years will depend to a large extent upon the availability of sufficient pipeline of the right diameter, and the ability of the relevant ministries involved to co-ordinate the laying of the pipelines at a fast enough rate.

In the absence of data on 1975 regional production achievements, from which it would have been possible to compare results against plans, it is difficult to see how Soviet crude production in 1980 can be less than 640m tons, and it is not at all improbable that this figure will be substantially exceeded.

The export position

The oil export position is less easy to predict with any accuracy in view of the greater number of uncertainties attached to it as distinct from the gas and coal situation. This will depend upon the amount of oil actually left available for export after all domestic consumption, waste and losses, and imports have been taken into consideration.

Table 3.6 shows the calculation of the relevant statistics for 1970, 1973 and 1974. It can be expected that there will be small improvements in controlling loss and wastage, but the volumes upon which even reduced percentages must be calculated will have increased, and so the net position will probably be little different, relatively, to that already obtaining. What matters is the total 'apparent' consumption.

Table 3.6

The Soviet oil balance 1970, 1973, and 1974
(Million tons)

	1970	1973	1974
Crude oil + condensate production	353·0	429·0	458·8
Total exports:	95·8	118·3	116·2
of which re-exports	3·5	13·2	4·4
Net exports	92·3	105·1	111·8
Retained (used) in the USSR	260·7	323·9	347·0
Imports (products)	1·1	1·5	1·0
Total apparent consumption	261·8	325·4	348·0

Source: Derived from Tables 2.5, 2.9, and 2.10.

The increase in the average annual rate of apparent consumption is some 7·4 per cent, and this would give a 1980 figure of about 536m tons. It is likely, however, that conservation measures and improved efficiencies would bring the average annual increase nearer to 7 per cent, which would give a 1980 usage of 517m tons.

The production of crude oil and condensate in 1980 should be at least 640m tons, leaving a minimum surplus of 123m tons for export. It will be shown in Chapter 8 on the Comecon energy situation that the East European members will use between 120 and 128m tons of oil in 1980 and their own production will be in the region of 19m tons (see Tables 8.25–8.27). It would therefore be possible for the Soviet Union to supply the total Comecon requirements if this became necessary, and still have a surplus of at least 15m tons available for export to other parts of the world.

There have been no indications from Soviet sources of the extent to which the USSR will supply the requirements of the other members of Comecon during the next five years, although East European sources claim that contracts have in fact been signed covering the 'steady increase of Soviet supplies', which would in any case be highly unlikely to be less than the 1975 figure of 57·3m tons of Soviet oil plus some 10m tons of Soviet 're-export' oil mainly for Bulgaria. There is a rumour from Polish sources that Soviet supplies to Comecon will increase by about 3·5 per cent annually over the next five years, and if this rate is applied to the straight Soviet deliveries, this would give a 1980 figure of 68m tons. Deliveries to Bulgaria in total on Soviet account are unlikely to be less than 17m tons, of which only, say, 5m will be included in the above-mentioned 10m, and so the total Soviet commitments to Eastern Europe of Soviet-produced and acquired oil will probably be around 80m tons; the East European countries may therefore have to find about 20m tons for their own account. This line of reasoning would give the Soviet Union about 45m tons available for export to the rest of the world, but it is likely that it will still have to supply around 10m tons to other Comecon members unless, for example, relations between Cuba and its American neighbours, e.g. Venezuela and Mexico, improve to the point where Cuba can obtain supplies from them, although the Soviet Union would probably still have to finance such a supply. This leaves the Soviet Union with not less than 35m tons of its own oil with which to earn hard currency, etc. plus, of course, any additional quantities which it can obtain from Iraq and other Middle Eastern producers. This compares with a 1975 figure of about 55m tons and would represent a significant loss in hard currency earning potential, particularly if world oil prices were to fall. It should be remembered in this connection, however, that exports of natural gas to Western Europe will be increasing rapidly during the next five years and will eventually begin to compensate for the losses on the oil front.

Notes

[1] For a considerably fuller account see I.F. Elliot, *The Soviet energy balance* (1974).

[2] *Vyshka,* 4 Dec. 1970, p. 1; *Neft. khoz.,* June 1968, pp. 1–8.

[3] *Ek. neft. prom.,* 1973, no. 7, pp. 22–4 and no. 10, pp. 6–9.

[4] *Ek. neft. prom.,* Mar. 1968, pp. 16–19; *Izvestiya Sibirskogo otdeleniya* AN SSSR, Jan. 1973, pp. 43–8.

[5] *Gaz. prom.,* Aug. 1967, p. 52.

[6] *Ek. gaz.,* Oct. 1969, pp. 8–9; *Gazovoe delo,* Sept. 1972, pp. 51–3.

[7] R.E. Ebel, *Communist trade in oil and gas* (1970), pp. 105 and 440.

[8] *Tribuni lyudi,* Jan, 1975.

[9] *Ek. neft. prom.,* 1973, no. 10, pp. 6–9.

[10] *Nar. khoz. Kazakhstan,* Oct. 1971.

[11] Appendix D contains data on manpower and equipment of the energy industries.

[12] *Neft. khoz.* 3 (1974); *Sots. ind.,* 6 June 1974; *New Times,* Apr. 1974; *Neftyanik,* Apr. 1973, pp. 5–7 carry information on different aspects of the above problems.

[13] *Ek. gaz.,* 11 (1974).

[14] *Burenie,* June 1975, pp. 5–11; *Ek. neft. prom.* June 1972, pp. 21–7 and 35–40.

[15] *Sots. ind.,* Mar. 1974, p. 2; *Stroitelstvo truboprovodov,* June 1967, pp. 1–3 and Apr. 1973, pp. 13–16.

[16] Bush, in NATO (1974), p. 61; R.N. North, *Soviet Studies,* Oct. 1972.

[17] *Geologiya nefti i gaza,* Nov. 1967, pp. 34–48.

[18] *Stroitelnaya gazeta,* 20 Mar. 1966, p. 2.

[19] *Pravda,* 16 Jan. 1967, p. 2.

4   The natural gas industry

History

The development of the natural gas industry did not really get under way until the 1950s and can be said to have suffered somewhat from being a poor relation and offshoot of the oil industry. Exploration was initially concentrated around large deposits in the west and south-east of the Ukraine but, as with oil, the majority of the significant new deposits which were discovered since 1965 were situated thousands of kilometres away to the east, in the deserts of Central Asia and in the inhospitable and undeveloped regions of Siberia, often in permafrost conditions. More recently, huge deposits have been found in eastern Siberia in Yakutia, where geographical and climatic conditions are even more adverse than in western Siberia, and where there is virtually no infrastructure on which to base their development.

Problems of distance and location similar to those already encountered by the oil industry face the gas industry. 75·5 per cent of the basic resources of natural gas lie in the eastern part of the country, up to 3,000 km away from the major consuming regions of European Russia.

Reserves

Ultimately recoverable reserves of natural gas are estimated to be over 100,000 billion cu. metres, and proven reserves in categories A + B + C1 had reached about 22,000 billion cu. metres in 1974, about one-third of the world's reserves. It was planned to prove up 25,000 billion cu. metres by the end of this decade although this figure seems likely to be exceeded. Only about 2,400 billion cu. metres have so far been produced in the Soviet Union and the proven reserves-to-production ratio for 1974 was approximately 77:1. The size of natural gas reserves in the Soviet Union has encouraged some Soviet planners to forecast an annual production of over 1,500 billion cu. metres by the year 2000. The growth in reserves of natural gas is shown in Table 4.2.

Table 4.1

Production of natural gas 1970, 1974, and 1975, by region
Original and revised plan
(Billion cu. metres)

	1970	1974	1975 Orig. plan	Rev. plan
European USSR and Urals of which				
Ukraine	61·0	58·0	62·0	57·5
Azerbaidzhan	6·0	6·0*	6·0	6·0*
Komi ASSR	7·0	16·7	16·0	17·2
Orenburg	1·0	15·0	26·0	17·4
North Caucasus ⎫ Stravropol ⎬ Volga—Urals ⎭	64·0	55·4*	54·0	54·0*
Sub-total	139·0	151·1	164·0	152·1
East of Urals of which				
Western Siberia	4·0	23·5	44·0	34·5
Central Asia incl.	47·0	81·6	105·8	90·7
Uzbekistan	32·0	37·2	33·7	36·2
Turkmenistan	13·0	39·0	65·1	47·5
Kazakhstan	2·0	5·4	7·0	7·0*
Others	8·0	4·5*	6·2*	7·7*
Sub-total	59·0	109·1	156·0	132·9
GRAND TOTAL	198·0	260·6	320·0	285·0

*Estimated
Note: Some quantities of gas are produced by oil associations and are included in the totals.
Sources: Ek. gaz.; Elliot, p. 51.

Table 4.2

Expansion of natural gas reserves (A + B + C1) 1960–75
(Billion cu. metres)

Year (Jan.)	Reserves	Year (Jan.)	Reserves
1960	2,202·4	1968	7,752·5
1961	2,336·1	1969	9,470·0
1962	2,547·4	1970	12,091·8
1963	2,786·5	1971	15,500·0
1964	3,061·6	1972	18,000·0
1965	3,219·7	1973	19,900·0
1966	3,565·9	1974	22,400·0
1967	4,431·7	1975*	24,400·0

*Five-year plan
Sources: Ek. gaz.; Neftyanik, 1 (1975); Elliot, p. 21.

Table 4.3

Location of natural gas reserves (A + B + C1) by region 1960–74
(Per cent)

	1960	1965	1970	1974
European USSR and Urals including	70·4	55·6	21·8	19·6
North Caucasus	27·8	21·0	5·1	
Transcaucasus	5·2	1·9	0·3	
Ukraine	24·8	18·0	6·0	
Komi	–	0·6	3·3	
Volga–Urals	12·6	14·1	7·1	
East of Urals including	29·6	44·4	78·2	80·5
Western Siberia	2·0	8·9	58·6	62·7
Eastern Siberia	1·0	1·4	3·0	3·1
Kazakhstan	–	1·4	1·5	14·7
Central Asia	26·3	31·3	14·7	
Far East	0·3	1·4	0·4	

Sources: L.M. and M.M. Umanskii, Ekonomika neftyanoi i gazovoi promyshlennosti (1974); Plan. khoz.

Production and performance

Consumption increased at a rate of about 8 per cent during the five-year period 1971–75, while production is likely to have shown an annual growth of about 8·8 per cent over the same period. The sectoral breakdown of consumption is shown in Table 4.4.

In contrast to the oil industry, the gas industry has consistently failed to meet its planned targets over the last decade, and the 1971–75 five-year plan period was no exception (see Tables 2.4 and 2.5). In 1967 the then minister of the industry forecast that by 1975 the level of extraction and production of gas was projected to increase to 400 billion cu. metres, although if the manufacture and deployment of 'ultra-powerful' gas lines was not successful, production in 1975 might only be 360 billion cu. metres. Following the failure of the gas industry to meet its 1966–70 five-year plan targets by over 15 billion cu. metres in the last year, the 1975 final targets were scaled down to lie within the range of 300–320

Table 4.4

Sectoral utilization of natural, associated and artificial gas
1963, 1965, and 1970

	1963		1965		1970 (est.)	
Indicators	Billion cu. metres	%	Billion cu. metres	%	Billion cu. metres	%
Production	89·8	100·0	128·3	100·0	197·9	100·0
Usage						
Everyday/domestic	9·5	10·4	13·2	10·3	20·2	10·3
Industrial, including	53·7	58·9	79·4	59·7	100·4	51·1
Metallurgical	11·2	12·3	21·9	17·0	36·1	18·8
Non-ferrous	–	3·5	2·7	2·7	5·4	2·7
Chemical	4·5	4·9	7·3	5·7	14·3	7·7
Engineering	8·0	8·8	9·3	7·2	12·7	6·9
Building materials	9·8	10·7	10·2	7·9	10·2	5·6
Others	20·2	22·1	28·0	21·9	21·7	11·4
Power stations	24·3	26·6	31·6	24·7	60·5	30·8
Others	3·9	4·3	6·8	5·3	16·8	8·5

Source: N.V. Melnikov, *Mineralnoe toplivo (1971).*

Table 4.5

Natural gas production, planned and actual,
and annual percentage increases 1960–75
(Billion cu. metres)

	Plan		Actual*	Ann. % increase
	Orig.	Rev.		
1960	60·0	53·0	45·3	28·0
1961		60·1	59·0	30·2
1962		70·5	73·5	24·6
1963		91·6	89·8	22·2
1964			108·6	20·9
1965	150·0	129·4	127·9	17·6
1966	142·0	148·0	143·0	12·0
1967	158·3	160·0	157·4	10·1
1968	170·3	171·3	169·1	7·4
1969	191·1	184·0	181·1	7·1
1970	225–240	198·0	197·9	9·3
1971	211·0	211·0	212·4	7·3
1972	229·0		221·4	4·2
1973	250·0	238·0	236·3	6·6
1974	280·0	257·0	260·6	10·6
1975	300–320	285·2		9·2

*This table does not include extraction of gas from coal and shale, which
accounts for a further 1½–2 billion cu. metres per year.
Source: Derived from Tables 2.2, 2.4, and 2.5.

billion cu. metres. However, the original 1973 plan was under-fulfilled by
14 billion cu. metres and the original 1974 plan (280 billion cu. metres)
was itself revised downwards to 257 billion, a target which was in fact
exceeded. The 1975 annual plan was subsequently put at 'over 285 billion
cu. metres', but production was well below the lowest figures of the
original five-year plan range. Cumulatively, the gas industry may have
failed to supply the economy with as much as 60 billion cu. metres during
1971–75.

Criticism of the Soviet gas industry's performance and shortcomings has
never been hard to come by, and in 1965 there was already criticism of
the fact that the reserves-to-production ratio in a number of regions had
fallen well below that considered normal (20:1).[2] One of the most

important reasons for the non-fulfilment of the plans for increment to the gas reserves was stated as being the sharp under-fulfilment of plans for prospecting and exploratory drilling. During the last ten years, however, there has been a marked increase in the rate at which the proven reserves have been added to if the Soviet Union is looked at as a whole, although practically all of the increase has come and, is likely to continue to come, from the remoter areas of Siberia and Central Asia. In 1972, one of the main reasons for the failure of the ministry to meet its production targets for the 1966–70 five-year plan was that planned increments to gas reserves in those regions situated in, or near to the zone of mass consumption of gas, namely the Ukraine, North Caucasus, etc. were not met. Moreover, in the traditional gas-producing regions of Krasnodar, Stavropol, Saratov, and Volgograd, reserves which had been accumulated earlier had to be eaten away; so much so that during 1966–70, the extraction of gas exceeded by 2–5 times the expansion in commercial reserves, and a large number of new deposits were only brought into production after extremely long delays. There were delays in the expansion of pipeline capacity and in the construction of compressor stations and facilities for the processing and treatment of gas before its transportation over increasingly long distances, and by 1970, not only were opportunities for growth in new gas-producing areas not realized, but over-production occurred in the older areas.[3] In fact, the total capacity of compressor stations completed between 1966 and 1970 was only equal to the capacity completed during the previous five years, and the carrying capacity of gas pipelines actually in operation was significantly under-utilized. When, by early 1973, it became clear that the 1971–75 targets for natural gas production were not going to be met, the ministry came in for comprehensive criticism for its failures to meet its plan targets for the transport of marketable gas and for allowing costs to escalate. The basic reason for the under-fulfilment of the production plan was the failure of the construction and installation organizations of the relevant ministry to complete, within the time schedule, a number of facilities for the extraction and transportation of gas. Thus the 1972 plan for the construction and bringing into operation of compressor stations on transmission gas pipelines was fulfilled by only 40 per cent; that for completion of new pipelines was fulfilled by only 80 per cent. The planned throughput of the main pipeline from Central Asia to the 'Centre' was not reached in 1973 due to delays in its construction. Further delays were caused by the delivery of machinery and equipment which was chemically unsuited to handling gas from certain Uzbek deposits which contain hydrogen sulphide.[4] The gas-producing associations, gas field administrations, and pipeline construction administrations were all criticized for not fully utilizing the internal reserves available to them, for not energetically introducing new techniques and for not improving their activities connected with the extraction and transportation of crude oil. The accident rate at many fields and on many major pipelines was described as being still too high, leading not only to the loss of gas but to enforced 'down' periods for basic equipment and machinery. There have been interruptions in the delivery of gas through Central Asia–'Centre', Bukhara–Urals, Ukhta–Torzhok, and several other pipeline systems. The preparation of gas for long-distance transport is also far from satisfactory, and moisture and condensate accumulating on the inner walls of the pipelines cause a reduction in the carrying capacity. Repair and maintenance at compressor stations is below standard and inadequate.[5]

Other criticisms centre upon the designing organizations of the gas industry which delay the issuing of plans and documents, the technical decisions contained therein not always being 'rational'. The better designs are not put into multiple circulation fast enough, and the gas-producing associations and pipeline administrations have not been competently fulfilling the function of contractors in supplying documents and technological equipment for the facilities which are being built.

Towards the end of 1972, major changes were made in the structure of the gas industry (see Appendix C), because it had grown far too big, exceeding the very largest world companies of a similar type. For this reason the Ministry of Construction of Enterprises for the Oil and Gas Industries was formed,[6] and while it is perhaps too early to expect immediate improvements in the performance of the gas production industry since that time, it is clear that all is still not going well. In 1973 the ministry had completed only 5,400 km of transmission gas pipelines as against the plan of 8,500 km. 31 compressor stations went into operation as against a plan figure of 55, and 15 gas treatment units were completed as against a planned 22.[7] In some instances the fault was with the suppliers, who were unable to provide the requested equipment and materials, but at a majority of the construction sites the suppliers delivered on time though completion of the facilities was hampered. One main reason is the shortage of materials, and particularly of equipment needed to carry the pipe to the route of the line. Whereas the welders could weld more than 7 km of pipeline per day, the trucks could only transport about 2·4 km to the construction site. There are considerable shortcomings in the supply of special heavy duty vehicles required for movement of the large-diameter pipelines.

It can be seen that the gas industry is experiencing many of the same problems as those facing the oil industry, and there are, indeed, many common problems such as distance, infrastructure, and the shortage of pipeline. Development of the Soviet gas industry started very much more recently than that of the oil industry, and there are signs that, not only was rather more expected from it than it could reasonably have been hoped to provide in a relatively short time, but also that, in emerging as an offshoot, as it were, of the oil industry, it was competing with the latter for many of the same categories of capital and human resources, without having had the opportunity to develop a material and technical base of its own. Hence, the lowering of sights and under-fulfilment even of diminished production targets in recent years. The gas industry is producing as much as it physically can at present, and the main restrictions on that production are clearly not so much due to the geological availability of gas resources but rather to their geographical distance from the consuming areas and the inability of the infrastructure to bridge that distance at a fast enough rate.

The problem of separating and transporting natural gas liquids has been referred to above (p. 41), and similar difficulties are encountered in the collection of natural gas associated with oil-producing wells. Production of associated gas is around 46 billion cu. metres annually, but in 1974 some 19 billion cu. metres of this had to be flared as a result of inadequate pipeline networks.

Transportation and storage

The long distances over which Soviet gas supplies have to be transported necessitates the installation of large numbers of compressor stations in order to maintain the pressures required for designed throughput volumes. Although machinery and equipment for these compressor stations is manufactured in the Soviet Union, it is not yet available on a sufficient scale; hence it is necessary to import gas-treating plant from the West.

While much of the Soviet Union's gas reserves is of relatively 'sweet' gas, containing almost pure methane or a very high percentage of methane and other hydrocarbons, some major deposits have a high sulphur content, notably the prolific and relatively conveniently situated Orenburg field from which it is planned to make some 15 billion cu. metres annually available to the other East European Comecon countries by the end of the decade with their assistance in constructing pipelines and infrastructure in the USSR (see Appendix E). Serious problems have been encountered in the removal of sulphur from the Orenburg gas, and equipment and technology have had to be imported from Western Europe.[8]

The storage of gas from the eastern parts of the country in underground reservoirs in the European part is being actively developed, particularly in the regions around Moscow; twenty-five underground storage facilities are now in existence.[9]

The authorities realized that enormous pipeline distribution systems would have to be set up and it was planned that pipes of 2·5 metres in diameter, capable of moving between 80 and 100 billion cu. metres of gas per year, would be used. But it has not so far proved possible to produce and deploy such pipelines; indeed, the largest pipelines currently in use are only 1·42 metres in diameter. The main constraint upon production is therefore recognized as the inadequacy of the distribution system, and although huge fields are now waiting in Siberia and Central Asia to begin production, the failure to construct adequate pipelines for transportation means that natural gas has not yet been able to play as large a part in the fuels—energy balance of the Soviet Union as had been planned.[10] Such pipelines as have been constructed in the northern parts of the country,

Table 4.6

Cumulative growth in major gas pipelines 1960—75

Year	Length in 000 km (end of year)	Throughput in bn cu. metres
1960	21·0	32·8
1961	25·3	37·4
1962	28·5	50·8
1963	33·0	69·4
1964	36·9	87·5
1965	41·8	112·1
1966	47·4	119·8
1967	52·6	133·8
1968	56·1	145·8
1969	63·2	166·0
1970	67·5	181·5
1971	72·5	209·8
1972	77·7	219·9
1973	83·5	231·1
1974	90·5	
1975 plan	98·3	

Sources: Ek. gaz.; Nar. khoz.; Elliot.

where some of the severest temperature and wind problems have been encountered, have not always stood up to these conditions and have had to be rebuilt, adding to the delays in bringing the gas to the consumers. At the receiving end of the pipeline there are often insufficient connections and appropriate burners, etc. to enable potential domestic consumers to make use of the gas which does arrive.

The 1980 position

The 1980 position in the gas industry is far harder to assess than the position in the oil industry, given the consistently poor performance over recent five-year plan periods. Developments in 1973–74 indicated that solutions were being found to some of the major difficulties in expanding the rate of production. Significant in this respect was the up-grading of the 1975 production target to 'over 285 billion cu. metres', after it had been revised downwards in 1973 from 300–320 to 280 billion cu. metres. Annual increases in production have gone up from 13 billion cu. metres in 1971 to a planned 27 billion cu. metres in 1975, and the average annual rate of increase is currently running at over 8 per cent, a considerable improvement on the earlier years of the 1971–75 five-year plan. An 8 per cent increase annually over the next five years would produce a 1980 production figure of 419 billion cu. metres, or the same as would be achieved if annual production increases could be held at the 1975 level of 27 billion cu. metres.

It seems extremely likely that gas production in 1980 will not be less than 400 billion cu. metres and it could well lie in the range of 430–440 billion cu. metres. An adequate supply of pipelines is once again seen to be the crucial factor affecting production, although there are other items of equipment, such as compressors and gas treatment units, the supply of which will also be vital, and for which the Soviet government has made it clear there is a substantial demand from Western suppliers.

The export position

The significance of the failures of the gas industry to meet its planned targets for 1975 is harder to assess. Availabilities for export to meet contracted volumes for both Eastern and Western Europe will be assured, but possibilities for stepping up exports to the West and of negotiating new contracts must have been seriously limited. Such deals as have been

68

negotiated or renegotiated have all involved the delivery of pipeline and equipment for use in the domestic gas industry, and there is no doubt that production is being seriously held up by the shortage of the means of transporting, storing, and distributing the gas. Considerable emphasis was laid earlier in the five-year plan period on the need to provide significantly larger volumes of gas for domestic purposes, the demand for which is far from satisfied. It had been planned to substantially increase the amount of gas used in industry in order to reduce coal consumption and improve efficiency and flexibility.

Table 4.7

Trade in natural gas 1971 and 1974
(Billion cu. metres)

| | Imports | |
	1971	1974
Afghanistan	2·5	2·8
Iran	5·6	9·1
Total	8·1	11·9

| | Exports | |
	1971	1974
Austria	1·4	2·1
Bulgaria		0·3
Czechoslovakia	1·6	3·2
Finland		0·4
FRG		2·1
GDR		3·0*
Italy		0·8
Poland	1·5	2·1
Total	4·6	14·0

*Estimated
Source: Vnesh. torg.

Table 4.8

Estimated natural gas exports 1980
(Billion cu. metres)

By country		Pipeline	
Comecon			
Bulgaria	6·3	Transit/Bratstvo	28·0
GDR	5·0	Orenburg	15·5
Hungary	3·8	Finland	1·4
Romania	2·8	Bulgaria	6·8
Czechoslovakia	6·0		
Poland	4·5		
Sub-total	28·4		
Western Europe			
Finland	1·4		
Italy	7·0		
Austria	2·4		
France	4·0		
West Germany	8·5		
Sub-total	23·3		
Total	51·7	Total	51·7

Notes

[1] For a full account see Elliot, pp. 14–18.
[2] *Gaz. prom.,* 8 (1965), pp. 1–3.
[3] *Ek. gaz.,* Feb. 1973, pp. 1–2.
[4] *Gaz. prom.,* Dec. 1972, pp. 5–18.
[5] *Ek. gaz.,* Feb. 1973, pp. 1–2.
[6] *Stroitelstvo truboprovavodov,* 4 (1974).
[7] *Sots. ind.,* 1 Mar. 1974, p. 2.
[8] *Pravda,* 3 and 4 Feb. 1973, p. 2.
[9] BBC, *Summary of World Broadcasts,* pt 1, 31 Aug. 1975.
[10] *Sots. ind.,* 1 Mar. 1974.

5   The coal industry

History[1]

Before the October revolution of 1917, coal production in Russia, mainly from mines in the Donets basin, had risen from about 4·5m tons in 1895 to 34·5m tons in 1916, mainly as a consequence of the expansion of the railway network which almost trebled in size during that period. Immediately after the revolution, production fell sharply as a result of the civil war and the take-over by the State of the country's entire coal industry, 60 per cent of which had been owned by foreign investors, mainly from Western Europe. By the outbreak of World War II production of coal in the Soviet Union had risen to 166m tons, and additional major fields near Kuznetsk, Karaganda, and Moscow had been brought into operation. The Donets coalfields were occupied by the Germans during the early part of the war and total production fell to 75m tons in 1942, but rose again to 150m tons in 1945, and to 510m tons by 1960, when the share of coal in the fuels—energy balance was 52 per cent.

Reserves

Total geological reserves of coal may be as high as 8,700 billion tons, including both hard and brown coals existing to a depth of 5,500 ft. Only about one-twentieth of this — some 470 billion tons — is expected ultimately to be recoverable, and only just over half is likely to be minable given existing or foreseen developments in mining technology. Western sources claim that only 250 billion tons are 'measured', that is to say, actually allocated to groups A + B + C1. Nevertheless, in terms of global resources this means that the Soviet Union probably possesses two-thirds of the calculated world total reserves of coal, and two-thirds of the Soviet reserves are of hard coal. Such measured reserves would allow production at the current level of 684m tons (the largest in the world) for over 360 years. A recent Soviet source states that production in the year 2000 will reach 1 billion tons. Coal is by far the Soviet Union's largest energy resource and accounts for nearly 90 per cent of its total fuel reserves. Unfortunately, coal reserves suitable for open-cast mining are situated in the Asiatic sector of the country, whereas 80 per cent of industry and 75 per cent of the population is in the European sector.

Table 5.1

Hard and brown coal reserves by basin
(Billion tons)

| Basin | Total geological reserves to 1,800 metres | | Balanced reserves to 1,200 metres | Proved to A+B+C1+C2 |
	Hard	Brown	Hard	Brown
Donets	219·1	21·5	53·0	—
Pechora	344·5	—	13·8	0·5
Moscow	—	24·3	—	6·1
Lvov-volynsk	1·7	—	0·7	—
Dnieper	—	4·2	—	2·5
Kizel	1·1	—	0·6	—
Chelyabinsk	—	1·6	—	0·9
South Ural	—	1·8	—	1·3
Karaganda	50·0	1·2	13·6	0·4
Ekibastuz	12·2	—	9·4	—
Maikyuben	—	21·0	—	4·9
Turgai	—	36·5	—	6·7
Kuznets	849·4	55·9	167·2	23·3
Kansk—Achinsk	1·8	1,218·5	1·6	83·4
Minusinsk	36·9	—	2·4	—
Irkutsk	84·7	4·2	19·1	2·8
Tunguska	1,553·2	190·8	3·0	0·9
Lena	1,141·7	1,505·5	1·7	1·7
South Yakut	40·0	—	5·2	—
Transbaikal	1·2	7·2	1·3	5·7
Taimyr	555·4	28·1	0·7	—
Bureya	25·0	—	2·0	—
Suchan	1·4	—	0·4	—
Central Asia	26·6	14·2	2·6	4·3
USSR	5,182·5	3,487·0	311·2	157·4

Source: Elliot, p. 137.

Production

Table 5.2 shows that 60 per cent of current coal production is from the older established regions of European Russia – the Ukraine, notably the Donets Basin – but production here is beginning to decline, and future production increases will depend on the eastern fields and long-haul coal from the Kuznetsk and Ekibastuz deposits. The growth of Soviet coal production since 1960 and annual percentage increases are shown in Table 5.3.

During the 1973–75 five-year plan, Soviet coal production has increased by 75m tons, at a time when no particular attention was apparently being paid to the coal industry in comparison with the other energy industry sectors. The average annual increase has been rising in recent years and is currently about 2·3 per cent. Annual volume increases are between 15m

Table 5.2

Coal production by basin and field 1970, 1974, and 1975
(Million tons)

	1970	1974	1975 (plan)
European USSR and Urals	353·8		
Donets	216·1	219·5	230·3
Pechora	21·5	23·3	
Moscow	36·2	35·0	
Lvov–Volynsk	10·6		
Others	23·2		
Urals	46·2		
East of Urals	270·3		
Kuznetsk	110·5	128·3	132·3
Karaganda	38·4	45·2	44·8
Ekibastuz	22·5		48·3
Eastern Siberia	56·8		
Far East	30·6		
Central Asia	8·3		
Kansk–Achinsk			26·0
Others	3·2		
TOTAL	624·1	684·0	700·0

Sources: Ek. gaz.; Elliot, p. 161.

Table 5.3

Coal production planned and actual, and annual
percentage increases 1960–75
(Million tons)

	Plan		Actual	Ann. % increase
	Orig.	Rev.		
1960	536·3	515·0	509·6	1·0
1961	554·6	511·7	506·4	−1·0
1962	571·5	512·8	517·4	2·2
1963	586·4	522·0	531·7	2·8
1964		554·0	554·0	4·2
1965	612·0		577·7	4·3
1966	598·0		585·6	1·4
1967		591·0	595·2	1·6
1968*			594·2	—
1969	595·0	593·4	607·8	2·3
1970	665–675	618·0	624·1	2·7
1971	620·4	633·0	640·9	2·7
1972	634·0	650·0	655·2	2·2
1973	651·5	665·0	667·6	1·9
1974	670·2	679·0	684·0	2·4
1975	675–685	700·0		2·3

*The 1968 coal plan was not published with other fuel plans, and all indications are that coal output had fallen far behind original targets.
Source: Derived from Tables 2.2, 2.4 and 2.5.

and 17m tons, and Soviet coal industry officials have talked about increasing coal production by 100m tons every five years. If a 2·3 per cent average annual increase was maintained until 1980, production would probably be around 785m tons, but it should be perfectly possible, given the necessary additional emphasis and investment, for a figure of over 800m tons to be reached, particularly if transportation and automation problems can be effectively solved.

Performance

Coal production in the seven-year plan period up to 1965 consistently failed to reach the planned targets (by up to as much as 54m tons in 1962

– see Table 5.3 p. 74), and even the revised 1960 plan was under-fulfilled by 5m tons. However, the revised annual plan for 1967 was over-fulfilled, and although the 1966–70 five-year plan targets proved substantially too high, annual plans were over-fulfilled in 1969 and 1970. Production in the current 1971–75 plan easily exceeded the original and revised five-year plan targets, by 21m tons in both 1971 and 1972, and by 16m tons in 1973. The 1974 plan was exceeded by 14m tons, and the 1975 target range of 685–695m tons was easily surpassed, and, cumulatively, the coal industry probably delivered some 70m tons of coal above plan to the economy by the end of 1975. The annual plan for 1975 was for the production of 700m tons.

The industry's spectacular increases in production during the first three years of the 1971–75 five-year plan period were not quite maintained during the last two years, but there is no question that the original five-year plan target for 1975 was substantially exceeded. The rate of average annual increases in production speeded up since 1972, and this again reflects the significant slowing down of the rate of change of the share of coal in the fuels–energy balance.

Problems facing the industry

Coal's ability to help meet the country's energy demand will depend to a considerable extent upon developments in the field of long-distance transmission of electric power. There are indications that the Soviet coal industry has been revitalized over the past few years and this is beginning to reveal shortages in coal face equipment and skilled personnel.[2] Open-cast mining is developing rapidly, and while it yielded only 24 per cent of production in 1965, it will produce 30 per cent in 1975,[3] and the comparatively low investment required, with the possibility of using powerful machinery, place open-cast coal on a par with oil and gas.

At present, only about half of Soviet coal production is being treated to remove dust and stones, etc. and a lot of the coal being delivered to consumers is of the wrong quality, containing much non-combustible or waste material which is uneconomic to transport. Considerable progress is being made in the manufacture and distribution of coal in the form of briquettes, etc. The prominence which is currently being given to the introduction of new, highly productive, coal-face machinery and fully automated production units indicates that the Soviet coal industry is technologically some way behind that of industrialized countries in the West, and productivity per man–shift in the hard coal mines of European

Russia, which is higher than that of the Siberian coalfields, is only about two-thirds of that in the UK.[4] The development of new coal-producing capacity takes longer per ton of SFE than the development of new oil and gas capacity and this complicates the task of the planners working on the future optimization of the fuels—energy balance. Coal will continue to play a vital role as an under-boiler fuel for many years to come.

As far as the coal industry is concerned, the main obstacles to any rapid development of production have less to do with availability of reserves, and more with the provision of an adequate distribution network and with the equipping of the most productive mines with new high-speed, high-output machinery and with a greater degree of automation. The location of Soviet coal reserves is, once again, the main problem in that something like four-fifths of these reserves, including those most suitable for the development of open-cast mining, are in the more distant and underdeveloped Asiatic regions, while production at the older fields has in many cases reached a plateau or is beginning to decline. Future production increases will therefore depend upon the more easterly situated fields. Unfortunately, the cheapest and most easily accessible of these deposits — at Kansk—Achinsk — is of relatively low calorific content, and tends to ignite spontaneously so that it is impractical to transport over distances in excess of 400 or 500 km. The transport over very long distances — several thousand kilometres — is only possible for hard coals, and the brown coals will have to be used to generate electricity locally, where, however, there is at present virtually no industry to provide a market outlet. The transmission of electricity westward to the industries of the Urals and beyond is clearly a possibility but will depend to a great extent upon successes in overcoming construction difficulties in the long-distance transmission by cable. Failing this, the effective use of the cheap Kansk—Achinsk coal may have to rely upon the development of treatment facilities to turn it into briquettes and semi-coke, although such fuels will be many times more expensive when used in European Russia than they would be when used in the region where they are produced. Indeed, expenditures upon transmission of locally generated electric power would exceed extraction costs by at least five times.

Soviet coal production is generally more labour-intensive than in the West, and its preparation for transportation and specific end uses is relatively unsophisticated. As is the case in the oil and gas industries, other ministries are failing to deliver the right amount of the right equipment in time, and technical specifications are not being met; nor are the requirements for spare parts. It is likely that transportation problems will be the most difficult to solve since they involve decisions relating to the location or relocation of the main coal-consuming industries.

Exports

Unlike oil and gas, coal has not been developed as a major energy export commodity apart from small quantities of high quality coking coal for Japan and Western Europe, but it is considered as a basic energy supplier, particularly for the intended eastwards movement of industry and urban development planned for the next few decades. Some 25m tons of coal annually are exported, mainly to the GDR, Bulgaria, and Czechoslovakia, and this figure could well increase. About 10m tons are imported from Poland, and it would make logistic sense to increase this volume to supply the westernmost parts of the country.

Table 5.4

Exports of hard coal coke 1971 and 1974
(Thousand tons)

	1971	1974
Eastern Europe		
Bulgaria	246	294
Czechoslovakia	75	76
GDR	1,294	1,036
Hungary	628	656
Romania	1,080	1,175
Other socialist countries		
Cuba	54	51
Mongolia	1	1
North Korea	159	106
Yugoslavia		140
OECD		
Austria	—	84
Denmark	10	45
Finland	579	597
Sweden	147	170
Others		
Algeria	26	109
	4·4m tons	4·6m tons

Note: In 1971 794,000 tons and in 1974 674,000 tons were imported from Poland.
Source: Neftyanik, 1 (1975).

Table 5.5

Exports of hard coal and anthracite 1971 and 1974
(Thousand tons)

	1971	1974
Eastern Europe		
Bulgaria	5,981	5,943
Czechoslovakia	2,915	2,749
GDR	3,854	4,119
Hungary	346	322
Poland	1,192	1,134
Romania	406	514
Other socialist countries		
Cuba	78	76
Mongolia	2*	1*
North Korea	500	228
Yugoslavia	1,144	1,418
OECD		
Austria	755	769
Belgium	194	389
Denmark	529	321
Finland	511	500
France	1,420	1,553
Greece	39	32
Italy	1,769	1,640
Japan	2,450	3,234
Netherlands	neg.	9*
Sweden	327	527
West Germany	31	242
Others		
Egypt	499	455
Tunisia	22†	9†
Total	24·9m tons	26·2m tons

*Hard coal only.   †Anthracite only.

Note: In 1971 8,388,000 and in 1974 9,712,000 tons were imported from Poland.

Source: Neftyanik, 1 (1975).

Transportation

Long-distance transportation of coal has to be by rail, and the capacity of the Soviet railway system is already severely stretched; moreover wastage from coal falling out of the railway trucks or being blown away is quite considerable.

Table 5.6

Transportation of coal 1960—73

	1940	1950	1960	1965	1970	1971	1972	1973
Rail (000m ton/ kilometres)								
Hard coal	100·8	168·0	318·9	374·4	426·6	441·0	449·7	460·0
Coke	6·1	10·2	15·0	22·5	23·5	25·9	25·4	26·6
Rail (millions of tons transported)								
Hard coal	145·3	255·0	468·2	552·6	613·9	636·5	652·2	672·3
Coke	7·3	11·1	24·3	30·4	33·3	33·8	33·6	34·1
Ship (millions of tons transported)								
Hard coal (total)	1·8	3·8	7·1	8·2	9·3	8·7	8·4	8·6
Hard coal (coastal)	1·6	2·4	5·7	5·1	4·8			
River, incl. coke	2·2	4·4	11·0	14·4	17·6	18·6	18·8	20·4

Sources: Nar. khoz.; Elliot, p. 173.

Notes

[1] For a full account, see Elliot, pp. 122–32.
[2] Radio Moscow, 16 May 1973.
[3] *Ek. gaz.*, Feb. 1975, pp. 1–2.
[4] Beamish-Crooke, in NATO (1974), p. 1.

6 Electricity, hydro-electric power, and nuclear energy

Electricity production

In 1973, output of electricity rose by 6·8 per cent, attaining 915 billion kWh. However, the gap between the growth of output of electric power and of generating capacity continued to widen. According to the 1971–75 five-year plan, output should have risen at a rate of 7·6 per cent and capacity at a rate of 7·0 per cent; in fact, over the past three years, output rose at an annual rate of 7·2 per cent but capacity at only 5·9 per cent. At the end of 1973, total capacity of electric power stations reached 195·6m kilovolts, of which 160·3 represented atomic and thermal power and 35·3 hydro-electric. Table 6.1 shows electricity production and annual percentage increases 1960–75.

According to the 1971–75 five-year plan directives, the capacity of atomic power stations was due to account for 12 per cent of the planned new power station capacities (some 66,000 MW), representing an increase from 920 MW to some 8,000 MW. Between 1970 and 1972 output of atomic power stations rose by 2·2 times (from 3·5 to 7·7 billion kWh). The 1973 plan provided for an increase of 52 per cent and the 1974 plan envisages a rise of 38 per cent.

During the 1971–75 five-year plan the production of electric power has exceeded the plan's annual targets although by declining amounts. The 1974 planned target of between 975 and 985 billion kWh was fulfilled, but the original planned target of 1,065 billion kWh for 1975 was not reached and the range 1,030–1,070 milliard kWh was only met at the lower end by a small margin since the 1975 annual plan is now 1,035 billion kWh.

Hydro-electric power

In 1965 hydro-electric power production, amounting to 81·4 billion kWh, accounted for 16 per cent of the total electricity output. In 1970 hydro-electric power production had increased to 124·4 billion kWh but its

Table 6.1

Electric power production, planned and actual, and annual percentage increases 1960–75
(Billion kWh)

	Plan Orig.	Rev.	Actual	Ann. % increase
1960	291		292·3	10·0
1961			327·6	12·1
1962		366	369·3	12·7
1963	408	412	412·4	11·7
1964			458·9	11·3
1965	500–520	510	506·7	10·4
1966	561		544·6	7·5
1967		598	587·7	7·9
1968	650		638·7	8·7
1969	687		689·0	7·9
1970		740	740·9	7·5
1971	790		800·4	8·0
1972	850		857·4	7·1
1973	913	915	914·7	6·7
1974	985	975	975·0	6·6
1975	1,035–1,065	1,035		6·2

Source: Derived from Tables 2.2, 2.4, and 2.5.

percentage share of electricity output was still only 16·8 per cent, and its share in total energy production was only 3·6 per cent in 1970. In 1975 it is planned that hydro-electric power should contribute some 165 billion kWh, or just under 16 per cent of planned electricity production for that year. It is estimated that hydro-electric power production could potentially amount to ten times current output. Potential output for the biggest rivers (in billion kWh) is: Yenisei 158; Lena 144; Angara 941; Volga 54; Ob 51; Vitim 50; Nizhnaya Tunguska 41; Kolima 40; Indigirka 40; Narin 36; Amu Darya 36.[1]

The rate of increase of hydro-electric power production is higher than that of energy production in general during the last ten years, and recent comments from Soviet sources indicate that efforts will be made to step it up still further throughout the rest of this decade.

The contribution of hydro-electric power to overall energy production can perhaps best be estimated by considering the quantity of standard fuel needed to produce an equivalent number of kWh if burnt in a conventional thermal power station. This figure has, in fact, been steadily declining during the past fifteen years and whereas every kWh of power produced in 1960 required 468 grammes of standard fuel, it required only 367 grammes in 1970, and by 1975 the figure was planned at 340 grammes.[2]

It is assumed that much of the hydro-electric power production in the Soviet Union is consumed locally, and since future developments are likely to be concentrated in the more northerly and easterly parts of the country, on the Yenisei and Lena rivers and in the Far East, it is likely that hydro-electric power will play an increasing part in the provision of energy for the eastward movement of Soviet industry and urban development aimed at in the longer term.

Nuclear raw materials[3]

The Soviet Union is known to have substantial reserves of uranium ores and production in 1970 was estimated at 8,000 tons.[4] However, little information is available regarding the quality of the ores or about Soviet processing capacity for peaceful purposes.

During the 1960s, in the Soviet Union as in other industrially advanced nations, effort in the field of peaceful uses of nuclear energy was directed towards the creation of different types of reactor and the selection of a few of these for further development. The early part of the 1970s has seen the introduction on a commercial scale of the successful prototypes. Particular attention is being paid to the introduction of nuclear energy in the energy deficit parts of the country, such as the European regions. As a first stage, in these regions and in the Urals and the Caucasus, there will be established a system of large thermal neutron atomic electric power plants. In the second stage, the nuclear plants to be built will be fast neutron reactors. Atomic plants of the first stage, the construction of which will be continued through 1980 to 1985, with a gradual shift to the construction of plants of the second stage, will, in addition to producing electricity, produce plutonium for the second-stage plants. By the year 2000, nuclear power will become part of a unified system of electric power generation, and the authorities intend to ensure that electric power on a large scale is sensitive to changes in competitive prices for natural uranium. The basic energy resources of the USSR up to the year 2000 will be organic fuels, and nuclear electric power will be developed in those regions where the economic effect gained from its utilization can be maximized. Thus in European Russia thermal nuclear reactors will remain economically expedient, and the fast neutron reactors will therefore be progressively integrated into an already existing nuclear power system.

Such rapid expansion of nuclear generating capacities will only be realizable if the nuclear power units themselves are of large capacity, for example 'channel' reactors of 2,000–3,000 kW. Meanwhile, the main problems are those of standardization and unification of construction and engineering solutions. Specific demands presented by materials and equipment, the special character of their operation, servicing, and repair, require the development of specialized machine builders to ensure the reliability and economic viability of nuclear power stations.

Nuclear reactors will also be used for the production of heat, fresh water, and various chemicals. The Shevchenko fast neutron reactor on the Caspian Sea will be used for fresh water production for irrigation and industrial purposes.

For the development of the rational economy of the USSR in the distant future, so much fuel and energy will be needed that a sharp change in the structure of the resource and operational base is unavoidable. The basis of such a change may be atomic energy which, by the year 2000, will become a well developed branch of the fuels—energy and electric power supply of the country.

In October 1973 it was stated that by 1975, nuclear power stations would be producing 25 billion kWh compared with 3·5 billion in 1970.[5] Although the total electricity production was over 1,000 billion kWh in 1975 and the nuclear contribution thus very modest, 'the future lies with nuclear stations'.

At the end of 1973 there were 14 nuclear power plants in operation with a capacity of 2,630 MW and the target for 1975 was for capacity of 6,000–8,000 MW. A further 16 plants are under construction, with a capacity of 7,300 MW, and the construction of 17 more is being planned, with a capacity of 19,000 MW. Most of the existing plants are based on the Soviet pressurized light-water reactor. It is believed that the Russians have been experiencing some difficulty in the development of their fast breeder reactors, and they have recently signed an agreement with West Germany for four of the German type of heavy-water reactor to be constructed in the Baltic region, the first of which will come on stream in the early 1980s.

It does not seem as if nuclear energy will begin to play a significant role in the overall Soviet energy situation until the mid-1980s at the earliest.

Notes

[1] M. Pervukhin, in *Plan. khoz.*, 7 (1974).
[2] *Ek. gaz.*, Jan. 1975, pp. 1–2.
[3] See Albonetti and Nicholson, in NATO (1974).
[4] Scanlan, ibid., p. 92.
[5] *Vyshka,* 26 Oct. 1973.

7 Minor fuels

Coke

Soviet exports of hard coal coke amounting to 2·6m tons in 1960 had almost doubled to 4·2m tons in 1970; most of it went to the East European Comecon countries (see Table 5.5). Exports are not expected to exceed 5m tons annually during the next five years. Some 700,000 tons of hard coal coke were being imported annually during the 1960s, a level which can be expected to continue throughout the current decade.

Oil shale

The only hydrocarbon production in the north-western areas of the Soviet Union, apart from some oil in Kaliningrad, comes from the high grade oil shales of Estonia, where mining has taken place since the nineteenth century. New production capacity has been added recently, raising the volume of shale mined to 25m tons in 1973. Oil produced from these operations amounts to some 3·5m tons per year. Table 7.1 shows the distribution of known oil shale reserves which would be recoverable under present conditions, and Table 7.2 shows production of oil shale from 1960 to the present day. Some two-thirds of shale output is used to produce electric power in thermal stations.[1]

The heat value of Estonian shale is about one-fifth that of crude oil and one-third that of good-quality coal.

Most of Russia's Baltic-area oil-shale output is still used raw as boiler fuel at two big Estonian electric power stations with a combined capacity of 2·9m kW. But the Russians emphasize that more than 40 valuable chemical products and fuels are produced from the shale. Besides pipeline gas, gasoline, kerosene, fuel oil, diesel oil, lubricants and asphalt, products derived from Soviet shale include benzene, toluene, xylene, solvent, butyl alcohol, phenols, acetone, detergents, ammonia, pesticides, herbicides, tanning agents, aniline dyes, flotation agents, plasticizers, polyesters, synthetic fibres, plastics, synthetic rubber, adhesives, paints, varnishes, ion-exchange resins, sulphur, hyposulphite, electrode coke, mineral fertilizers, mineral 'wool', and pharmaceuticals.

Table 7.1

Distribution of known oil shale reserves recoverable
under present conditions

Area	A + B + C1 reserves		C2 reserves
	(Million tons)	%	(Million tons)
RSFSR	2,567·5	39·0	5,130·9
Leningrad Oblast	1,120·1	17·0	1,955·6
Kostroma Oblast	6·1	0·1	36·2
Kuibyshev Oblast	728·7	11·1	1,895·2
Ulyanovsk Oblast	48·2	0·7	112·4
Saratovsk	143·8	2·2	2·2
Orenburg Oblast	376·0	5·7	457·3
Kemerovo Oblast	41·8	0·6	90·0
Irkutsk Oblast	90·5	1·4	—
Bashkir ASSR	10·7	0·2	32·0
Komi ASSR	1·6	neg.	550·0
Estonian SSR	3,931·8	59·8	4,667·4
Kazakh SSR	54·0	0·8	163·7
Kirgiz SSR	21·9	0·3	43·3
Tadzhik SSR	3·9	0·1	26·1
USSR	6,579·1	100·0	10,031·5

Source: Elliot, p. 202.

Table 7.2

Shale production 1960–75
(Million tons)

Year	USSR	Kuibyshev Oblast		Leningrad Oblast	Estonia
1960	14·1	1·4		3·5	9·2
1965	21·3	1·3		4·1	15·8
1966	21·4	1·1		4·2	16·1
1967	21·6	1·2		4·3	16·1
1968	21·9	1·1		4·3	16·4
1969	23·0	1·2		4·3	17·5
1970	24·3		5·4		18·9
1971	26·1		5·3		20·8
1972	29·3		5·5		23·7
1973	31·1		5·8		25·3
1974	33·5*		7·5*		26·0
1975 (plan)	37·0	1·2		5·8	30·0

*Estimated
Source: Elliot, p. 205.

Part of the ash accumulated at electric power stations is used to make cement, to lime acid soils, and to manufacture wall panels.

Output of Estonian shale gas declined slightly from about 20·5 billion cu. ft in 1970 to 20·1 billion in 1973 as increasing quantities of cheaper natural gas were transmitted into the Baltic area from other parts of the USSR.[2]

Peat[3]

Although peat accounts for less than 2 per cent of fuel produced in the USSR, it retains considerable importance as a local fuel and agricultural raw material. Peat-fired power stations, situated mainly in the north-west and the Urals, account for more than 50 per cent of consumption. Agriculture accounts for another 20 per cent, where peat fulfils a variety of functions, not least as a much needed fertilizer. Production of peat briquettes reached 5·3m tons in 1970 and is planned to increase to 15m tons by 1980. Peat production fluctuates widely, but reserves are sufficient to allow a considerable increase in output and the trend seems to be that whilst its share in the fuels balance will continue to fall (eventually to less than 1 per cent), it will continue to be of local importance. Table 7.3 shows peat production by republic 1960–75 and Table 7.4 shows the location of reserves and potential production.

Table 7.3

Output of fuel peat by republic 1960–75
(Thousand tons)

Year	USSR (total)	RSFSR	Ukraine	Belorussia	Lithuania	Latvia	Estonia
1960	53,625	36,816	4,664	8,312	1,554	1,795	467
1965	45,747	29,402	4,343	8,366	1,248	1,649	670
1970	57,500	39,449	4,030	9,232	1,481	2,148	974
1971	54,300	33,700	4,523	11,252	1,492	2,285	1,048
1972	68,900						
1973	82,400						
1974							
1975 plan	97,300						

Source: Elliot, p. 191.

Table 7.4

Location of peat reserves and potential production

Area	No. of peat bases	Exploitable reserves (million tons of air-dried peat, water content of 40%)	Potential ann. output (million tons)
Belorussia	8	1,007·4	33·3
Ukraine	1	67·0	2·2
Lithuania (with Kaliningrad)	2	330·0	2·3
Latvia	1	900·0	7·0
Estonia	1	210·0	7·0
RSFSR	64	25,778·7	713·0
Leningrad	11	2,385·4	79·2
Moscow	6	872·7	29·1
Priorskii	2	59·0	1·9
Upper Volga	8	629·0	20·7
Volga-Vyatskii	6	406·9	13·6
Northwest	10	719·7	23·2
Komi ASSR	4	410·6	13·7
West Urals	2	402·0	13·4
Middle Urals	9	8,705·2	288·5
West Siberia	3	10,740·0	214·8
Far East	3	448·2	14·9
USSR	77	28,293·1	764·8

Source: Elliot, p. 187.

Notes

[1] Elliot, p. 207.
[2] *Oil and Gas Journal,* 6 Oct. 1975.
[3] For a full account see Elliot, pp. 179–96.

8 The European Comecon countries

The energy situation in the Comecon countries of Eastern Europe – Poland, Czechoslovakia, the GDR, Romania, Hungary, and Bulgaria – contrasts markedly with that in the Soviet Union. Although these countries were, as a whole, in energy balance in 1960, they moved into energy deficit in about 1963, and by 1970 were already dependent upon imports for about 11 per cent of their consumption. This percentage rose to about 20 per cent in 1975 and may well exceed 25 per cent by the end of this decade.

No one country, with the exception of Romania, has sufficient hydrocarbon resources to enable it to meet domestic requirements, let alone to make net exports. Only Poland has sufficient coal resources to enable it to make net exports, and none of the countries has adequate supplies of the three major sources of energy – coal, oil, and natural gas – to enable it to create an optimum fuels–energy balance without recourse to imports. Poland is the only country which is a net energy exporter at the present time although its economy is becoming increasingly dependent upon oil and natural gas imports. Romania has recently become a small net importer of energy and is likely to continue in this position.

Energy consumption per capita ranges from about 3·5 tons of standard fuel per annum in Hungary and Romania to about 6·8 tons in Czechoslovakia, with Poland approaching 5 tons. Between 1960 and 1970 energy consumption in these East European countries grew by an average of 4·6 per cent per annum and 1971–75 plans foresaw a similar although perhaps marginally slower growth rate until the end of 1975.

Energy production, however, is increasing at a much slower rate, at around 3·7 per cent, and apart from Poland, where there are good prospects for substantially increased hard coal and natural gas production, no country is likely to be able to improve its production rates significantly.

There are small but unquantified reserves of uranium ores, mainly in the GDR, Romania, and Czechoslovakia. Production of ores in 1970 has been estimated at 600 tons.[1]

Reserves

Commercially recoverable coal reserves in Eastern Europe amount to 4 billion tons of hard coal and 27 billion tons of brown coal (see Table 8.1).

With the exception of Polish coal, proven energy reserves in Eastern Europe are quite insignificant when compared with those of the Soviet Union, and in most cases they are already being exploited at a maximum rate which may have to be reduced by the end of this decade unless substantial new reserves are discovered. Prospects for discovering new reserves are not exciting, although exploration and prospecting has not been proceeding at an optimum rate in recent years because of shortages of manpower and equipment. There are probably some oil reserves in the offshore regions of the Baltic and the Black Sea, but it is not expected that these will make a substantial difference to the general energy situation for the foreseeable future.

Hydrocarbon imports

Imports of hydrocarbons from the Soviet Union have been facilitated by the construction of the Druzhba or 'Comecon' oil pipeline and the Bratstvo gas pipeline, and electricity imports and sharing between Comecon members is made possible by the Mir power grid. The maximum throughput

Table 8.1

Total estimated East European energy reserves

	Hard coal (billion tons)	Brown coal and lignite (billion tons)	Crude oil (billion tons)	Natural gas (billion cu. metres)
Poland	165·0	36·1	0·1	0·1
Czechoslovakia	6·4	9·0	neg.	0·1
GDR	0·2	25·0	neg.	0·4
Romania	0·9	3·9	1·5	0·4
Hungary	0·4	3·2*	0·2	0·1
Bulgaria	0·1	4·2	0·3	neg.
Total	173·0	81·4	2·1	1·1

*Known reserves.

of the Druzhba pipeline of 50m tons per annum was, however, reached in 1975 and, at the time of writing, there has been no firm indication that any increase in capacity is planned. This pipeline feeds the GDR, Poland, Czechoslovakia, and Hungary; Bulgaria has to rely entirely upon tanker deliveries. Agreement has been reached between Czechoslovakia, Hungary, and Yugoslavia for the construction of an oil pipeline from the Adriatic coast of Yugoslavia, near Rijeka the 'Adria' (see Appendix F), which is intended to deliver 5m tons per annum each to Czechoslovakia and Hungary by 1977–78, and Poland and Romania are believed to have expressed interest in receiving additional supplies through extensions to this southern route. The Bratstvo gas pipeline is to be augmented during the 1976–80 five-year period by the construction of another line from the recently discovered Orenburg gas deposit (see Appendix F), 1,000 km to the south-east of Moscow, and supplies of Soviet gas to Bulgaria already come through a separate line.

Up-to-date data on the energy industries of Eastern Europe are extremely hard to come by, particularly concerning consumption and reserves, and much of the following information comes from Soviet material, although Hungarian, Polish, and Romanian sources have from time to time proved valuable. There are even fewer data available on the GDR and Bulgarian energy industries than for the other countries.

Energy accounting techniques and conversion factors used by the East European Comecon countries are similar to those used by the Soviet Union, although in the case of coal different conversion factors are used in each country to arrive at the SFE, since most of the coal produced in Eastern Europe is either brown coal or lignite of rather low calorific value.

The significance of the East European Comecon countries' energy situation to the main theme of this book lies in their substantial dependence for supplies of oil and natural gas on the Soviet Union at a time when many observers are suggesting that there may not be as much surplus Soviet energy available for export in future as there has been over the last ten to fifteen years. Could the Comecon countries reduce their dependence upon Soviet supplies? Could they obtain supplies from other sources? Which countries would be in the most difficult position?

Comecon statistical data

The energy consumption, production, growth rates, and import and export trade of the six European members of Comecon are shown in Tables 8.2–8.6 which emphasize the importance of coal in the fuels–energy

Table 8.2

East European energy production 1960, 1965, and 1970
(Million tons of standard fuel)

	1960				1965				1970			
	Oil	Gas	Coal	Other	Oil	Gas	Coal	Other	Oil	Gas	Coal	Other
Poland	0·3	0·6	83·3	2·0	0·5	1·6	99·0	1·9	0·6	5·4	120·9	2·4
Czechoslovakia	0·1	1·2	48·0	2·2	0·2	0·2	56·9	3·1	0·3	1·3	61·0	3·2
GDR	0·1	–	71·7	–	0·3	0·1	79·8	0·3	0·3	1·4	81·6	0·9
Romania	16·8	12·4	3·4	3·1	18·6	21·0	5·6	3·1	19·6	30·0	10·1	3·8
Hungary	1·7	0·3	12·6	1·3	2·5	1·5	14·2	1·6	2·5	3·9	12·9	2·2
Bulgaria	0·3	–	6·4	1·3	0·3	0·1	9·4	1·4	0·4	0·7	10·4	1·2
Total	19·3	14·5	225·4	9·9	22·4	24·5	264·9	11·4	23·7	42·7	296·9	13·7
	269·1				323·2				377·0			
Ave. ann. increase %	1960–1965 = 3·8%				1965–1970 = 3·1%							

Table 8.3

East European energy production 1970, 1973, and 1974

	Hard coal (million tons)			Brown coal and lignite (million tons)			Oil (million tons)			Natural gas (billion cu. metres)		
	1970	1973	1974	1970	1973	1974	1970	1973	1974	1970	1973	1974
Poland	140·1	156·6	162·0	32·8	39·2	39·8	0·4	0·4	0·4	5·2	5·8	5·7
Czechoslovakia	28·2	27·8	27·9	81·8	81·2	82·2	0·2	0·2	0·2	1·2	1·0	0·7
GDR	1·0	0·8	0·6	260·6	246·2	243·4	0·2	0·2	0·2	1·2	7·0	8·0
Romania	6·4	7·2	7·1	14·1	17·7	19·8	13·4	14·3	14·5	25·0	28·0	30·1
Hungary	4·2	3·4	3·2	23·8	23·4	22·5	1·9	2·0	2·0	3·5	4·8	5·1
Bulgaria	0·4	0·4	0·3	28·9	26·5	24·0	0·3	0·2	0·1	0·5	0·2	0·2
	182·0	197·3	201·1	442·6	435·5	431·7	16·4	17·3	17·4	35·6	47·3	49·8

Table 8.4

East European energy consumption 1960, 1965, and 1970
(Million tons SFE)

	1960								1965				1970							
	Oil	%	Gas	%	Coal	%	Other	%	Oil	Gas	Coal	Other	Oil	%	Gas	%	Coal	%	Other	%
Poland	3·4	4·5	0·8	1·1	69·2	92·0	2·0	2·6	6·6	2·0	82·2	1·9	11·7	10·0	6·5	5·5	98·1	82·6	2·4	2·0
Czecho-slovakia	3·9	7·1	1·2	2·2	47·5	88·0	2·2	2·7	8·3	1·2	58·0	3·1	14·7	18·0	3·0	3·6	62·3	75·5	3·2	2·9
GDR	1·7	2·1	0·1	0·1	79·1	97·7	—	—	5·7	0·1	89·1	0·3	13·3	12·7	1·4	1·3	88·2	85·0	0·9	0·1
Romania	8·3	29·5	12·1	43·0	4·6	16·4	3·1	11·0	10·6	20·4	5·5	3·1	15·6	25·8	29·8	49·3	11·3	18·2	3·8	6·3
Hungary	3·7	18·5	0·5	2·5	14·6	72·6	1·3	6·5	5·9	1·7	17·0	1·6	8·8	31·2	4·1	14·5	14·1	50·0	2·2	4·8
Bulgaria	1·7	18·1	—	—	6·4	68·0	1·3	14·0	5·2	0·1	11·2	1·4	12·0	40·0	0·7	2·4	15·7	53·5	1·2	4·1
Total	22·7	8·4	14·7	5·5	221·4	82·3	9·9	3·7	42·3	25·5	263·0	11·4	76·1	17·7	45·5	10·7	289·7	68·5	13·7	3·2
	268·7								342·2				425·0							

Ave. ann. increase %: 1960–65 = 4·9% 1965–70 = 4·4%

	Totals (MTSFE)		Ave. ann. % growth rates
	1960	1970	1960–70
Poland	75·4	118·7	4·6
Czecho-slovakia	54·8	83·2	4·3
GDR	80·9	103·8	2·5
Romania	28·1	60·5	8·0
Hungary	20·1	29·2	3·5
Bulgaria	9·4	29·6	12·0
	268·7	425·0	

Table 8.5

East European net import (export) of major fuels 1970, 1972—74

	Hard coal and anthracite (million tons)				Brown coal (million tons)				Natural gas (billion cu. metres)				Crude oil and products (million tons)			
	1970	1972	1973	1974	1970	1972	1973	1974	1970	1972	1973	1974	1970	1972	1973	1974
Poland	(27·7)	(31·5)	(34·7)	(38·9)	(4·0)	(4·1)	(5·0)	(5·2)	1·0	1·5	1·7	2·1	8·1	10·3	12·9	12·4
Czechoslovakia	1·6	2·2	1·9	1·4	(1·1)	(1·2)	(1·3)	(1·5)	1·3	1·9	2·3		10·8	13·6	15·4	
GDR	8·2	7·6	7·9	—	—	4·1	5·0	3·9	(neg.)	(neg.)	0·8		10·4	15·4	16·0	
Romania	0·7	0·8	1·4	1·5	(1·1)	(1·2)	(1·3)	(1·4)	(0·2)	(0·2)	(0·2)		(3·1)	(2·1)	(1·7)	
Hungary	2·0	1·7	1·5	—	—	—	—	—	0·2	0·2	0·2		4·1	5·4	6·4	7·7
Bulgaria	5·0	5·8	5·9	—	—	—	—	—	0·2	0·2	0·2	0·2	8·4	10·6	12·0*	

* = approx.

Table 8.6

East European imports of crude oil and products from the Soviet Union as percentage of total crude oil and products imports 1960—74

	1960		1965		1970		1973		1974	
	(m tons)	%	(m tons)	%	(m tons)	%	(m tons)	%	(m tons)	%
Poland	2·1	84	4·7	85	8·6	91	12·3	87	11·9	88
Czechoslovakia	2·7	100	6·4	94	10·5	97	14·3	93	14·8	100
GDR	2·2	85	5·4	95	9·3	89	13·0	81	14·4	91
Romania	—	—	—	—	—	—	—	—	—	—
Hungary	1·4	88	2·5	89	4·8	91	6·3	84	6·7	94
Bulgaria	0·8	80	3·4	92	7·0	92	9·3	77	10·9	92
TOTAL	9·2	88·5	22·4	91·4	40·2	87·8	55·2	79·5	58·7	83·5

balances. The tendency in most of the countries is to reduce the share of solid fuels and to increase the share of oil and natural gas. (In Romania the tendency is the reverse.)

In Tables 8.2—8.24 the sources used are the statistical yearbooks of the individual countries, *Statisticheskii Ezhegodnik Stran-Chlenov* (SEV Yearbook), *Vneshnaya torgovlya,* UN Yearbooks of Coal and Electrical Energy Statistics for Europe.

Poland

Of all the European members of Comecon, Poland is perhaps best placed as regards energy resources (Table 8.1), having proven reserves of hard coal estimated at between 165 and 180 billion tons, and of brown coal estimated at 36 billion tons. Natural gas reserves are put at some 140 billion cu. metres and reserves of oil at about 0·1 billion barrels. Poland is the fourth largest producer of coal in the world, exceeded only by the United States, the Soviet Union, and China, and is currently the second largest exporter of coal after the United States. Approximately one-quarter of Poland's hard currency earnings come from coal exports (see Table 13.3). It is therefore understandable that the percentage of hydrocarbons in the Polish energy consumption balance was only 8·4 per cent in 1965 and about 15 per cent in 1970. However, the basic tendency in the structural changes forecast in the fuels—energy balance is the expected growth in the relative share in liquid fuel from 13·7 per cent in 1975 to 18—19 per cent in 1980, and of natural gas from 9·4 per cent in 1975 to 15·5 per cent in 1980.[2] The basis for fuel and energy developments in Poland will, of course, continue to be coal, since gas and oil production are far too small to satisfy domestic demands and prospects for significant increases in either crude oil or natural gas production are not at all promising. Oil demand is in fact increasing by some 10 per cent whereas oil production seems likely to remain at its current level of about 0·4m tons per annum for the foreseeable future, unless new reserves are discovered in the offshore regions in the Baltic. Natural gas production has been increasing at about 7 per cent over the last few years and it was originally planned to produce about 13 billion cu. metres in 1975, although this target proved unrealistically high. For some years Poland has been importing about 1·5 billion cu. metres of natural gas from the Soviet Union, and a further 2·8 billion will become available on completion of the Orenburg pipeline. Most of this, as with much of Poland's natural gas, will be used for industrial purposes, particularly in the petrochemicals industry and in the manufacture of fertilizers.

Poland is undertaking an extensive programme of exploration for new reserves of hydrocarbons but progress has been hampered by a shortage of equipment and by a history of inadequate geological exploration of the country's resources generally. Under a ten-year technical and scientific agreement signed in April 1974 with Sweden, provision was made for joint oil prospecting and drilling rigs for use in the Baltic area.

The country has been heavily dependent (87 per cent in 1973) upon the Soviet Union for supplies of crude oil and products, even though some of the other Comecon members, e.g. Romania and Czechoslovakia, have been supplying small quantities of products. It was planned to deliver some 12·5m tons of Soviet crude to Poland in 1975, and a long-term agreement covering the 1976—80 period is reported to have been reached which will result in steadily increasing annual deliveries. Poland has also been making arrangements with some of the OPEC producers in the Middle East for additional supplies during the next five years, the terms of some of which were agreed upon before the autumn of 1973 and were based upon barter payments.

Per capita consumption of energy is currently about 4·6 tons of standard fuel per annum, of which 0·6 tons is liquid fuels and it is hoped to raise the total to nearer 10 tons per annum in the not too distant future.

Polish refining capacity was estimated at 9·5m tons in 1972 and the throughput in 1975 was about 14m tons. By 1980 capacity is scheduled to be between 25 and 30m tons, with extension being made to the 10m-ton refinery at Plock and the construction of new refineries at Gdansk (6m tons) and Blachownia (3m tons). Supplies to the Plock refinery come through the Druzhba pipeline from the Soviet Union and supplies for Gdansk will come via tanker, partly from the Middle East and partly from the Soviet Union. Supplies for the Blachownia refinery might one day come through an extension of the planned Adriatic pipeline, although plans for this have not yet been formulated. It is possible that the envisaged increase in oil consumption will be somewhat delayed in view of increased prices, a development which has already led to the introduction of measures to economise on oil usage and to limit its substitution for coal to those areas where coal is demonstrably less effective.

There are no commercial reserves of peat in Poland but it possesses significant hydro-electric power potential. Nuclear energy is not expected to contribute to the overall energy supply position until well into the 1980s. Poland exported some 1·8 billion kWh of electricity, net, in 1973 to Czechoslovakia, the GDR, Romania, Hungary, Austria, and Switzerland. It may export to West Germany and West Berlin if transit arrangements with the GDR can be negotiated and an uninterrupted supply to the customer guaranteed. Small quantities of electricity are imported from the USSR. A country-wide grid is in an advanced stage of development.

The following tables show energy production and consumption and the import and export trade in major fuels.

Table 8.7

Poland: production of major fuels 1960—75

	Oil (million tons)	Natural and associated gas (billion cu. metres)	Hard coal (million tons)	Brown coal (million tons)	Electricity (billion kWh)
1960	0·2	0·5	104·4	9·3	29·3
1965	0·3	1·4	118·8	22·6	43·8
1970	0·4	5·2	140·1	32·8	64·5
1971	0·4	5·4	145·5	34·5	69·9
1972	0·3	5·8	150·7	38·2	76·5
1973	0·4	6·0	156·6	39·2	84·3
1974	0·4	5·7	162·0	39·8	91·6
1975 (plan)	0·4	11·0	170·0	36·0	96·0

Table 8.8

Poland: apparent consumption of major fuels 1960—74

	Oil (million tons)	Natural gas (billion cu. metres)	Hard coal (million tons)	Brown coal (million tons)	Electricity (billion kWh)
1960	2·5	0·7	87·7	3·8	29·6
1965	4·7	1·8	99·0	17·4	43·3
1970	8·5	6·2	112·4	28·8	64·4
1971	9·4	6·9	116·5	30·9	69·8
1972	10·6	7·3	119·2	34·1	76·3
1973	13·3	7·7	121·9	34·2	82·5
1974	12·8	7·8	123·1	34·6	88·8

Table 8.9

Poland: net import (export) of major fuels 1960—74

	Oil, products and synthetics (million tons)	Gas, natural and associated (billion cu. metres)	Hard coal (million tons)	Brown coal (million tons)	Electricity (billion kWh)
1960	2·3	0·2	(16·7)	(5·5)	0·3
1965	4·4	0·4	(19·8)	(5·2)	(0·5)
1970	8·1	1·0	(27·7)	(4·0)	(neg.)
1971	9·0	1·5	(29·0)	(3·6)	(0·1)
1972	10·3	1·5	(31·5)	(4·1)	(0·2)
1973	12·9	1·7	(34·7)	(5·0)	(1·8)
1974	12·4	2·1	(38·9)	(5·2)	(2·8)

Czechoslovakia

Czechoslovakia is a land-locked country, and although it has hard coal reserves estimated at some 6 billion tons and reserves of brown coal of approximately 9 billion tons, it is deficient in hydrocarbon reserves, which may amount to no more than 1,000 billion cu. metres of gas and insignificant quantities of crude oil (Table 8.1).

Energy demand increased by an average annual rate of 3·7 per cent between 1966 and 1970 and this rate will probably have been maintained throughout the 1971—75 five-year plan period. Domestic energy production is quite unable to satisfy the increase in demand and imports of energy accounted for some 20 per cent of total demand in 1971, a share which is expected to rise to over 40 per cent in 1980.

Crude oil production is running at about 0·2m tons per annum and is unlikely to exceed 0·4m tons by 1980. Consumption, on the other hand, is rising rapidly. It was only 2·7m tons in 1960 but rose to 11·0m tons in 1970, and the 1975 figure was likely to have been about 16·5m tons. Imports of oil come almost entirely from the Soviet Union (14m tons in 1974) through the Druzhba pipeline, but its capacity will be inadequate to meet a 1980 expected requirement of some 25m tons, and this is why Czechoslovakia has agreed to participate in the construction of the Adria pipeline (see Appendix E) through which it will expect to receive supplies, starting in 1977—78, which will rise, ultimately, to 5m tons per annum.

Natural gas production has been steady at about 1·2 billion cu. metres per annum; although there has been talk of increasing production to twice that level by the end of the decade, the bulk of requirements will have to be met by imports from the Soviet Union, which amounted to 1·4 billion cu. metres in 1970, and was expected to reach about 2·6 billion cu. metres in 1975. It is planned to more than double imports by 1980, 2·5 billion cu. metres of which will be coming via the newly planned Orenburg pipeline.

Domestic hard coal production seems to have levelled out at about 28m tons per annum and it is not expected that this total will be surpassed. Imports of hard coal from Poland are running at about 1·5m tons per year. Brown coal production, on the other hand, has steadily increased from 58m tons in 1960 to 81m tons in 1970 and, possibly, 85m tons in 1975, but it is not expected that there will be any substantial increase during the next five years.

Czechoslovakia has significant reserves of uranium ore although no data are available on the exact volumes, and the total production is transferred to the Soviet Union for processing into industrially usable forms. The Soviet Union is co-operating with Czechoslovakia on the provision of equipment for two atomic powers plants, each of 440 MW capacity, and the first of these should be completed by 1977. There should be four units of a similar capacity in operation by 1980, when 8 per cent of total electricity generation is optimistically expected to come from nuclear energy. A further ten nuclear power stations should be brought into production by 1990.[3]

Oil refinery capacity in Czechoslovakia is estimated at 17m tons at the present time, the major refineries being Slovnaft at Bratislava, with a throughput of some 8·5m tons, Zaluzi, with a throughput at Most of 5·0m, and Kralupi, with a capacity of 3·5m tons which came on stream in 1974. Capacity is expected to grow to nearer 25m tons by 1980 and this should reduce the need for product imports currently running at about 1·5m tons per annum, although these may continue for logistic reasons in the same way that Czechoslovakia's own exports of about ½m tons per annum may continue. Synthetic oil is manufactured at the Most plant which was built during World War II.

Energy production and consumption and the import—export trade are shown in Tables 8.10—8.12.

The GDR

Apart from some 25 billion tons proven reserves of brown coal and lignite, and some 4,000 billion cu. metres of natural gas, the GDR is not well

100

Table 8.10
Czechoslovakia: production of major fuels 1960–75

	Oil (million tons)	Gas, natural and associated (billion cu. metres)	Hard coal (million tons)	Brown coal and lignite (million tons)	Electricity (billion kWh)
1960	0·1	1·4	26·4	59·5	24·5
1965	0·2	1·0	27·8	73·2	34·2
1970	0·2	1·2	28·2	81·8	45·2
1971	0·2	1·2	28·8	84·8	47·2
1972	0·2	1·2	27·9	85·6	51·4
1973	0·2	1·1	27·8	81·8	53·5
1974	0·2	0·7	27·9	82·2	56·0
1975 (plan)			26·4	84·6	60·0

Table 8.11
Czechoslovakia: apparent consumption of major fuels 1960–74

	Oil, products and synthetics (million tons)	Gas, natural and associated (billion cu. metres)	Hard coal (million tons)	Brown coal and lignite (million tons)	Electricity (billion kWh)
1960	2·8	1·4	26·6	58·1	24·2
1965	7·0	1·0	29·8	72·2	34·9
1970	11·0	2·5	29·8	80·7	48·6
1971	12·8	2·6	30·8	83·6	51·7
1972	13·8	3·1	30·1	84·4	55·0
1973	15·6	3·4	29·7	80·5	57·8
1974			29·3	80·7	60·5

Table 8.12
Czechoslovakia: net import (export) of major fuels 1960–74

	Oil, products and synthetics (million tons)	Gas, natural and associated (billion cu. metres)	Hard coal (million tons)	Brown coal and lignite (million tons)	Electricity (billion kWh)
1960	2·7	(neg.)	0·2	(1·4)	(0·3)
1965	6·8	(neg.)	2·0	(1·0)	0·7
1970	10·8	1·3	1·6	(1·1)	3·4
1971	12·6	1·4	2·0	(1·2)	4·5
1972	13·6	1·9	2·2	(1·2)	3·6
1973	15·4	2·3	1·9	(1·3)	4·3
1974			1·4	(1·5)	4·5

supplied with energy reserves, those of crude oil being negligible and those of hard coal put at not more than 0·2 billion tons (Table 8.1).

Energy demand grew by 4·1 per cent per annum between 1966 and 1970 and is currently running at about 3·8 per cent per annum. Energy production, on the other hand, has only been increasing by about 2·4 per cent in recent years and has in any case been insufficient to meet domestic requirements. Crude oil production has been running at 0·3m tons per annum and is likely to continue at this level for the foreseeable future. But demand for crude oil has risen from 4m tons in 1965 to about 15m tons in the early 1970s, 80 per cent of which is supplied by the Soviet Union down the Druzhba pipeline. In recent years, however, increasing quantities have been coming from Middle Eastern producers, chiefly Iraq.

Following the discovery of substantial reserves of natural gas near Magdeburg in the mid-1960s, production has risen from 0·1 billion cu. metres in 1965 to 8 billion cu. metres in 1974, and a production of between 11 and 14 billion cu. metres is considered achievable in the near future. Nevertheless, Magdeburg gas is of relatively low calorific value, and is mixed with town gas. Imports of approximately 5 billion cu. metres annually from the Soviet Union are contemplated until the end of the decade.

Production of hard coal at 0·6m tons per annum is insufficient to meet domestic requirements and the GDR imports 7m or 8m tons annually from Poland and the Soviet Union. Brown coal production rose steadily to a peak of 261m tons in 1970 and was then allowed to decline until the energy crisis in autumn 1973 caused plans to be revised; planned production in 1975 has returned to approximately the 1970 levels. The mining of coal will now be maintained at at least the current level during the rest of this decade, although this will present problems, since the most accessible but older open-cast pits are becoming exhausted, and the overburdens encountered in the newer fields are increasing in thickness. Considerable investment will be entailed in the working of the newer pits, and in some cases this will mean the destruction of roads, railways, and, indeed, whole villages. 80 per cent of the country's electric power is produced from lignite and the major part of the increase in electric power generation planned for the future is to come from thermal power stations. By the end of this decade it is anticipated that coal will supply some 60 per cent of energy requirements and crude oil and natural gas 36 per cent. Nuclear power will contribute increasing (though small) quantities during the next five years, the first nuclear station (150 MW) having entered into operation in 1966.

Refinery capacity in 1975 is estimated at 18m tons, based on two refineries: at Schwedt, connected both to the Druzhba pipeline and to the port of Rostock, and at Leipzig. Consumption of oil in 1980 is estimated at 22m tons, and there will have to be expansion of refining capacity.

An unknown quantity of synthetic oil is manufactured at the Leunawerke plant from brown coal and is believed to be exported to the German Federal Republic.

Tables 8.13–8.15 show production, consumption, and net energy trade.

Table 8.13

GDR: production of major fuels 1960–75

	Oil (million tons)	Gas, natural and associated (billion cu. metres)	Hard coal including anthracite (million tons)	Brown coal including lignite (million tons)	Electricity (billion kWh)
1960	0·1	–	2·7	225·5	40·3
1965	0·2	0·1	2·2	250·8	53·6
1970	0·2	1·2	1·0	260·6	67·7
1971	0·2	2·8	0·9	262·8	69·4
1972	0·3	5·0	0·8	248·5	72·8
1973	0·2	7·0	0·8	246·2	76·9
1974	0·2	8·0	0·6	248·6	80·3

Table 8.14

GDR: apparent consumption of major fuels 1960–74

	Oil, products and synthetics (million tons)	Gas, natural and associated (billion cu. metres)	Hard coal including anthracite (million tons)	Brown coal including lignite (million tons)	Electricity (billion kWh)
1960	2·7	0·1	10·8	231·0	39·9
1965	5·9	0·1	11·7	256·0	53·7
1970	10·6	1·2	9·2	260·6	68·1
1971	11·3	2·9	8·9	262·8	69·9
1972	15·6	5·0	8·4	252·6	73·8
1973	16·2	7·8	8·7	251·2	78·2
1974			7·8	253·1	81·5

Table 8.15

GDR: net import (export) of major fuels 1960–74

	Oil, products and synthetics (million tons)	Gas, natural and associated (billion cu. metres)	Hard coal including anthracite (million tons)	Brown coal including lignite (million tons)	Electricity (billion kWh)
1960	2·6	0·1	8·1	5·5	(0·4)
1965	5·7	neg.	9·5	5·2	0·1
1970	10·4	neg.	8·2	–	0·4
1971	11·1	0·1	8·0	–	0·5
1972	15·4	(neg.)	7·6	4·1	1·0
1973	16·0	0·8	7·9	5·0	1·3
1974			7·2	5·2	1·2

Romania

In contrast to the other European Comecon members, Romania has relatively strong reserves of hydrocarbons, estimated at 1·5 billion tons of crude oil and 4,000 billion cu. metres of natural gas, but rather weak reserves of coal – those for hard coal being estimated at 0·9 billion tons and those for brown coal and lignite at 3·9 billion tons (Table 8.1).

The demand for energy increased at an average annual rate of 6·3 per cent between 1966 and 1970, and the rate for the 1971–75 five-year period is somewhat lower at 5·5 per cent. Energy production only increased by 4·3 per cent between 1966 and 1970 and is currently increasing at an even slower rate.

Romania's energy industry has been based mainly upon hydrocarbons, which provided 75·5 per cent of total fuel consumption in 1970. However, it is planned to raise the share of solid fuels from only 18·7 per cent in 1970 to nearer 24–25 per cent in 1980, and to increase the share of hydro-electric power and nuclear energy from a 1970 level of 1·5–8·5 per cent in 1980.

Romania's reserves of oil are sufficient to allow production at the current rate of 14·5–15·5m tons per annum to be maintained for the next decade or so, but unless substantial new discoveries are made, a decline in production can be expected thereafter. Throughout the 1960s, domestic requirements for oil were significantly below domestic production, allowing for substantial net exports of oil products, and it is only in recent years that domestic demand coupled with export requirements has exceeded domestic supply. This has been brought about not only because of the growth in demand for internal consumption but also by the maintenance of the export of oil products, currently running at about 5·5m tons. The result is that Romania has now to import some 5—6m tons of crude oil, which comes entirely from non-Comecon sources such as Iran and Libya, in order to maintain both product exports, which earn much-needed hard currency, and maximum throughput for the refineries, which now have a combined capacity of over 20m tons per annum.

Natural gas production has also been sufficient to meet domestic demand during the last ten to fifteen years and to allow for a small (0·2 billion cu. metres per annum) export to Hungary from the Transylvanian fields. Gas production has risen from about 10m cu. metres in 1960 to 25m cu. metres in 1970, but there are now considerable doubts about whether production can be significantly raised above this level; planned production for 1975 was only 26·8m cu. metres at the outside.

Over recent years Romania has been stressing the production of oil and gas, although their reserve positions are relatively weak in the total energy picture. In 1970, for example, natural gas accounted for just over half of the total output of primary energy but its reserve position was just over one-quarter of total potential. Petroleum production contributed some 33 per cent of primary fuels output but oil only accounted for one-tenth of fuel reserves. In contrast, coal accounted for more than three-fifths of reserves but contributed only 15 per cent of fuels output at that time. The global energy situation has caused the Romanian planners to re-think the energy situation and it is clear that the country will be unlikely to return to a position of energy surplus or balance. A considerable effort will be expended on stepping up geological research and in employing improved drilling technology which will allow an increase of deeper drilling at depths beyond 3,000 metres. Romania will step up off-shore exploration in the Black Sea, if possible with foreign partners, and will also be pre-pared to take part with foreign enterprises in the search for and develop-ment of oil resources in other parts of the world.[4] New techniques for the secondary recovery of oil are to be increasingly utilized at fields which are currently in production.

The use of gas in the chemical industry will be increased, and while proved reserves are probably sufficient to allow production at the current level to continue for several decades, it will be necessary to discover new deposits and to enhance production from existing fields by secondary recovery means.

Apparent reserves of coal might cover domestic needs for up to 200 years, and coal will now acquire greater significance in the Romanian economy. Production is currently running well behind plan and a substantial boost in output is scheduled for the 1976–80 period. Measures are envisaged to raise electric energy output through the use of coal and hydro-electric power potential and also through the use of other energy sources such as nuclear power, bituminous shales, etc. (The share of hydro and thermal power plants working on coal is to increase from 46·5 per cent in 1975 to at least 60·7 per cent by 1980, whereas the share of hydrocarbons used for electricity generation will go down from 50·3 to 34·9 per cent during the same period.) Romania possesses significant reserves of shale oil near Banat and shale is expected to fuel its first thermal station by 1978. In future, requirements of electric power are to be met to an even greater extent by nuclear resources, a fact which calls at present for speeding up implementation of the programme for the design and manufacture of equipment and the construction of nuclear electric power plant. The first nuclear plant, which will be a 440 MW Soviet model, will come into operation between now and 1980; and after 1980 all plants will be over 1,000 MW units. Romania apparently has reserves of uranium ores and intends to expand uranium mining and to process its own nuclear fuels. [5]

Romanian planners say that only one-fifth of hydro-electric power potential is now being utilized; it could provide some 11 per cent of the country's primary energy requirements by 1980 through a network of plants which could be constructed on the Danube and on other rivers. The concentrated switching of thermal power stations from natural gas and oil to solid fuels will require substantial investment and will involve some disruption of the electricity supply, and this is already reflected in a scaling down of the projected electricity production plans in 1974 and 1975.

Romania has introduced some of the strictest measures for conserving hydrocarbons, [6] particularly oil and oil products, and these have already brought about a saving of 1·5m tons in 1974. There will be a reorientation of industrial planning to give priority to those sectors which are low power consumers, while the growth of sectors which are big energy consumers will be limited. Priority will also be given to the domestic manufacture of machinery and equipment required by the coal mining and electric power industries.

Tables 8.16–8.18 show energy consumption and production and details of imports and exports.

Hungary

Although limited supplies of oil can reach Hungary by barge up the Danube, it is to all intents and purposes a land-locked country and dependent upon

Table 8.16

Romania: production of major fuels 1960–75

	Oil (million tons)	Gas, natural and associated (billion cu. metres)	Hard coal including anthracite (million tons)	Brown coal including lignite (million tons)	Electricity (billion kWh)
1960	11·5	10·3	4·5	3·7	7·7
1965	12·6	17·5	4·6	5·6	17·2
1970	13·4	25·0	6·4	14·1	35·1
1971	13·8	26·7	6·8	13·8	39·5
1972	14·1	27·7	6·6	16·5	43·3
1973	14·3	29·2	7·2	17·7	46·8
1974	14·5	30·1	26·9		49·3
1975 (plan)	14·6	26·8	29·8		56·5

Table 8.17

Romania: apparent consumption of major fuels 1960–73

	Oil, products and synthetics (million tons)	Natural gas (billion cu. metres)	Hard coal including anthracite (million tons)	Brown coal including lignite (million tons)	Electricity (billion kWh)
1960	5·5	10·1	4·9	3·7	7·7
1965	6·8	17·3	5·1	5·6	16·6
1970	10·4	24·8	7·1	14·1	32·8
1971	11·4	26·5	7·5	13·8	36·3
1972	11·9	27·5	7·4	16·5	39·7
1973	13·6	29·0	8·6	17·7	43·2

Table 8.18

Romania: net import (export) of major fuels 1960–73

	Oil, products and synthetics (million tons)	Natural gas (billion cu. metres)	Hard coal including anthracite (million tons)	Brown coal including lignite (million tons)	Electricity (billion kWh)
1960	(6·0)	(0·2)	0·4	—	(0·03)
1965	(5·8)	(0·2)	0·7	—	(0·6)
1970	(3·0)	(0·2)	0·7	—	(2·3)
1971	(2·4)	(0·2)	0·7	—	(3·2)
1972	(2·2)	(0·2)	0·8	—	(3·6)
1973	(0·7)	(0·2)	1·4	—	(3·6)

pipeline and rail supplies. Of all the European Comecon countries it is perhaps worst off in terms of indigenous reserves of energy, even though it occupies second place to Romania as an oil-producing country, with an annual output of about 2m tons. Proven reserves of energy are estimated at about 0·4 billion tons of hard coal, 3·2 billion tons of brown coal, 0·2 billion barrels of oil and 1,000 billion cu. metres of natural gas (Table 8.1). Whereas oil production will probably be held at its current level until the end of the decade, after which it will decline, natural gas production is increasing by some 6 or 7 per cent annually and has not yet reached optimum production rate. Coal production, which ranges between 26m and 27m tons annually, is likely to remain at this level during the next few years, but is scheduled to reach 40m tons per annum by 1985. Power stations now utilize some two-thirds of the country's coal output while industrial uses, transportation, and domestic consumption are declining.

Total oil refinery capacity in 1975 was 9·5m tons and is planned to increase to over 13m tons in 1980.

In 1950 some 11 per cent of Hungary's energy demand was met by imports, and by 1960 the share was 26 per cent. In 1970 imports accounted for 37 per cent and it was planned that their share would have risen to 50 per cent by 1980, although in 1974 44 per cent of demand was already coming from imports.

Over 80 per cent of Hungary's oil imports come from the Soviet Union via the Druzhba pipeline, with small quantities from Iraq and other OPEC countries. Agreements have been reached with the Soviet Union for the import of increasing quantities of crude oil during the 1976—80 five-year plan period and some 10m tons will probably be flowing down the second string of the Druzhba pipeline to Hungary by 1980. Some imports will, however, also be necessary via the Adria pipeline (see Appendix E), and Hungary will probably ultimately receive about 5m tons per annum by this route.

Domestic natural gas production of 5·3 billion cu. metres is now supplemented by imports of 0·2 billion cu. metres from Romania and, beginning in 1975, by some 1 billion cu. metres from the Soviet Union via the Bratstvo pipeline. Hungary imports some 1·5m tons of coal, 1·2m tons of coke and about 0·5m tons of coal briquettes annually and about 1m tons of oil products. Nuclear energy will not contribute to the overall domestic supply position until after 1980, when the first nuclear power plant will be brought into operation.

New thermal power stations are to be constructed to meet constantly growing electric energy requirements. The operation of coal-based thermal power stations is to be concentrated near well mechanized, highly productive, and mainly open-cast mines. A 2,000 MW energy combine is to be built to use fuel from the open-cast lignite mine near Buekkabrany. Construction and extension of two thermal power stations using waste distillate from oil refineries will help to cover demand for electricity over the next five years. A 750 kilovolts long-distance power line is to be built within the Comecon Mir power grid which will increase electricity imports from the Soviet Union to almost double their current level of 750 MW.

Preparatory work for the first Hungarian nuclear power stations has started at Paks in southern Hungary. The first phase of construction will comprise two reactor sets of 440 MW capacity which will start operation in 1980 and 1981. The final capacity of the station is planned to be over 4,000 MW.

The share of coal as an energy source in Hungary is expected to drop from 34 to 26 per cent between 1965 and 1980, and the share of crude oil to rise from 39 to 41 per cent and of natural gas from 20 to 25 per cent. Other energy sources will continue to contribute between 7 and 8 per cent, and latest estimates indicate that energy imports will in fact rise from their current level of 48 to 57 per cent in 1980. The consumption of energy in Hungary is expected to increase by between 3·5 and 4·0 per cent annually through to 1980, although consumption of electricity is increasing by 7·8 per cent. Production, consumption, and imports and exports are shown in Tables 8.19—8.21.

Table 8.19

Hungary: production of major fuels 1960—75

	Oil (million tons)	Natural gas (billion cu. metres)	Hard coal (million tons)	Brown coal and lignite (million tons)	Electricity (billion kWh)
1960	1·2	0·3	2·8	23·7	7·6
1965	1·8	1·1	4·4	27·0	11·2
1970	1·9	3·5	4·2	23·8	14·5
1971	2·0	3·7	3·9	23·5	15·0
1972	2·0	4·1	3·7	22·2	16·3
1973	2·0	4·8	3·4	23·4	17·6
1974	2·0	5·1	3·2	22·5	18·9
1975 (plan)	2·0	5·6	26·6		

Table 8.20

Hungary: apparent consumption of major fuels 1960—74

	Oil, products and synthetics (million tons)	Natural gas (billion cu. metres)	Hard coal (million tons)	Brown coal and lignite (million tons)	Electricity (billion kWh)
1960	2·1	0·5	4·2	23·6	8·1
1965	3·4	1·3	7·1	26·9	12·5
1970	6·0	3·7	6·2	23·7	17·8
1971	7·0	3·9	5·8	23·4	19·3
1972	7·4	4·3	5·4	22·1	20·7
1973	8·4	5·0	4·9	23·3	22·3
1974	9·7	5·4	4·7	22·4	23·4

Table 8.21

Hungary: net import (export) of major fuels 1960—74

	Oil, products and synthetics (million tons)	Natural gas (billion cu. metres)	Hard coal (million tons)	Brown coal and lignite (million tons)	Electricity (billion kWh)
1960	0·9	0·2	1·4	(0·1)	0·5
1965	1·6	0·2	2·7	(0·1)	1·3
1970	4·1	0·2	2·0	(0·1)	3·3
1971	5·0	0·2	1·9	(0·1)	4·3
1972	5·4	0·2	1·7	(0·1)	4·4
1973	6·4	0·2	1·5	(0·1)	4·7
1974	7·7	0·2	1·5	(0·1)	4·5

Bulgaria

Bulgaria is particularly poorly provided with energy resources, its reserves being estimated at 0·1 billion tons of hard coal, 4·2 billion tons of brown coal, 0·3 billion barrels of oil, and negligible quantities of natural gas (Table 8.1). As a result, imports of energy accounted for over 60 per cent of consumption in 1970, and by 1980 this share could be as high as 75 per cent.[7] Over 90 per cent of oil supplies come directly from the Soviet

Union or on Soviet account from the Middle East OPEC countries, but Bulgaria does import small quantities on its own account, mainly from Iraq.

Crude oil production did reach 0·5m tons in 1967 but is now running at about 0·2m tons and it is unlikely that more than 0·5m tons will be produced by 1980, unless substantial new deposits are discovered.

Natural gas production started in 1965 but reached a plateau of 0·5 billion cu. metres annually in 1968, a level which has fallen slightly since that time and which is unlikely to rise again in the foreseeable future. Imports of natural gas started in 1974, via pipeline from the Soviet Union, and reached 3m cu. metres in 1975. Imports via this pipeline can increase substantially over the next five years since the capacity is put at 10·0m cu. metres per annum.

Domestic production of hard coal has stabilized at about 0·5m tons per annum and is not expected to exceed this level. Bulgaria has been importing hard coal from the USSR during the past ten years and some 6m tons were imported annually in the 1970s. Brown coal production has been increasing steadily over recent years but seems likely to level off at around its current level of 25m tons per annum.

There are deposits of oil shale in Bulgaria and it is planned to develop these with assistance from other Comecon partners and from West Germany.

Refinery capacity is estimated at 12m tons in 1975, and this is expected to rise to between 18m and 20m tons by 1980. Some 2m tons of oil products has been imported annually, mainly from the Soviet Union, but it is likely that, in view of Bulgaria's own surplus refining capacity, such imports of products will be curtailed.

Energy demand in Bulgaria grew by almost 11 per cent annually between 1966 and 1970, although the rate fell to an average of about 9 per cent during the 1971–75 five-year plan period. The envisaged growth in the total demand for fuel and energy is planned to be accompanied by changes in the fuels—energy structure, whereby the relative share of solid fuels is to be substantially reduced and that of petroleum products and natural gas increased accordingly. Such changes are, of course, totally dependent upon imported oil and gas.

The first nuclear power station should have commenced production by the end of 1975 and when the plant is fully on stream it should have a capacity of 880 MW based on two 440 MW units. This particular plant, at Kozlodui, will eventually have a capacity of 1,760 MW by 1978, and is expected to produce 11·3 billion kWh per annum. Whereas in 1971 solid fuels provided 73 per cent of electricity generated, with liquids providing 16·2 per cent and hydro-electric power 10·3 per cent, by 1980 nuclear power will account for over 50 per cent of electricity generation, when Bulgaria will become the leading East European nuclear power producer, and new plants are planned to be built totalling 2,000 MW capacity during the next five years.

Production, consumption, and the import—export trade, are shown in Tables 8.22—8.24.

Table 8.22

Bulgaria: production of major fuels 1960—75

	Oil	Gas, natural and associated	Hard coal including anthracite	Brown coal including lignite	Electricity
	(million tons)	(billion cu. metres)	(million tons)	(million tons)	(billion kWh)
1960	0·2	—	0·6	15·4	4·7
1965	0·2	0·1	0·6	24·5	10·2
1970	0·3	0·5	0·4	28·9	19·5
1971	0·3	0·3	0·4	26·6	21·0
1972	0·2	0·2	0·4	26·9	22·3
1973	0·2	0·2	0·4	26·5	22·0
1974	0·1		0·3	24·0	26·8
1975 (plan)					30—31

Table 8.23

Bulgaria: apparent consumption of major fuels 1960—75

	Oil, products and synthetics	Gas, natural and associated	Hard coal including anthracite	Brown coal including lignite	Electricity
	(million tons)	(billion cu. metres)	(million tons)	(million tons)	(billion kWh)
1960	1·2	0·2	0·7	15·4	4·7
1965	3·8	0·3	3·2	24·5	10·3
1970	8·7	0·7	5·4	28·9	19·6
1971	10·3	0·5	6·4	26·6	21·2
1972	10·8	0·4	6·2	26·9	23·3
1973	12·3	0·2	6·3	26·5	25·3
1974			6·3	24·0	28·6

Table 8.24

Bulgaria: net import (export) of major fuels 1960–75

	Oil, products and synthetics (million tons)	Gas, natural and associated (billion cu. metres)	Hard coal including anthracite (million tons)	Brown coal including lignite (million tons)	Electricity (billion kWh)
1960	1·0	0·2	0·1	–	0·0
1965	3·6	0·2	2·6	–	0·0
1970	8·4	0·2	5·0	–	0·1
1971	10·0	0·2	6·0	neg.	0·2
1972	10·6	0·2	5·8	–	1·0
1973	12·1	–	5·9	–	3·3
1974		0·5	6·0	–	3·3
1975 (plan)		3·0			

East European energy planning

With the exception of Poland, the energy resource bases of the European Comecon countries allow very limited flexibility in the planning of production increases of oil, coal, and natural gas, and output of these appears already to have reached maximum levels commensurate with the reserves positions. Planned increases in energy consumption hitherto have therefore been based upon planned increases in imports of hydrocarbons, in keeping with the overall policy of improving the fuels–energy balances by decreasing the historically heavy dependence upon coal. Poland has always foreseen a steady increase in its output of hard coal, directed particularly at the export market, but longer-term plans show that a massive increase in both oil and gas consumption has been scheduled.[8]

A guaranteed supply of hydrocarbons from the Soviet Union, based on stable prices and calculated regular volume increases, has clearly been fundamental to Comecon energy planning and will continue to be so, and although the prices themselves will not be stable in future, the rules for calculating their gradual escalation are now established. The five-year economic plans of the East European countries must clearly reflect Soviet capabilities and intentions in the field of energy supplies, to the extent that the ability of any one Comecon country to switch from dependence upon Soviet supplies or to make good sudden shortfalls is extremely limited, and will remain so as long as the chronic shortage of hard currency throughout Eastern Europe continues. Although there has been a reduction in the percentage share of individual Comecon countries' imports of oil coming from the Soviet Union in recent years, from almost 100 per cent in some cases down to below 80 per cent in others (Table 8.6), there is no question that the countries of Eastern Europe, with the exception of Romania, will continue to be heavily dependent upon the Soviet Union for hydrocarbon supplies for the foreseeable future. During the early years of the 1970s considerable efforts were made by these countries, apparently at the suggestion of the Soviet Union, to make arrangements with oil-producing countries of the Middle East for increasing volumes of crude oil in exchange for economic aid, barter, etc., but the annual volumes actually involved seldom amounted to more than 500,000 tons here and 1½m tons there. No arrangements for the supply of natural gas from any countries other than the Soviet Union have yet been negotiated. It should be emphasized that all the Comecon countries except Romania have, to a greater or lesser extent, invested substantial sums of money in the development of the Soviet energy industries (even Romania now seems to be following suit and is providing equipment to build the Orenburg gas pipeline — see Appendix F). They are significant suppliers of pipeline and other equipment necessary for that development. Not only are their relevant industries geared to meeting Soviet needs in this respect but their oil-refining and petrochemical industries are, for the most part, totally geared to receiving piped supplies of Soviet hydrocarbons which could not in the short term, physically, be replaced by supplies by any other route.

Oil price rises and related problems

The domestic energy supply situation in a number of the East European countries was already giving rise to adjustment problems even before the oil price rises at the end of 1973, as a result of a sharp slow-down in expansion of, and in some cases such as the GDR, a decline in, indigenous coal output aimed both at raising economic efficiency and improving the construction of energy-consuming installations and the development of the petrochemical industry. Towards the end of 1973 Bulgaria, Czechoslovakia, Poland, and Romania introduced energy conservation measures in varying degrees of severity.[9] Romania was the first country to institute an oil conservation programme which included rationing petrol for passenger vehicles, reducing speed limits, the introduction of restrictions on heating and lighting, and a general 30 per cent reduction in the use of electricity by households. Bulgaria introduced a rationing system for passenger vehicles and a reduction in speed limits. The use of fuel oil in administrative buildings was also restricted by 15 per cent and steps were taken to restrict the use of diesel oil in agricultural enterprises. In Poland, prices of petrol were increased by 100 per cent and a speed limit of 80 km per hour for all vehicles was instituted. State-owned passenger cars and small trucks and buses were ordered to reduce their petrol consumption by 30 per cent and were prohibited from driving on Sundays. Czechoslovakia introduced a reorganization of working hours and the working week, in order to reduce peak loads in electric power stations. In almost all countries, the economic plans for 1974 emphasized the need to reduce fuel consumption, and in some countries programmes were elaborated to speed up the development of indigenous energy sources, although this is not likely to have any great effect upon the growth of import requirements.

As has been indicated, supplies of oil from the Soviet Union to the Comecon countries used to be based upon prices fixed at the time of the generation of the five-year plans, and in the case of the 1971–75 period, those prevailing for 1968 to 1970 were taken. As a result of the quadrupling of world oil prices at the end of 1973, the Comecon countries found themselves in a favourable situation regarding Soviet supplies, since prices were not due to be renegotiated until the preparation of the next five-year plans for 1976–80, due to take place in 1975. Nevertheless, with the exception of Bulgaria and Czechoslovakia, East European importers of Soviet oil did apparently pay some 10 per cent more for it in 1974 than in 1973.[10] The Soviet Union has managed to increase its prices for 1975 deliveries to Comecon nearer to those prevailing on the world market (although they are still well below world prices), and while the Comecon countries tried to resist all such efforts, it transpired that in January 1975 an increase of 130 per cent in the price was agreed upon, from 16 to 37 transferable rubles per ton. Although there will be small variations in supply prices to countries for logistical reasons, a similar price level will apply throughout the bloc.

The energy-saving measures introduced in the Comecon countries in the last two years may partly have been due to attempts to reduce import of oil from non-Soviet sources, and partly to dislocation in the sources of supply such as occurred during the early part of 1974. However, actual availability of supplies of Soviet oil will be less of a problem to the Comecon countries in the long term than the consequences of the price increases. These consequences are more important, not only with regard to that part of imports which is obtained on world markets but also regarding that part which is obtained within the area, since, while the problem of price relationships between goods traded in the area is undoubtedly complex, Comecon governments may find it difficult, even if desirable, to isolate these problems from those prevailing on world markets. Any particular change between relative raw materials and finished product prices on world markets cannot fail to have significant repercussions also on the terms under which such goods are traded within the area. In 1972, with an average price per ton of imports of oil products from the Soviet Union ranging between 17 and 20 rubles, the net oil import bill of Bulgaria is estimated at some $190m; that of Czechoslovakia at $310m, of East Germany at $220m, of Hungary at around $106m, and of Poland at around $205m. Rough calculations indicated that these figures, expressed in terms of the national income equivalent for the various countries, would range from 0·5 per cent in Poland to some 2 per cent in Bulgaria. In terms of the threefold increase in world market prices which took place in 1973, this would mean an additional burden ranging from an equivalent of some 1 per cent of national income in Poland to 4 per cent in Bulgaria. The balance-of-trade effect can be determined with greater precision. Using the same figures, the estimated impact of a threefold increase in oil prices ranges from an overall import equivalent of an additional 7 per cent in Hungary to an equivalent of 15 per cent in Bulgaria. Faced with a greatly increased fuel bill, giving rise to significantly changed relationships between the cost of imports and the cost of development of indigenous sources of supply, governments may now opt not only for energy-saving patterns in production, but also for a substantial departure from the traditional pattern of change in the structure of energy resources. Planned increases in brown coal production in East Germany and of hard coal production in Poland and Romania are pointers in this direction, although it is doubtful, in view of the considerable investments which have already been made in order to improve the fuels—energy balance, that such measures will have more than a marginal impact upon the Comecon energy situation for some time to come.

The 1975 position

The estimated 1975 position as shown in Table 8.25 indicates an overall energy deficit of some 95m tons of SFE, and in terms of basic units this could manifest itself as 67·5m tons of oil and 14 billion cu. metres of natural gas, offset by some 18m tons of hard coal exports from Poland. The Soviet Union has apparently agreed to supply Comecon with 57·3m tons of oil of Soviet origin,[11] so that at least 10m tons will have had to come from elsewhere, some of it on Soviet account, to meet the requirements

Table 8.25

East European 1975 estimates of production and consumption of major fuels
(Million tons SFE and basic units where stated)

	Oil		Natural gas		Hard coal		Brown coal		Others	Total
	(Million tons)	(MTSFE)	(Billion cu. metres)	(MTSFE)	(Million tons)	(MTSFE)	(Million tons)	MTSFE	MTSFE	MTSFE
Production										
Poland	0·4	0·6	11·1	13·2	167·0	133·6	36	11·2	3·5	162·1
Czechoslovakia	0·2	0·3	1·1	1·3	28·0	22·4	90	41·4	1·0	66·4
GDR	0·3	0·4	8·0	9·5	1·0	1·0	250	77·5	1·0	89·4
Romania	14·5	20·7	27·2	32·4	9·0	6·3	25	7·5	2·5	69·4
Hungary	2·0	3·0	5·3	6·3	5·0	4·5	22	7·5	1·0	22·3
Bulgaria	0·4	0·6	0·5	0·7	0·5	0·5	33	11·5	0·5	13·8
Total	17·8	25·6	53·2	63·4	210·5	168·3	456	156·6	9·5	423·4
Percentages		6·0		14·9		76·8			2·3	100·0
Consumption (Domestic usage)										
Poland	14·5	20·7	12·5	14·8	125·0	100·0	33	11·0	3·5	150·0
Czechoslovakia	17·5	25·0	4·8	5·7	29·5	23·6	90	41·4	2·0	97·7
GDR	14·5	20·7	13·0	15·5	5·7	4·5	250	77·5	1·0	119·2
Romania*	16·6	23·7	27·0	32·3	12·0	8·5	25	7·5	2·5	74·5
Hungary	8·1	11·5	6·5	8·1	6·5	4·9	22	7·5	3·5	35·5
Bulgaria	14·1	20·2	3·6	4·3	7·0	5·0	33	11·5	0·5	41·5
Total	85·3	121·8	67·4	80·7	185·7	146·5	453	156·4	13·0	518·4
Percentages		23·3		15·5		58·7			2·5	100·0

*Romania's refinery throughput is some 22m tons, and exports of 5·6m tons of products make up the difference. Hard coal consumption includes imports of anthracite and coking coal.

of Bulgaria and the GDR. These calculations of Soviet supplies do not take into account the Romanian position; Romania will probably have exported some 6m tons of products to the West and will have had to import some 7m tons from the Middle East. Exports of small quantities of oil products by the other East European countries to the West, for primarily logistic reasons, are accounted for in the oil demand picture, and as things stand at present it looks as though their total oil import requirements from the OPEC countries will have amounted to less than 15m tons in 1975, and may have been substantially lower, particularly if the energy saving measures referred to above proved reasonably effective.

The 1980 position

In the absence, at the time of writing, of 1976—80 five-year plan material from any of the European Comecon countries except for Romania, it is very difficult to estimate what the 1980 position will be, but Tables 8.26—8.28 represent an attempt to show how the energy situation in Eastern Europe is likely to develop.

Table 8.26

Estimated East European energy production 1980

	Oil		Gas		Coal	Total
	(million tons)	(MTSFE)	(million cu. metres)	(MTSFE)	(MTSFE)	(MTSFE)
Poland	0·4	0·6	18·0	22·3	171	193·9
Czechoslovakia	0·5	0·7	2·4	2·8	72	75·5
GDR	0·2	0·3	14·0	16·6	86	102·9
Romania	15·5	22·2	24·0	28·0	18	68·2
Hungary	2·0	2·8	6·0	7·1	10	19·9
Bulgaria	0·5	0·7	1·0	1·2	14	15·9
Total	19·1	27·3	65·4	78·0	371	476·3
Percentages		5·7		17·1		77·2

Note: Production of minor fuels and of hydro-electric and nuclear power is estimated at 17m tons SFE (3·2 per cent); total production is therefore 493·3 MTSFE.

Table 8.27

Estimated East European energy demand 1980

	Oil		Gas		Coal	Total
	(million tons)	(MTSFE)	(billion cu. metres)	(MTSFE)	(MTSFE)	(MTSFE)
Poland	25	35·8	24	28·6	114·4	178·8
Czechoslovakia	25	35·8	7	8·6	74·4	118·8
GDR	22	31·5	17	20·0	85·8	137·3
Romania	22	31·5	27	32·0	18·0	81·5
Hungary	15	21·5	9	11·4	11·4	44·3
Bulgaria	19	27·2	8	10·0	17·2	54·4
Total	128	183·3	92	110·6	321·2	615·1
Percentages	29·9		17·9		52·2	

Note: Total demand, including 17m tons SFE from minor sources (2·6 per cent), is therefore 631·1m tons SFE

Table 8.28

Estimated individual East European deficits (surpluses) oil, gas and coal 1980

	Oil		Gas		Coal	Total
	(million tons)	(MTSFE)	(billion cu. metres)	(MTSFE)	(MTSFE)	(MTSFE)
Poland	24·6	35·2	6·0	6·3	(56·6)	(15·1)
Czechoslovakia	24·5	35·1	4·6	5·8	2·4	43·3
GDR	21·8	31·2	3·0	3·4	(0·2)	34·4
Romania	6·5	9·3	2·8	4·0	–	13·3
Hungary	13·0	18·7	3·0	4·3	1·4	24·4
Bulgaria	18·5	26·5	7·0	8·8	3·2	38·5
Total	108·9	156·0	26·4	32·6	(49·8)	138·8

By 1980 the overall energy deficit will probably have grown to about 138m tons of SFE, and the overall oil deficit, based upon pre-energy crisis long-term plans for imports and refinery capacities etc., could be in the region of 109m tons of crude oil. It is quite possible that energy-saving measures will result in the deficit being kept nearer to 100m tons of crude oil, although there seems no way in which a gas deficit of some 27 billion cu. metres can be reduced. Poland itself should have a surplus of at least

50m tons of hard coal, at least half of which should be available for export to the West, and it will remain in a net energy surplus position, with coal probably accounting for a slightly larger share of demand than shown, and oil slightly less. Romania seems likely to hold its current position of being marginally in deficit, but all the other countries will increase their dependence upon imported energy, Hungary and Bulgaria to a substantial degree. The above estimates allow for a small reduction in the average annual rate of energy demand over current average levels and a rather larger increase in the rate of energy production, notably in Poland, the GDR, and Romania.

No difficulty is foreseen in the availability or distribution network for natural gas supplies from the Soviet Union in view of the substantial efforts which the Comecon countries have already put into the Bratstvo pipeline and which they will put into the building of the Orenburg line.

The oil supply position

The question of crude oil supplies does, however, pose some questions. The maximum capacity of the Druzhba pipeline – 50m tons – was reached in 1975, and there are no indications at present that its throughput is to be added to during the rest of the decade although plans for a third string are believed to have been discussed. Work on the Adria pipeline (see Appendix E) has already commenced, with financial assistance from Kuwait and Libya, and it will come on stream some time between 1977 and 1979. Its maximum throughput to be reached in the early 1980s will, however, only be 34m tons per annum, and it was originally intended that only 5m tons each would go to Czechoslovakia and Hungary with the remainder being retained in Yugoslavia. It now seems that Yugoslav demand will be unable to cope with the additional 24m tons, at least until the early 1980s, and additional quantities could therefore be available for the Comecon countries. Romania is known to be discussing the possibility of taking some of the throughput via a spur-line from near Belgrade, and Poland has also expressed an interest. If as much as 15m tons per annum were to enter Comecon by this route, bringing pipeline supplies to 65m tons annually, this would still leave 35m tons to bring in via some other route. Bulgarian requirements of 18m to 19m tons will presumably continue to be delivered by tanker as they are at present, and Romania would also continue to import its requirements in this way. This still leaves at least 10m tons unaccounted for, mainly required by Poland and the GDR, and this will also have to be delivered by tanker.

Consideration of the source of East European oil import requirements in 1980 also raises a number of questions. 50m tons will clearly come down the Druzhba pipeline from the USSR, and Bulgaria will presumably take about 15m tons of Soviet or Soviet-financed crude from the Black Sea. Tanker deliveries of Soviet oil to the GDR and Poland will be made across the Baltic from the Ventspils export terminal, but it begins to look as though some 25m tons will not be coming from the Soviet Union direct, yet while a substantial part of this may be supplied from the Middle East on Soviet account, the Comecon countries would face a size-able balance-of-payments problem if they had to import even 15m tons from OPEC at the current level of world prices, i.e. at a cost somewhere in the region of $1·2 billion. Unlike the Soviet Union, the European Comecon countries have no reserves of gold or any significant gold pro-duction, and if the OPEC countries were to insist upon their East European customers paying for their oil imports in hard currency, the latter would have a number of fairly unpleasant choices before them. In the first place, they could reduce consumption of petrol by private indi-viduals even more sharply, and they could introduce stricter measures to bring about fuel saving in the public sector. Second, they could delay the change-over in the fuels—energy balance from coal to oil and gas, although they have in many cases already built, or are building and planning to build, substantial additional refinery capacity and petrochemicals complexes which it would be uneconomic to abandon or to operate at reduced throughput. They could also with Soviet help devote much more effort towards increasing nuclear energy production. The maintenance of, let alone any increase in, the rate of coal output will require increasingly heavy capital investment in machinery and transportation facilities, and would take a number of years to make a substantial impact upon reversing the trend towards oil and gas usage. Third, the European Comecon countries could still further step up their investment in the development of Soviet energy resources, although this would mean that a greater pro-portion of their better quality industrial production would have to be earmarked for the Soviet Union instead of for export to the West to earn hard currency or reduce domestic consumption. The result would be that the Comecon industries would become even more closely integrated with and dependent upon the Soviet Union, although, as a corollary, the Soviet Union would have to commit a greater proportion of its surplus hydro-carbon production for export to Comecon rather than being free to increase its activities in the international energy market in order to earn additional hard currency for itself.

A fourth alternative for the European members of Comecon would be to find some way of encouraging the OPEC countries to accept substantially increased technological and industrial aid over the longer term, for repayment either in crude oil or by guaranteeing sales of crude oil to Eastern Europe at substantially reduced prices. In this connection Comecon would be competing with the industrialized countries of Western Europe, America, and Japan, and there seems no major reason why the OPEC countries should prefer East European industrial co-operation, even taking into consideration possible deliveries of armaments, etc. However, since Comecon requirements for oil imports from OPEC would be very small compared with Western demand, and since OPEC countries would probably wish to secure political and economic influence in as many different parts of the world as possible, they might well be prepared to continue to tolerate a considerable element of barter in the case of their oil supplies to Eastern Europe.

Probable developments

It seems likely that the East European countries will attempt all of these alternatives to a greater or lesser extent. They have, as mentioned above, already introduced energy economy measures aimed at creating savings by as much as 1½m tons of oil annually. Coal production in 1974 exceeded the planned targets by significant amounts in both Poland and the GDR. Most countries have expressed the intention to use oil and gas imports in future for chemicals and lubricants production and not for raising steam. There have been numerous expressions of confidence in the togetherness of the European Comecon bloc as regards energy matters, and in addition to the major new plans for further integration of Comecon's energy industries, 'satisfactory' long-term oil supply agreements with the Soviet Union have been concluded by Hungary, Czechoslovakia, the GDR, and Poland. Exact long-term volumes have not been revealed, but it is now known that the Soviet Union charged around $50 a ton in 1975; this price will rise to at least $80 by 1980 unless world prices decline, and volume increases will possibly be confined to some 3–4 per cent per annum instead of the 8–10 per cent rates recorded during the 1971–75 five-year period. Finally, delegations from all the East European countries have indeed been visiting the OPEC countries seeking special long-term arrangements for oil supplies against industrial and economic assistance. Co-operation with Western concerns in these efforts has even been discussed, although how successful such ventures are proving is not known at the time of writing.

122

Soviet and East European energy in relation to the rest of the world

The Soviet Union is the world's largest coal producer, and produces some 15·6 per cent of the world's oil. In 1970 the world demand for energy was some 6,570m tons of SFE (excluding China) and the Soviet and East European consumption was about 1,570m tons or 23·9 per cent. In 1980, global demand (excluding China) is put at 10,760m tons SFE and that of the Soviet Union and Eastern Europe at 2,535 tons or 23·6 per cent.

In 1972, in the world outside China, Eastern Europe, and the Soviet Union, solid fuels accounted for 20 per cent of demand, petroleum fuels 53 per cent, natural gas 19 per cent, hydro-electricity 7 per cent, and nuclear power 1 per cent. The proportion of oil varied from country to country, meeting 40 per cent of demand in the United States, 58 per cent in Western Europe, and about 75 per cent in Japan. It was estimated in 1973 that by 1980 the share of solid fuels will have fallen to 15 per cent, that that of petroleum will have risen by 55 per cent, that natural gas will occupy 17 per cent, hydro-electricity 6 per cent, and nuclear electricity 7 per cent. By comparison, in 1975 coal supplied about 58·7 per cent of East European Comecon demand, oil 23·4 per cent, natural gas 15·5 per cent, and others, including hydro-electric and nuclear, 2·5 per cent. In 1980 coal's share will have dropped to 52·4 per cent, that of oil will have risen to 28·1 per cent, and that of natural gas to 17·1 per cent. For the Soviet Union, the 1975 estimated shares are: solid fuels 37 per cent, petroleum fuels 35·8 per cent, natural gas 22·9 per cent, hydro-electric 3·8 per cent, nuclear 0·5 per cent. For convenience, the figures are shown in Table 8.29.

Table 8.29

Estimated demand for major fuels 1975 and 1980
(percentages)

	Rest of world (excl. China)		Soviet Union		Eastern Europe	
	1975	1980	1975	1980	1975	1980
Solid fuels	20	15	37·0	31·6	58·7	52·4
Petroleum fuels	53	55	35·8	39·1	23·4	28·1
Natural gas	19	17	22·9	24·1	15·5	17·1
Hydro-electric	7	6	3·8	3·9	2·5	2·4
Nuclear	1	7	0·5	1·3		

Conclusions

The overall energy position up to 1980 in the Soviet Union and Eastern Europe as a whole at least appears to be reasonably satisfactory. Imports of oil from the rest of the world could be between 20 and 25m tons in that year while exports should be not less than 35m tons. Imports of gas from the rest of the world could still be only 15 billion cu. metres annually while net exports will have exceeded this figure. There should be net exports of coal of between 25m and 35m tons. The ability of Comecon to import more oil from OPEC will depend not only upon financial considerations and the world price of oil but also upon physical limitations such as the availability of oil pipeline and rail tank-car capacity, and the throughput of oil storage and handling facilities at the main Comecon ports. Natural gas import and export capabilities will depend upon the rate at which the necessary pipelines can be constructed from e.g. Iran, on the one hand, and to e.g. Scandinavia and West Germany, on the other. It is reasonably certain that, given the extremely un-promising development to date of 'big' schemes involving the participation of American, Japanese, and other consortia in the development of Soviet energy resources, such schemes will not affect the position by 1980.

It is not yet completely clear how the Soviet Union will apportion its surplus crude oil as between its Comecon allies and the rest of the world, but, to the extent that evidence is becoming available that it has decided not only not to reduce supplies to the European members of Comecon but to increase them (albeit at a slower rate) to meet the bulk of their higher requirements estimated for the 1976—80 five-year plan period, its latitude for exporting to the rest of the world is clearly limited. However, the fact that it has apparently agreed to stand by its Comecon allies, and their terms of trade with the Soviet Union are adversely affected by their now having to pay at least double the prevailing price during the last five years, implies that the Soviet authorities are more concerned about the well-being of the other East European economies than about maximizing their own hard currency earnings. This seems to give the lie to those Western commentators who predicted that the Soviet Union would indeed divert supplies away from Comecon to the dollar area, and particularly to the United States.

It is also not yet clear to what extent the Soviet Union will assist in the financing of those imports from OPEC which its allies, particularly Bulgaria, will have to make, and in what way this financing will be carried out once the credit which it has built up with the Middle East oil-producing countries, particularly Iraq, by the provision of economic assistance and military aid in the past, runs out.

124

One other important area of uncertainty is the extent to which the Soviet Union can achieve or, indeed, exceed the crude oil production target for 1980, estimated at not less than 640m tons. Its ability to do so will, to a certain extent, depend not only upon its being able to overcome the infrastructural and logistical problems referred to above, which may not actually be so very different in kind or in magnitude from those which it has always faced and, apparently, managed to overcome in the past, but also upon its own assessment of the optimum rate at which already discovered reserves should be exploited in the light of the annual increments which it is possible to make to the total volume of exploitable reserves. According to the most reliable information available in the West, if the Soviet Union has been able to maintain the same rate of annual additions to reserves which it managed between 1966 and 1970, throughout the 1971—75 five-year plan, then there is no reason why the target of 640m tons should not be within reach. The difficulty is to know to what extent criticisms of the rate at which new reserves are being proved up are based upon actual shortcomings in performance or upon failures to meet over-optimistic expectations. Sufficient data are simply not available in the West to resolve this particular problem, but it may be said that any, even massive, Western assistance which might be forthcoming immediately could have very little effect upon the 1980 target, although it could substantially alter the picture for the period thereafter. The feasibility of the 1980 target is therefore seen as depending upon Soviet assessments of oil reserves already proven and, indeed, under production development, particularly those in western Siberia. There appear to be considerable misgivings in Soviet oil industry circles about what will happen *after* 1980, and it is for this reason that substantial Western assistance for exploration both on-shore in eastern Siberia and in the Volga—Urals region, and off-shore in the Far East and north, is currently being sought, and quite large deals could well be on the cards if payment could be arranged in terms of deferred supplies of hydrocarbons discovered as a result of such Western assistance.

In the event that a lower 1980 oil production target is announced in the 1976—80 five-year plans, the indications at present are that growth in Soviet domestic consumption of oil could be curtailed (and more coal used particularly for electricity generation), and that exports to the dollar area would be more likely to be affected than would supplies to the Comecon allies.

At the time of writing, the likely course of action of the Soviet Union in the energy fields over the next five years will include the following elements: in the first place, efforts will be made to maximize production in all the sectors of the energy industry. In the case of oil, this may well involve the acquisition of Western technology and equipment for secondary recovery methods. Imports of pipelines from the West, currently running at about 2m tons per annum, will also be keenly sought to supplement the Soviet production of over 14m tons. Exploration ventures, both off-shore and on-shore, will be entered into both with Western and Comecon organizations, and the Soviet Union is likely to purchase substantial quantities of relevant equipment, including computers.

In the second place, the Soviet Union will guarantee at least a major part of the increases in energy requirements of its East European Comecon allies for the next five years. In return, it will ask for and receive increased commitments by its allies to supply equipment and machinery related to the energy industry, and to invest in and participate in the development, particularly in the field of transportation and distribution, of Soviet energy resources. Energy interdependence between the Soviet Union and its East European allies will be considerably strengthened, with emphasis being placed upon international Communist solidarity.

In the third place, the Soviet Union is likely to continue its efforts to secure access to off-shore supplies of oil and possibly gas primarily in the Middle East, in exchange for economic assistance and political–military aid. If exports of Soviet oil to the rest of the world do have to be somewhat reduced, it would seem that there could arise a surplus of Soviet tanker tonnage which could be put at the disposal of friendly oil-producing countries at a time when there is already a serious surplus of Western tonnage which is likely to continue for many years.

In conclusion, it seems that up till 1980 the Soviet Union (and its East European allies) will be able to remain relatively aloof from the energy turmoils of the rest of the world, although it may miss out on opportunities to boost its hard currency earnings from energy sales to the West and can be expected to seek compensation accordingly from its allies, who will not be in a good position to resist. The position after 1980 looks somewhat less favourable from the Soviet point of view, particularly as far as oil is concerned, and some form of co-operation with the West, sooner rather than later, would appear to be a prudent step for the Soviet Union to take, even though it will not be forced to do so.

A NOTE ON NON-EUROPEAN MEMBERS OF COMECON

None of the non-European Comecon countries, Cuba (which joined in 1972), North Korea, North Vietnam,[12] and Mongolia (a member since

Table 8.30

Non-European Comecon members' production of major fuels 1960–76

	1960	1965	1970	1971	1972	1973	1974	1976 (plan)
Oil (m tons)								
Cuba	neg.	0·1	0·2	0·1	0·1	0·1		
Mongolia	neg.	neg.	—	—	—	—		
Gas[1] (bn cu. metres)								
Cuba	—	—	—	—	neg.	neg.		
Mongolia	neg.	neg.	—	—	—	—		
Hard coal[2] (m tons)								
Cuba	—	—	—	—	—	—		
Mongolia	—	0·1	0·1	0·1	0·1	0·1		
North Korea[3]	10·6	17·9	27·5		30·7			50–53
N. Vietnam[3]	2·6	3·4			3·2			
Brown coal[4] (m tons)								
Cuba	—	—	—	—	—	—		
Mongolia	0·6	0·9	1·9	2·0	2·1	2·2		
Electricity (bn kWh)								
Cuba	2·2[5]	2·9	4·0	4·2	4·6	5·8		
Mongolia	0·1	0·3	0·5	0·5	0·6	0·7		
N. Korea	9·1	15·1	16·5		19·0	19·6		28–30
N. Vietnam	0·3	0·5			0·8		1·0	

[1] Natural and associated.
[2] Including anthracite.
[3] Unspecified coal.
[4] Including lignite.
[5] Estimated.

Sources: SEV Yearbook; R.A. Scalapino and C. Lee, *Communism in Korea* (1972), pt 2, pp. 1223 and 1244; *Bolshaya Sovetskaya Ensiklopedya Ezhegodnik 1974;* J.S. Chung, *The North Korean economy* (1974), p. 87.

1962), produces more than negligible quantities of oil or natural gas. Apart from North Korea, which produces some 30m tons of coal per annum, they rely to a very great extent upon supplies of energy from the Soviet Union, which supplied them with 7·5m tons of oil and oil products in 1970. This figure had risen to 8·5m tons in 1973, primarily because of Cuba's increased requirements, since supplies by the USSR to North Korea and North Vietnam actually fell over the same period, although they rose again in 1974. Cuba, North Korea and Mongolia also import small quantities of Soviet hard coal and coke. North Vietnam and North Korea also receive some 1·5m tons of crude and products from China.

The Soviet Union has supported Cuba with deliveries of crude oil throughout the time of the embargo of the Organization of American States upon vessels of other countries trading with Cuba, although it is known that such a commitment is proving onerous in Soviet oil trading circles, and there are indications that it would prefer to see Cuba supplied from the South and Central American oil-producing countries such as Mexico or Venezuela, on an exchange basis under which the Soviet Union would perhaps supply the producers' customers with oil or other commodities in say Western Europe.

It seems unlikely that the Soviet Union will relinquish its task of supplying Mongolia, North Korea, and North Vietnam, particularly as alternative suppliers would be hard to find and would almost certainly involve increased supplies from China.

Such scant information as is available on the energy situations and trading positions of these countries is set out in Tables 8.30 and 8.31.

Table 8.31

Soviet exports of fuel to non-European Comecon countries 1960—74

	1960	1965	1970	1971	1972	1973	1974
Crude oil, and products * (m tons)							
Cuba	2·1	4·7	6·0	6·4	7·0	7·4	7·6
Mongolia	0·1	0·2	0·3	0·3	0·3	0·3	0·3
North Korea	0·2	0·4	0·8	0·7	0·4	0·6	0·9
North Vietnam	0·1	0·1	0·4	0·4	0·2	0·2	0·3
Hard coal[†] (000 tons)							
Cuba	7	—	51	78	56	62	76
Mongolia	53	134	2	2	2	2	1
North Korea	—	—	587	500	356	269	228
Hard coal coke (000 tons)							
Cuba	—	31	38	54	57	54	51
Mongolia	neg.	2	1	1	1	1	1
North Korea	—	—	106	159	135	122	106

* Including synthetics.   [†] Including anthracite.

Sources: Bolshaya Sovetskaya Ensiklopedya Ezhegodnik 1974, p. 245; Le plan quinquennal de la République démocratique de Vietnam 1961—5; Vnesh. torg.

Notes

[1] Scanlan, in NATO (1974), p. 92.

[2] *Ek. prom.*, Dec. 1971, p. 12 V6.

[3] Ibid., Aug. 1972, p. 8 V3.

[4] Speech by N. Ceausescu at 11th Congress of Romanian CP.

[5] See *Ek. prom.*, Jan. 1969, p. 1 V88.

[6] UN, *Economic Survey of Europe 1967*, p. 111 n. 64.

[7] *Ek. prom.*, Sept. 1971, p. 9 A13.

[8] *Nafta*, Oct. 1969, p. 298.

[9] *Economic Survey of Europe 1973*, p. 111 n. 64.

[10] Unit values calculated from *Vnesh. torg.* This figure could be misleading as price rises could be due to changes in product mix. There is some rise in unit prices every year but usually only amounting to 1 or 2 per cent.

[11] *Tribuni lyudi*, Jan. 1975.

[12] North Korea and North Vietnam are not actually members although they have a special status which amounts to limited participation in some of Comecon's work.

PART II

International Implications

9 Introduction and intra-Comecon relationships

It has been indicated in Part 1 that improvements in the fuels—energy balance of the Soviet Union planned to be brought about by the progressive substitution of coal by oil and gas are likely to be retarded, and the trend may even be reversed for the time being, in view of the relatively greater speed with which existing proven coal reserves can be mobilized in the short term. In the other European Comecon countries, however, it is less likely that a similar trend reversal can take place, since not only are coal reserves inadequate to support such a development, but their fuels—energy balances — except in Romania — are in any case so heavily weighted in favour of coal that improvements in economic efficiency would be seriously impaired, and previous substantial investments aimed at increasing the share of oil and gas would be under-utilized.

It has likewise been indicated that considerable doubt exists in the minds of Soviet *oil* industry officials about the ability of existing Soviet proven reserves of crude oil to sustain envisaged increases in production after 1980, and there is concern that the discovery of new commercial reserves is not proceeding at a fast enough rate, so that if major new discoveries are not made within the next few years, production increases may well decline from their expected annual level of 35m tons. No such concern about commercial availabilities exists in the *gas* and *coal* industries, but the main problems facing these ministries have to do with transportation and distribution and shortages of the necessary equipment and pipeline etc.

It has been seen in Chapter 1 that both Western commentators and East European official spokesmen tend to give undue prominence to individual 'good' and 'bad' developments at any given time, and all too often there are reports of 'desperate' shortcomings, 'massive' requirements for Western assistance, 'enormous' new discoveries, and, 'multi-billion dollar' East—West energy deals.

This Part will therefore attempt to place the Soviet and East European energy situation into global perspective, and to examine its implications for Soviet relations with the industrially developed countries of the West, Comecon—Soviet interrelationships, and Soviet and East European relationships with the countries of the Middle East and various developing nations. An attempt will also be made to see if there are pressures developing as a result of the Soviet and East European energy situation which might encourage the Soviet leadership to experiment in influencing the international situation in one direction or another.

Any first-time observer of the current position of the Soviet oil industry would easily be convinced, from a study of the contemporary literature, that the entire apparatus was shuddering to a halt, having outgrown its strength in an attempt to give more to the national economy than anyone could reasonably have expected of it. It has been pointed out, however, that many of these problems were in fact facing the Soviet oil industry ten years ago, but, in spite of all the shortcomings, it managed to forge ahead and, indeed, surpass the United States in its annual production. The planners still intend to increase the share of oil in the country's fuels—energy balance, pointing out that every 1 per cent increase in that share can bring about a saving of about 1 billion rubles. 2·7 billion rubles were invested in the oil industry in 1975 (equivalent to 5·5 rubles per ton produced) and exports of oil and products to the West in 1975 will have earned the Soviet Union over $3·0 billion even without any appreciable rise in volume, and oil will remain the USSR's major currency earner. Clearly the Soviet oil industry is not going to be allowed to crumble, and it is indeed seen as one of the pillars of the Soviet economy. It has been shown (pp. 32—3) that there is scope for interchangeability of fuels within the Soviet economy, should this become necessary, although, until the performance of the gas industry improves substantially, the options will be limited to coal and oil, and the volume involved in substitution will probably not be more than 5—10m tons in any one year.

It is quite revealing to see what happens if current trends in Soviet and East European oil production and consumption are extrapolated through to 1985. It should be stressed at this point that no sophisticated mathematical techniques have been employed in looking at the future development of Comecon's energy, since their validity, in a situation where important economic decisions are liable to be heavily influenced by ideological and political considerations, is questionable. It is quite possible that the application of Input—Output analysis to the Soviet economy would yield some valuable information on, for example, the interchangeability of different types of fuel or the viability of energy-consuming industry plans in the light of fuel availabilities, but it would not be more likely to enable an analyst to predict the failure of the Soviet gas industry to meet its five-year plan production targets by over 15 billion cu.,metres per annum, or the success of west Siberian oil production in exceeding its original 1975 target by over 20m tons.

If the Soviet Union were to achieve its aims of raising the annual increases in oil production to 35m tons, then by 1985 it could be producing as much as 810m tons, requiring an average annual increase from 1975 of just over 5 per cent. If consumption increases could be reduced to 6·5 per cent annually, as a result of improvements in the natural gas supply and the increasing contribution from nuclear power, the Soviet Union could be consuming about 710m tons, leaving a surplus of 100m tons for export.

By 1985, however, the European Comecon countries, even if they were able to reduce the average annual rate of increase in oil consumption from the current 9 per cent down to say, 7 per cent, would be unlikely to be requiring less than 170m tons annually. Production of oil in Eastern Europe is considered unlikely to exceed its 1980 level of 20m tons, leaving an overall deficit of 150m tons. This would imply that, at some stage between 1980 and 1985, the Soviet Union would cease to be in a position where it could, even if it so wished, supply *all* its Comecon allies' requirements from its own surplus production, since even if it were to make available its entire 100m tons surplus to Comecon, the latter would still have to find 50m tons from elsewhere. Added to this, the Soviet Union would have to face up to the prospect of foregoing the benefit of some $3·0 billion annually which it now enjoys on account of its oil export earnings to the hard currency areas.

The above scenario is of course riddled with assumptions, but it does perhaps indicate the general direction in which the Soviet and East European oil situation is moving. The most unpredictable element in the above reckoning is Soviet production capability, certainly if left to rely upon the current level of purely domestic support and if the eagerly sought bonanza of the discovery of a new oil province of the same order of magnitude as western Siberia does not come about within the next few years. The rate of growth of Soviet oil consumption is perhaps more amenable to downward pressure, in view of the inherent degree of flexibility which the Soviet Union enjoys vis-a-vis inter-fuel substitutions. It is increasingly likely that by 1985 the Soviet gas industry will be well on the way to fulfilling its early promise, and increased availability could well be more than enough to satisfy part of the energy requirements hitherto satisfied by oil. It would be far harder for the other East European countries significantly to restrain their growth in oil consumption, although a greater proportion of their overall energy requirements could well be met by stepping up both imports of Soviet natural gas and the production of nuclear energy.

Intra-Comecon relationships

The importance of the Soviet oil industry to the well-being of the rest of the Soviet economy needs no further elaboration. Its importance moreover to the well-being of the economies of the other East European countries, apart from Romania, is also clear, as is the contribution which Soviet oil exports make to the hard currency earnings of the Soviet Union itself and to the saving of hard currency expenditure for the European Comecon bloc as a whole. The maintenance of an oil export surplus, both to meet most of Comecon's requirements and to earn hard currency, has therefore clearly been a basic Soviet policy, and is likely to continue to be so. It so happens that the sharp rise in world crude oil prices has come at a time when Comecon planners had already been made aware by the Soviet leadership that they would have to face difficulties over supplies from the Soviet Union for the rest of this decade and beyond. The price rise must have given the Soviet side a most welcome windfall for at least three reasons.

In the first place, it obliged those East European recipients of Soviet crude oil to re-evaluate any plans they might have had for substantially reducing their dependence upon Soviet oil, at least for the immediate future, by acquiring increasing quantities from elsewhere with their extremely restricted quantities of hard currency. Indeed, the sharp rise in oil prices will have strengthened the Soviet hand in seeking from its allies increased investment in the Soviet energy industries, and, for reasons which have previously been mentioned, will have favoured the whole, albeit slow, process of Comecon integration.

In the second place, it has, for the present, significantly reduced the strain upon Soviet oil exports to the rest of the world as a vital earner of hard currency with which to import the technology and equipment considered necessary by the Soviet leadership for the general improvement in the technical level of the Soviet economy — to the extent that the same volume of oil exported to the West after 1973 is now bringing in four times as much hard currency as it would have pre-October 1973, the Soviet trade balance with the industrially developed capitalist countries improved from a $1 billion deficit position in 1973 to a small surplus in 1974 (see Appendix G). The fact that the surplus was smaller than might have been expected in view of the fourfold oil price rise is explained by the substantial increase above previous levels in Soviet imports of machinery and equipment from the West in 1974. Since there are clearly limitations to the volume of Soviet crude available for export (total gross exports of oil fell from 118·3m tons in 1973 to 116m tons and exports to the industrially developed capitalist countries fell from 43·1 to 35·2m tons in 1974), the Soviet planners have been able, more easily, to countenance increased supplies for Comecon allies (at twice the price) as the urgent need for the Soviet Union to boost its hard currency earnings by means of increased volume exports of crude oil to the West was temporarily lifted.

Third, the boost in hard currency earnings from oil exports has meant that there has been less pressure upon the Soviet energy industries to enter into longterm schemes with Western organizations under conditions which would have been more likely to give a greater say in the operation and financial management of the schemes to the Western partners and, for a time, rather more of the relevant Western technology and equipment could be bought for cash or obtained with fewer strings attached.

An important additional factor is the increase in value imparted to the vast physical but otherwise economically valueless 'dead' assets comprising undeveloped or undiscovered oil and gas reserves in the north and east of the country.

Agreement now appears to have been reached between the Soviet Union and its oil-dependent allies in Eastern Europe upon the quantities and the prices of supplies over the next five years. This would suggest that the Soviet Union must have traded quite heavily on the fact that the East Europeans were, and are, in no position to acquire sufficient hard currency to purchase much additional oil from OPEC since, by the late 1970s, they will, if all goes according to plan, be paying the Soviet Union a price (in rubles) for its crude oil extremely close to, or if the world price of oil falls, possibly exceeding, world prices generally. This is because under the Comecon price revision, instead of prices being fixed for a five-year period (once they have been agreed upon and traded at that price), they will now be reviewed every year, and will be based upon the average of world prices taken over the previous five-year or possibly even three-year period. There is no indication at present from East European sources of just what quantities the Soviet Union will be supplying in 1980 to Eastern Europe, but, as is indicated on p. 57, it will still be likely to be around 70 per cent of the total requirements. For any quantities of Soviet crude purchased over and above the agreed quotas, the East European importers may have to pay the Soviet Union in hard currency, and the latter has apparently arranged for substantial lines of credit to be extended to some of the Comecon allies to enable them to adapt to this new oil situation. The Soviet Union clearly attaches considerable importance to the military security and political stability of the European members of Comecon, and to the need to maintain the economic well-being of these countries. An attempt has been made to demonstrate that the energy dependence of the other Comecon countries upon the Soviet Union is a continuing and growing phenomenon, and furthermore that the economic well-being of the East European countries would be seriously affected by any deterioration in their fuels—energy balances or by any significant reduction in their energy supply. The inability of the other countries of Comecon to finance more than a very small part of their imports of energy from hard currency sources, even at the relatively low volumes required today, needs no further elaboration. Although these countries will undoubtedly do all they can to secure supplies from OPEC in exchange for 'soft' currency payment in one form or another, any suggestion that the Soviet Union would require them to finance the bulk of their total import requirements by themselves would surely be regarded by them as unacceptable. The refining industries of the East European countries are to a very large extent geared to the receipt of Soviet oil along the established channel of the Druzhba pipeline; although by 1985 the 50m tons currently arriving via this route as it now stands will only represent something like a third of the import requirements, it would take several years before alternative supply routes could be developed, and it is far more likely that the throughput of the Druzhba pipeline will in fact be increased during the course of the next ten years.

At about the time of the invasion of Czechoslovakia in August 1968, there was some discussion among Western strategic analysts about the possibility that the Soviet Union might at some stage be obliged to use the threat of a cut in energy supplies to control one or other of its unruly satellites. Consideration was, at this time, given to the possibility of Western governments and energy companies making good the shortfall of energy in such an event, using the flexibility of the international oil industry as the basis of its operations. The international energy situation which has developed since October 1973 has quite clearly reduced the ability of the West to come to the aid of an East European country faced with a similar problem, and the East European countries themselves will no doubt have taken good account of this fact. They will also have realized, however reluctantly, that at least for the time being investment in the development of intra-Comecon energy resources distribution networks and production based on the Soviet Union provides the most rational course of action likely to guarantee them stable supplies of energy over the longer term. Marginal supplies, which will steadily increase in volume, will undoubtedly be sought from countries other than the Soviet Union, but Soviet help in financing and transporting these imports will still be required by most of the Comecon countries for a long while to come.

Looking now to the period after 1980 during which, it is suggested, the net Soviet surpluses of crude oil for export will decline, and probably be replaced by a need to import substantial volumes of crude oil from the OPEC countries, if not for its own use, then for the use of its Comecon allies, the problem then arises of how these imports are to be financed, assuming first that the world price of oil remains at approximately its current level and, further, that the oil-producing countries will continue to require the Soviet Union and its allies to pay for imports in hard currency. An import of some 80m tons of oil for example, in 1985, might cost the Comecon bloc some $6·5 billion (all projections are at 1975 prices), and this is to be seen in relation to current Soviet earnings of hard currency from oil exports of about $3·0 billion. There are, therefore, compelling reasons for the Soviet Union and its allies not only to restrain the growth in their oil consumption but to increase oil and other energy production by every available means. There is little if any evidence to suggest that the Soviet leaders or, indeed, the Soviet planners and energy industry officials were, in any way, expecting a global energy crisis and the subsequent fourfold increase in oil prices. They had, however, been encouraging their East European allies to attempt to secure at least a small part of their energy requirements from outside Comecon since, with the world price of oil as low as it was before 1973, the Soviet Union calculated that, by the time it had transported that oil increasing distances within its own borders from East to West, it was becoming economically less attractive to export it to Comecon than to use it in the high energy-deficit areas of European Russia.

10 Some considerations of détente and East-West relations

At a time when oil matters are big global news, rather more significance is often given to the Soviet and East European position than it possibly merits. Although Soviet crude oil sales are producing over 30 per cent of its total hard currency earnings, this percentage is expected to decline slowly over the next five years, as sales of other commodity groups increase in volume while the volume of crude oil sales will remain static or decline. Foreign trade (see Appendix G) has hitherto been a relatively small aspect of Soviet international relationships and is the equivalent of only 8 per cent of the estimated GNP (2·5 per cent if only trade with the developed West is considered). There are indications that as long ago as 1966 the Soviet leadership was contemplating a greater participation in international trade, particularly if this would mean that the Soviet economy would be able to obtain that technological boost which it so badly required if it was ever to reduce the perceived gap in economic performance between itself and the United States and other industrialized Western countries.

Détente[1]

It is difficult to say exactly when the process of détente can be said to have begun, for it had clearly been in progress for some time before the official pronouncements centred around the occasion of President Nixon's visit to the Soviet Union in 1972. Whether détente was conceived at some point in time as a master strategy upon which the development of Soviet relations with the West were to be based over the next decade or two, or whether it started to happen of its own accord at the same time as forces supporting the Cold War began to wither and fade away for lack of nourishment, will probably never be determined, but sometime between 1968 and 1971, when Mr. Brezhnev included détente in the 'peace programme' which he put before the 24th Soviet Communist Party Congress, the process got under way.

If possible economic motivations for détente are considered, it must be recalled that a fairly substantial degree of East—West economic

140

co-operation was already taking place in the late 1960s, the most notable example being the Fiat automobile factory deal. It is likely that during the eighth five-year plan period from 1966 to 1970, with the introduction of the economic reforms sponsored by Mr Kosygin, the leadership became convinced that the Soviet economy was failing to live up to the expectations voiced for it during the Khrushchev era. Far from it enabling the Soviet Union to 'overtake and outstrip' the industrialized West in economic terms, it was falling even further behind and would be increasingly unlikely to catch up unless it could secure substantial imports of superior Western technology and equipment. The internal ideological debate over whether it was right for the Soviet Union to resort to the capitalists for economic assistance or, at least, the import of capitalist technology, etc. seems temporarily to have been won sometime in the mid-1960s by the more pragmatic and economically minded in the Soviet hierarchy, and from that time onwards increasing purchases were made of those key items of Western equipment and know-how, mainly for cash and with the help of gold sales, since at that time Western governments were co-operating in refusing to extend much in the way of medium and long-term credit to the communist bloc, and certainly not on specially favourable repayment terms.

The alternative to imports from the West would be to call upon the Soviet economy for strenuous efforts, such as would be required to create the same level of general technological sophistication as that possessed by the West. Whether the Soviet economy would ever be able to respond adequately to such a call is highly debatable, but a radical reapportioning of the State budget would almost certainly be involved – a course of action more likely to prove acceptable to the Soviet leadership[2] during an extended and unshakeable period of détente. It could be argued that the ability of Soviet industry to meet such a challenge, even if massive investment were forthcoming as a result of its diversion away from other sectors of the Soviet economy, would also depend upon what would necessarily amount to a managerial revolution and the abandonment of some fundamental communist economic doctrines, a development which the current Soviet leadership would certainly be extremely unlikely to sanction. The whole question of any degree of dependence of the Soviet economy upon Western technological superiority has always been, as is mentioned elsewhere (see p. 148), very much a matter for the ideologists and politicians in the Soviet leadership rather than for the economists and pragmatists, although there are indications that the voices of the latter two groups are becoming increasingly heard in the councils of the Soviet leaders. Import-led growth has, indeed, been an abiding factor in Soviet economic thinking, although the degree of dependence of the overall economy upon imported technology and equipment has always remained very small, seldom rising above a few per cent.

Meanwhile, in the late 1960s, it had become increasingly clear that the Soviet Union was not in a position to earn as much hard currency through its exports to the West as it would need, if it were to be able to import the quantity of Western goods and technology which the economic pragmatists in the Soviet leadership felt that the economy could use. The Co-ordinating Committee in Paris was at that time operating a fairly effective embargo on the export to the Soviet Union and its allies of any goods and technology which might be capable of benefiting the 'strategic' sectors of their economies and the 'COCOM' list was 400 or 500 items long. The new Soviet leadership under Mr Brezhnev and Mr Kosygin must have realized that, although, the eastward flow of Western technology and equipment could be encouraged to grow by playing off one Western country against another, its rate of growth would remain inadequate as long as Soviet hard currency earnings remained small and as long as larger-scale credits were not extended by the West. Perhaps the problem was seen at that time as one of how to encourage the West to be more forthcoming with its loans and its machinery etc. in larger quantities, and at a faster rate than appeared likely to develop as a result of a less positive easing of international tension.

From a political viewpoint the Soviet leaders must have been increasingly uneasy about the growing magnetic attraction of an economically powerfully developing Western Europe upon the satellite countries of Eastern Europe, which were becoming increasingly restive and dissatisfied with their own rates of economic development. The Soviet Union therefore had pressing reasons for delivering a sharp reminder, by its handling of the events in Czechoslovakia in the autumn of 1968, that it regarded the maintenance of strict Communist Party control over the countries of Eastern Europe as of paramount importance, and not to be challenged from within or from without. The prospect of a militarily united Western Europe, backed by US nuclear and conventional forces and economically prosperous, must have greatly worried the Soviet leadership at a time when its own economy was showing signs of strain and when it was having some difficulty in maintaining a unified front in Eastern Europe. It may have also realized, at about this time, that it could never hope to achieve the kind of strategic superiority over the United States which military theoreticians might advocate in view of its technologically less advanced and less efficient economy. It must, however, have seen that the capitalist West was growing increasingly weary of the general state of international tension and the consequent need to spend large sums of money on defence or, in the case of the United States, on the conduct of the war in Vietnam. The Soviet leadership probably also perceived that the inherent internal contradictions between political parties in individual countries and between the countries of Western Europe themselves, and between Western Europe and the United States, would have more chance of bringing about cracks in the Western Alliance if the perceived communist threat were to recede and diminish.

It appears, therefore, that there may have been three separate strands of reasoning by the Soviet leadership leading towards the emergence of a 'détente' offensive, the first being the need to call a halt to the strategic arms race and the vital need to avoid any chance of a nuclear conflict with the United States, for which the latter would have been numerically and technically better equipped. The second strand of reasoning reflected the need of the Soviet Union to prevent, or at least retard, the further political and military development of Western Europe, which was seen as a very real threat to the stability of the communist regimes in the East European countries. There was also, of course, a fundamental and seemingly irrational fear of the regeneration of West German military and industrial power and revanchism, such as might openly dispute the right of East Germany to remain a separate country, etc. The third strand was probably based on economic considerations having not only to do with the increasingly shaky performance of the Soviet bloc in the 'race' with the capitalist West, but also reflecting a genuine desire on the part of the Soviet leadership to improve the lot of the Soviet citizen, not only for purely humanitarian reasons, but also because, in the final analysis, the Soviet leadership would be vulnerable in the event of any failure to fulfil its promises or to justify the expectations which the Soviet Union itself has been responsible for generating in the minds of the Soviet and East European masses. It is possible that there had developed at about the same time a fourth strand of thinking which related the need for more Western technology and equipment, and the extension of large amounts of Western credit, to the need so to improve the international climate that governments, financial circles, and businessmen in the West would be more inclined to look favourably upon extending what would clearly amount to economic assistance to the Soviet bloc.

In the early part of the 1970s, world events seemed to be helping the Soviet Union in its promotion of the idea of détente. There was the election of Chancellor Brandt in West Germany, and the subsequent development of his Ostpolitik. There was increasingly costly involvement of the United States in South East Asia and in the Middle East, and there were the controversies on both current economic and political policy within the European Economic Community and in connection with its possible future enlargement as well as the effect of this upon its future relationship with the United States. At the same time, all was not going at all well with the ninth Soviet five-year plan (1971–75), and the need for increasing quantities of economic and financial assistance must have become clear even for the most conservative elements in the Soviet leadership.

Even within the context of the possible economic motivations behind détente, energy matters probably played little if any part, at least until the early 1970s. By 1971 it was becoming clear to some people in the United States that that country would have to become increasingly dependent on imported hydrocarbons during the rest of the 1970s, and that this was clearly going to have an effect on US policy in relation to the development of events in the Middle East. At about this time it was also becoming clear in the Soviet Union that the energy production targets for the ninth five-year plan were not going to be met, and that this would have much wider implications for the longer-term development of the Soviet energy industries and, therefore, of the Soviet economy as a whole. It was inevitable that a possible commercial relationship between an expected American demand for imported hydrocarbons and a Soviet requirement for large volumes of credit and machinery and technology should emerge, and, by the time that the idea of East–West détente may finally be said to have achieved international recognition, on the occasion of the Nixon–Brezhnev meeting in May 1972, conditions seemed very promising for the conclusion of large-scale US–Soviet energy deals. These deals would have gone quite a long way to solving some of the developmental difficulties affecting the ability of the Soviet Union to sustain a stepped-up acquisition of Western technology and equipment, in spite of a foreseen reduction in Soviet exports of energy to the West. In an improved international climate the Soviet Union would acquire the credits with which to import the necessary hardware and technology for the development not only of its domestic energy networks but also, incidentally, for the creation of additional export volumes in due course, which would be used to pay back the credits and subsequently to earn additional quantities of hard currency. It began to look as though one particular area of détente was about to pay off handsomely, and, quite apart from the energy scene, the eastward flow of Western technology and finance was accelerating, if on a somewhat smaller scale than the Soviet leadership might have wished.

Whether any big US–Soviet energy deals would have gone ahead if the renewal of Arab–Israeli hostilities had not occurred in October 1973, with the subsequent development of the global energy crisis, no one will ever know, but the fact of the matter now is that tens of billions of dollars' worth of Western credit which might have been forthcoming in 1973, some of them earmarked for energy schemes, had not yet materialized in 1975, and are unlikely to do so in time to be incorporated into the tenth Soviet five-year plan period from 1976–80. In the event, the Soviet Union certainly found itself in 1974 and 1975 with over $2 billion more hard currency per annum than it might have expected, as a result of its substantial though slowly declining oil sales to the West. On the one hand, therefore, the Soviet Union was in a position to pay in cash for some equipment and technology which it would hitherto have either been unable to pay for, or would have had to obtain on credit or by means of sales of gold, stocks of which were possibly depleted as a result of a need to import massive quantities of US grain in 1972–73. On the other hand, the significant 'underpinning' of détente, which the successful development of such large-scale energy deals between the Soviet Union and the United States would have meant, has not yet materialized. It could be argued that the Soviet need for Western credits is, at least for some time to come, somewhat reduced. This need for Western credits is not a measurable entity however, and the need for Western technology, equipment, and consumer goods, though it can be related to a perceived gap in the standard of living and technical advancement between the countries of the industrialized West and the Soviet bloc as a whole, is not only determined by the rate at which the relevant imports form the West can be absorbed into the Soviet economy. It must also take account of domestic economic developments and political judgements upon the optimum degree of dependence on and ideological contamination by the capitalist West.

The Kremlin leadership does at the time of writing appear to be prepared to countenance a degree of East–West economic co-operation. A significant feature of such co-operation would be the provision of large-scale Western credits in the short term against repayment in the longer term by exports of energy and raw materials, the production of which, at least for export, could only be made possible as a result of the equipment, technology and, possibly, managerial expertise imported on the back of these credits. There is little doubt that, if the Soviet Union were able to generate larger amounts of hard currency by its export earnings to the West, it would rapidly increase the volume of its Western purchases for cash (instead of building up a a large reserve of hard currency in a time of high global inflation). Requirements for Western imports in excess of those financeable by Soviet hard currency earnings could, up to a point, be purchased by the sale of a proportion of the annual production of Soviet gold, now believed to be running at about 450 tons per annum, and worth about $2·0–2·5 billion on the world market at current prices of $160, per fine ounce. Soviet gold reserves are estimated at around 2,200 tons, and in recent years Soviet gold sales have increased substantially to assist in the purchase of the large quantities of grain from the United States which were necessary because of the failure of the Soviet grain harvest in 1972 to live up to expectations. Sales of Soviet gold in 1974 apparently returned to nearer their pre-1972 level, in the region of $700m per annum, but are believed to have increased again in mid-1975 as the result of another failure to meet grain production targets.

It is widely recognized that Soviet agriculture is one of the weakest sectors of the economy, and the Soviet leadership has put its collective weight behind a massive livestock improvement scheme aimed at creating a better balanced and more varied diet for the Soviet people, whose consumption of meat is very much lower than that of many countries in the industrialized West, particularly the United States. Since the livestock improvement programme depends so heavily on a satisfactory fulfilment of grain production plans, and since the grain harvest depends to such an extent on the vagaries of the climate, Soviet planners must make ample provision for emergency purchases of Western grain. They would there-fore, presumably, be rather reluctant to use Soviet gold sales to finance the import of commodities other than food, since it would be easier to make provision for their production and consumption by the Soviet economy, and thus their import and financing, etc., in the normal prep-aration of the State budget. The Soviet leadership is well aware of the shortcomings of Soviet agriculture, although repeated reorganizations and boosts given to this sector of the economy have failed, so far, to demon-strate that the fundamental problems have yet been overcome.

It is clear from the above that if Western credits are forthcoming — and at present there is every indication that the Soviet Union is regarded by Western financial circles extremely favourably from the point of view of credit rating — the Soviet Union will continue to have a strong interest in securing as much credit as it can afford to finance, in preference to financing its import of Western equipment and technology by means of gold sales or by the straightforward sale of raw materials such as crude oil and timber, the value of which will currently increase as long as world inflation continues.

Having correctly assessed that the easterly flow of advanced Western technology would only reach major proportions in a generally relaxed and tension-free international situation, the Soviet leadership encouraged the creation of the necessary conditions. Their ability to achieve this was probably enhanced by the disillusionment of the majority of US citizens both with their country's foreign policy, particularly in relation to the war in Vietnam, and with domestic affairs, culminating in Watergate. For example, the US leadership can hardly have been convinced that it was carrying the nation behind it in the early 1970s, particularly in its dealings with the Soviet Union, and it may have behaved rather less circumspectly in this relationship than would have been likely if it had not been so preoccupied with other external and internal factors which tended to detract from its self-confidence. The more hawkish and ideological elements in the Soviet leadership must also have viewed with a certain amount of satisfaction the numerous and increasing cracks which had, for some years, been appearing in what they regarded as the capitalist front arrayed against them, as instanced by trade disagreements between Japan and the United States, Western Europe and the United States, as well as the growing political and economic arguments arising out of the enlargement of the Common Market. However, the economists in the leadership may have been less pleased to see the economic difficulties of the industrialized West, perhaps being concerned that these would jeopardize the chances of the Soviet economy gaining access to the anticipated technology and finance, etc.

As mentioned earlier, the Soviet leaders realized that a substantial increase in general economic relations with the capitalist countries could have adverse repercussions on the inert and rather tranquil domestic situation, by creating a new level of expectation in the minds of the Soviet people. There is some evidence that, at the same time as increasing contact was made with the West, further steps were taken to ensure that dissident groups were kept under control, contact between Soviet citizens and visiting foreigners was reduced, and that the Soviet allies in Eastern Europe were made aware of the consequences of allowing their imaginations to run away with them on the question of independence. The situation today seems to be very much under Soviet control once again, and the flow of Western technology in many fields is gathering pace, although not perhaps quite as quickly as the Soviet leadership would have wished. The global energy crisis which developed at the end of 1973, and the subsequent maturing of recession conditions in the West, augmented by raging inflation and increases in prices of raw materials other than gas and oil, has led Western governments and potential Western partners in large-scale Soviet energy deals seriously to reconsider their position, and think twice about tying up scarce capital and manpower in the development of resources located in the depth of what has shown itself to be, ideologically and politically, a rather hostile country, over whose actions the West has no possible control unless it be the denial of trading opportunities and the supply of technology and credit, and so on. The very nature of the massive deals under consideration is such as to require the Western partner to come up with a lot of money and technology in the short term, to be repaid by raw materials etc., at a much later date. Thus, as has been pointed out elsewhere in this study, the Soviet planners for their part have, since 1973, been seriously reappraising the whole Soviet energy situation, consequent first upon the rather disappointing performance of the oil and gas industry during the first three years of the 1971–75 five-year plan, and second, because of doubts about the future ability of those industries to satisfy the envisaged future demands of the domestic economy and of the European Comecon countries. Included in the reappraisal has been a searching analysis of the possible role of Western assistance, both in extent and in mode of operation, and it is becoming clear that the more progressive elements of the Soviet scientific and commercial hierarchy have appreciated the fact that there will have to be changes in Soviet managerial and trading practices at least at enterprise level if effective Western assistance is to be encouraged.

The debate about the desirability and wisdom of allowing the Soviet economy to become increasingly, even if selectively, dependent on infusions of Western technology, to resuscitate the performance of a given sector, which is flagging as a result of inadequacies of Soviet research, development or management in a particular field, continues between different sections of the Soviet leadership. But the unequal development of technological innovation in the Soviet oil and gas industries, and the patchy introduction of even the most advanced Soviet developed technology throughout the many and geographically widely separated branches of those industries, are clearly giving rise to concern in this respect. The problem is that the more sophisticated Western technology likely to be available for exchange with the Soviet bloc is designed to operate in rather different managerial and infrastructural environments from those obtaining in that region, although it would of course yield some improvements in efficiency even under existing conditions. This applies particularly in the more remote and uninviting regions in the north and east of the Soviet Union where, in fact, the major effort in the development of energy resources to meet the future incremental demands of Comecon is being extended.

During the Stalin period the Soviet citizen was persuaded by a continuing campaign of terror to adopt a 'pioneering' spirit towards the opening up of new frontiers, both economically and geographically, and the suffering of hardships connected with the climate and with the absence of the normal trappings of civilization enabled prodigious deeds of construction to be performed in the decade before World War II. The Soviet citizen today, however, has, in general, reached that level of enlightenment and sophistication at which manifestations of the 'pioneering spirit' are more readily forthcoming at the promise of such improvements in the standard of living as the acquisition of a private car or of adequate unshared accommodation, than as a result of exhortations to put the Communist Party's recipe for life into practical effect.

The return on capital invested in the Soviet Union seems to be declining, at a time when reserves of cheap labour seem to have been exhausted, and the leadership is faced with a particularly difficult 'stick and carrot' problem over raising productivity. The sort of carrot which might be expected to produce the best results is tainted with many flavours distilled from the world of capitalism such as genuine material incentives and independence of thought coupled with access to unedited scientific and technical information. The re-application of 'the stick', when so much effort has been expended in recent years in trying to put the Stalinist past behind, would not only have a good chance of being counter-productive with the new generation of Soviet citizens, but it would also go a long way to nullifying those gains which the Soviet leadership may believe that it has made in its bid for the hearts and minds of the non-committed nations and the Third World in general. The provision of the material incentives necessary to bring about an increase in the productivity of the Soviet people will require a major improvement in the infrastructural level of the Soviet economy and this is clearly not within the capability of the existing political and managerial economic set-up.

The relevance of this to the Soviet energy industry is that it is becoming increasingly difficult for Soviet management circles to persuade enough people with the required skills to work, for a long enough period, on the major energy development schemes which are increasingly located in those remoter and harsher parts of the Soviet Union, where the prospect of ever experiencing adequate living conditions is equally remote, and where the thrill of receiving doubled or trebled wages is dissipated by the growing knowledge that there is all too little of real value which can be purchased with them.

From an ideological point of view, although justification can and is being found by the Party hierarchy in the writings of Marx and Lenin for such an intensified turning to the capitalist West for economic assistance, it is at the somewhat lower levels of economic administration that one can expect maximum resistance to the changes which would be necessitated by the introduction and incorporation of new Western technology and operational management. One problem facing the Soviet policy makers is

149

that if the substantial imports of Western technology which have to be made are to be used to optimum effect, there ought also to be changes in the Marxist–Leninist way of managing the economy, such managerial change having, of course, much wider ideological implications. The sophisticated technology which must be imported from the West will itself require corresponding managerial practices if it is to be fully effective in bringing about the necessary improvements in the technological infrastructure of the Soviet economy. There is naturally considerable opposition at the highest levels in the Soviet hierarchy to the ideological contamination of the Soviet way of life which the more orthodox members of the leadership foresee as an inevitable result of any large-scale 'industrial co-operation' schemes involving the admittance to Soviet territory of considerable numbers of 'free-thinking' capitalist workers and, more importantly, managers, especially under local conditions of poorly developed infrastructure and different standards of living, etc. While it is one thing to contain 1,000–2,000 Italian workers in the comparatively compact and civilized confines of Togliattigrad car factory in the southern European part of the country, it would represent far greater problems to the security and other authorities if thousands of, say, American oil or gas men were to be let loose in the vastness of Siberia to work on a pipeline scheme several thousand kilometres in length, to be constructed over a period of five or six years. The willingness of Mr Brezhnev and his colleagues seriously to countenance, however briefly, the possibility of setting up a number of such schemes in co-operation with the United States and other Western industrialized countries could be taken as evidence of a signficiant change in Soviet thinking. Whether this change, if change it be, has been brought about by economic pressures resulting from consistent and increasing failures in key sectors of the Soviet economy, or whether it has come as a result of enlightened and constructive thinking upon the whole future of Soviet international relations is difficult to determine at this stage. There is no guarantee that the change is irreversible or that it will survive a change in Soviet leadership. It is not impossible that it might, indeed, bring about a change in the Soviet leadership. But the question must be asked to what extent should potential Western partners rely upon the durability of the currently perceived Soviet policy towards substantial Western involvement in the development of the Soviet economy in general and of the energy sector in particular, and will it really lead to an economic underpinning of détente?

East—West relations

Although agreement between Comecon and the European Community on how to deal with each other on international trade and other levels had not, as of June 1975, yet been reached, and neither had agreement on European security and troop reductions in Europe, there has developed over the five years 1971—75 a growing measure of interdependence between Comecon and the industrialized countries of the West, and the communist nations appear to be moving towards acceptance of at least a medium-term reliance on Western technology, to enable them to boost their own economic performance and consequently to set themselves more lofty economic targets than might otherwise have been possible. In view of the chronic state of hard currency shortage in all the East European countries, with the possible exception today of the Soviet Union, new forms of East—West economic relationships have had to be developed over the last two decades, and are usually referred to under the general heading of 'industrial co-operation'. This phrase refers to those economic relationships and activities arising from contracts extending over a number of years between partners belonging to different economic systems which go beyond the straightforward sale or purchase of goods and services, to include a set of complementary or reciprocally matching operations (in production, the development and transfer of technology, marketing, etc); and from contracts between such partners which have been identified as industrial co-operation contracts by governments in bilateral or multinational agreements. This evolution of 'industrial co-operation' is clearly necessary if there are ever to be mutually advantageous new relationships between partners in countries with different systems.

It is perhaps worth repeating at this point that, with the possible exception of the recently concluded Sakhalin exploration deal (described on pp. 62—3), no major energy schemes with Western organizations such as would fit into the above projected developments have yet been signed or fully negotiated. It is unlikely therefore that any Western assistance would be able to contribute very much to Soviet crude production capabilities until the early 1980s, although it could help to improve the reserves-to-production ratio quite significantly. Moreover, even the largest schemes so far talked about involving Western participation would not result in the addition of more than, say, 20 billion cu. metres of gas or 25m tons of oil to the Soviet annual production totals.

It is difficult to escape the conclusion that, for the remainder of this decade at least, the development of the Soviet oil and other energy industries is going to rely almost entirely upon domestic effort, in spite of all the shortcomings mentioned in Part I. These shortcomings have almost certainly been taken fully into consideration by the Soviet planners. It is hard to see how, given the existing economic set-up in the Soviet Union, Western assistance could make a significant contribution to the overall picture except in rather specialized fields, such as some aspects of exploration, the provision of steel pipelines, and the introduction of certain secondary and tertiary recovery methods. Even this amount of assistance would, however, require the mobilization of international co-operation on a scale greater than almost any previously, even in the West, involving the creation of large international consortia of financial concerns, equipment suppliers, and energy companies, and a considerable degree of co-operation between governments of several Western countries. It is probably fair to state that at present the necessary stage of evolution of co-operation between countries of the West has not yet been attained, and co-operation between countries of East and West certainly has some considerable way to go before either side can derive the full economic benefits which must surely be realizable. The evolution of such co-operation will not take place overnight, and will very probably give rise to a great many initial problems of a political and strategic nature. It is probable nevertheless that such an evolution will get under way during the next few years; yet although it will quite possibly generate a number of multi-billion dollar deals, the economic significance of these for the time being in the overall pattern of international trade and, indeed, the international energy industry itself, should not be overestimated.

Within the framework of East—West technical and commercial co-operation there is a fundamental difference between the nature of the participants on either side. In the case of the Soviet Union and the countries of Eastern Europe, all the negotiators are, of course, representing the State — either the Ministry of Foreign Trade, or some other industrial ministry or its research establishments, or one of the new industry associations or trusts which embody, for example, the management from a number of factories in the same sector of industry, drawn from widely separated parts of the country although ultimately responsible to the industrial ministry. On the Western side the participants may vary from small private companies, through the multinational corporations, to quasi-governmental complexes such as those Japanese organizations in which the Ministry for International Trade and Industry (MITI) has a determining role. While the smaller Western companies, particularly those possessing a particular piece of highly specialized advanced technology, still have an important part to play in the development of East—West trade, such is the scale of the projects which are increasingly the subject of East—West co-operation that it is only the larger firms or, indeed, associations and consortia of these plus banks and construction companies, etc. which can, physically, handle them. The very largest projects are beginning to raise such questions of international finance, politics, and security that the involvement of individual Western governments to a greater or lesser extent is already taking place, and it seems likely that, in future, co-operation between Western governments may well be indispensable if the optimal degree of East–West commercial co-operation is to be realized. Nevertheless, in much of this current co-operation, decisions on whether or not to go ahead with any particular piece of business are still taken on purely commercial grounds by the management of the private Western companies involved, and the role of the Western governments is primarily one of creating and maintaining the necessary degree of diplomatic and political harmony, and of providing the necessary financial guarantees.

Industrial co-operation as described above embraces many different types of what might be called 'non-conventional' trade. Since East–West trade has developed at a rapid rate in recent years, it is now perhaps correct to draw a distinction between the more sophisticated and longer-term means of economic co-operation, such as would be involved in any major schemes for Western assistance in the development of Soviet or East European energy resources, and the straightforward purchase by the Soviet Union and its allies of key items of technology and equipment which could then be incorporated in and disseminated throughout the appropriate sector of industry by the ministry concerned. An example of this might be the acquisition from a Western equipment manufacturer of the most advanced geophones and recording equipment for seismic work, together with the operational techniques and computer processing know-how, acquired from an experienced Western seismic operator.

Once such equipment and know-how was purchased, disseminated throughout the industry, and put into operation, there would be no continuing need for involvement by the Western partners in the activities of the Soviet ministry concerned.

Soviet foreign trade ministry and oil industry officials have made it clear to Western energy companies that assistance in the exploration for e.g. oil, both off-shore and in eastern Siberia, would be welcomed, although there is far less evidence that physical (as opposed to financial and technological) assistance in the *development* of any previously discovered resources would be equally welcomed.

It is clear that many potential Western partners are still weighing up the pros and cons of becoming deeply involved economically with the Soviet Union over a long period, and it will not be until some clarification of current global economic and political uncertainties allows them to see some concrete advantages for themselves in this involvement that they will respond more wholeheartedly to Soviet overtures.

Notes

[1] Détente is commonly understood as referring to the atmosphere in which East—West discussions take place, but for the purposes of this book it is the actual *policy* as perceived by the Soviet Union which is under consideration.

[2] It may be relevant to point out that the next few years are likely to see changes in the Soviet leadership on age or other grounds, and such changes in the past have tended towards changes in emphasis in the policies pursued by the leadership.

11　Japan and China

It is appropriate at this stage to review the development of Soviet relations with the Western world in the field of energy, particularly those involving Japanese, American, and West European governments and consortia in the bigger energy schemes. It is also appropriate to consider the various economic and political factors influencing these schemes and the implications for future developments. The largest amount of data is available concerning the Japanese developments. This is partly because negotiations on them have been in progress for longer than those concerning schemes with other Western countries — a natural outcome perhaps of the considerable Soviet and Japanese complementarity of interests in the field of resources development. It is also partly perhaps because the high degree of government co-ordination and control, through MITI, of the response of Japan's industrial circles to Soviet approaches on industrial co-operation, has resulted in a more meaningful and streamlined dialogue between the administrative and business organizations of the two countries than that which tends to develop when many different firms from a Western country are all talking with different voices about the same project. The negotiations between Japan and the Soviet Union primarily involve the possibility of co-operation in the exploitation of Siberian and Far Eastern energy, mineral and timber resources.

Siberia and the Far East

The Tyumen scheme

Significant discussions between the two sides were inaugurated in Tokyo in 1966 at the first meeting of the Japan—Soviet Economic Committee which consists of Japanese businessmen and Soviet commercial representatives and which was created in September 1965 to exchange ideas on the direction and scope of future co-operation. The Soviet side proposed that Japan should participate in a project to develop the petroleum resources of the Tyumen region of western Siberia. Other projects discussed at that time included the exploration for oil, gas and other mineral reserves of the continental shelf off Sakhalin Island, the construction of pipelines, the development of Siberian copper deposits, the construction of port facilities in the Soviet Far East, and the development of Siberian timber and wood pulp resources. No concrete agreements were reached in 1966 although subsequent meetings of the Japan—Soviet Economic Committee led to the signing of a timber agreement in July 1968 and agreements on the development of port facilities at Wrangel Bay in December 1970 and on co-operation in wood chip and pulp production in December 1971. The 1968 agreement stipulated that Japan would supply credits worth $133m in equipment and $30m in consumer goods over a three-year period for development of the timber and wood-working industry on the Amur River. Repayments were to be made in the form of Soviet exports of timber during 1969—73. The terms of Japanese credit for the equipment were a 20 per cent deposit, with repayment of the balance over a five-year period at 5·8 per cent interest. Deferred payments were arranged on Japanese exports of $30m in consumer goods. The agreement on Japanese participation in construction of a new Soviet port on Wrangel Bay was a logical corollary to the discussions on joint development of raw materials since, the new port, the construction of which is well under way, will ultimately have facilities for handling annually 10m tons of coal, 800,000 tons of wood chips and other raw materials. The agreement provides for Japanese delivery of equipment, machinery, and materials to be used in the construction of the port. The Soviet purchasers will pay 12 per cent down and will receive a Japanese credit of $80m to be repaid in seven years at 6 per cent interest. The wood chip and pulp production agreement involves the Japanese provision of a credit of about $45m to be repaid over six years at 6 per cent interest. Regarding the Soviet proposal concerning the petroleum and natural gas resources of western Siberia, the Japanese delegation expressed polite interest in the projects in 1966, but made no serious moves to pursue the discussions until April 1971, partly because of political issues connected with the disputed Kurile Islands (see p. 165), but mainly because the size of the projects suggested by the Soviet Union at that time, and the amount of Japanese capital which would be required on deferred repayment terms which Japan was not then in a position to provide. In 1971 Japan was more interested in buying Soviet raw materials at favourable prices on a commercial basis and was also critical of the lack of clear-cut Soviet plans for the projects which they were proposing.

In April 1971 the Japanese leadership of the Japan—Soviet Economic Committee indicated that it was interested in resuming substantive talks on Tyumen, and asked the Soviet side to present a concrete proposal at the fifth session of the joint committee, originally scheduled for 1970 but now re-scheduled for February 1972. It was at this point, in the spring of 1971, that serious discussions concerning the Tyumen project were begun. In May, the Japanese ambassador to the Soviet Union discussed the project with Soviet Prime Minister Kosygin; in August, a leading Liberal Democrat Party member of the Diet, Zentaro Kosaka, discussed the issue with Deputy Prime Minister Baibakov, the chairman of Gosplan (the State planning institution), in Moscow; in early September the chairman of the petroleum sub-committee of the joint committee met in Moscow with the Soviet first Deputy Minister of Trade to pursue the Tyumen question further. The Soviet Minister of Trade, Mr Patolichev, visited Tokyo in December and discussed a possible Tyumen project with the Japanese Prime Minister and with the Ministers of Finance and Industry. The preliminary discussions leading up to the fifth meeting of the joint committee were held during the visit of Soviet Foreign Minister Gromyko to Japan in January 1972. During this visit Japan and the Soviet Union agreed to accelerate discussions concerning Japanese participation in Siberian development.

At the fifth joint committee meeting in Tokyo in February 1972 the Soviet Union presented five proposals for Japanese participation in Soviet resource development projects, all of which involved the granting of loans and credits by Japan for amounts far greater than had been the case in any of the previous agreements. Two projected proposals, involving oil in Tyumen and natural gas in Yakutia, entailed bank loans running into several billions of dollars. When Soviet representatives had first brought up the question of co-operation in western Siberia in 1966 they had asked for Japanese assistance in building a 7,800km pipeline from Tyumen to Nakhodka, but by the time of the fifth joint committee meeting in February 1972, the Russians had already completed the building of 3,400km of this pipeline, from Tyumen to Irkutsk. The proposal which the Soviet side now put forward was that Japan should provide a bank loan of over $1 billion to enable the Soviet Union to purchase large diameter pipeline and other equipment and materials necessary for constructing the remaining 4,178km of pipeline from Irkutsk to Nakhodka, and for constructing large storage facilities and a shipping terminal at Nakhodka. An increase in the capacity of the existing pipeline between Tyumen and Irkutsk would also be involved. Japan would provide the funds to buy the material although it would not participate in any of the construction itself. In return for all this, the Soviet Union offered to supply crude oil to Japan at the rate of 25–40m tons annually over a twenty-year period.

Over the years discussions of the Tyumen oil project have generated various proposals for Japanese shipment of machinery, equipment and materials on credit, to be repaid by Soviet deliveries of crude oil, but since the February 1972 meeting, the Soviet Union has changed the terms of its offer on Tyumen co-operation several times and, for example, most recently the Soviet negotiators proposed Japanese co-operation in the construction of a much shorter Baikal—Amur railway. This meant that supplies of oil for Japan would have to be transported for a major part of the journey from Tyumen by railway.

In June 1972, a Japanese technical mission visited Tyumen and concluded that, 'seen from the technical viewpoint, the Tyumen project is worth pursuing'. In October 1972 the Japanese Foreign Minister visited Moscow, and in March 1973 the Japanese Prime Minister, in a letter to Mr Brezhnev, called for negotiations for a peace treaty and stressed the importance of achieving an agreement on the Tyumen project for the long-term relations between the two countries. It was also proposed that a joint Japanese business—government delegation, headed by the Chief of the Petroleum Committee of the Japan—Soviet Economic Committee, Imazato, should visit Moscow in June to negotiate a basic agreement on the Tyumen project. Yet from the middle of May there was a sudden reversal from what had looked like rapid progress towards an agreement. This was probably a result both of the reappraisal by Moscow of the overall Soviet energy position, which was known to be well under way at this time, and of its deliberations on the desirability of building a railway from Baikal to Amur. On 25 May, therefore, the Soviet Union asked that the business—government visit be postponed and that the sixth meeting of the joint committee, which had been scheduled for July, should also be postponed until some time in the autumn. In August 1973 it was announced that the Soviet and Japanese top leadership of the committee would meet at the end of September in Tokyo, and that the sixth meeting would be held early in 1974. However, in September 1973, the Soviet Union suddenly announced that instead of the original proposal to supply Japan with between 25m and 40m tons of crude oil annually, it would now only be prepared to supply a maximum of 25m tons. It should be noted that this statement was made before the massive rises in the world price of oil which took place at the end of 1973, probably as a result of the growing realization in Soviet energy planning circles that they might well not be able to guarantee the supply of quantities in excess of 25m tons in view of rapidly growing domestic and bloc requirements. The Soviet Union also announced that, because of inflation and changing exchange rates, Japanese participation would be expected to amount to considerably more than the provision of $1 billion. In October 1973, the Japanese Prime Minister confirmed during a visit to Moscow that Japan was still interested in the development of Siberia, and he even promised government support for the Tyumen project once an agreement had been worked out between the Soviet authorities and the participating Japanese business leaders. On his return to Tokyo he indicated his willingness that the government should cover 80 per cent of the financing of a bank loan, as contrasted with a previous position that the government would assume no more than 70 per cent financing, and also indicated that the government would probably agree to keep the interest rate under 6 per cent, in line with what the Soviet Union had demanded.

In March 1974 the Soviet Union indicated that it had revised its earlier plans to transport oil from Tyumen to Nakhodka entirely through a pipeline, and stated that it now planned to transport the oil part of the way over a second trans-Siberian railway. If the Japanese wanted to participate in the Tyumen project at all they would now have to contribute to the building of the railway line. In addition, the price for the right to buy Tyumen oil had gone up from the original $1 billion to an estimated $3·3 billion.

The fact that the Soviet Union was now intending to link the Tyumen oil development to the construction of a second Siberian railroad intensified the already considerable Japanese concern with the political and military implications of the Tyumen development scheme. Although some Japanese business leaders professed to see the railway as simply another way to transport oil across Siberia, the Japanese government saw in the proposal strategic implications of the most serious nature, since not only would the supply position of the Soviet Far Eastern fleet be considerably enhanced, but the supply position of the Soviet military forces on the Far Eastern border with China would also benefit, a fact which would be far from acceptable to the Chinese government. Since this most recent Soviet proposal, the Tyumen project has to all intents and purposes, been shelved by the Japanese who are apparently awaiting modification of the proposal, and particularly some improvement in the volumes of crude oil which will be supplied. The Soviet offer as it reportedly now stands is for the supply to Japan of 5m tons of Tyumen oil in 1981, 10m tons in 1982, 15m tons in 1983, 20m tons in 1984, and 25m tons annually from 1985 until the year 2000.

The sixth meeting of the Japan—Soviet Economic Committee finally took place in Moscow at the end of 1974 and ended with a joint communiqué stressing the need for continued talks on the oil issue and on projects involving paper, natural gas, forestry projects, and Siberian coking coal. The Japanese declined to agree to extend the $3·3 billion in loans for the Tyumen oilfield development because of their concern over the proposed Siberian railway and its strategic and political implications, and also, perhaps, because the international oil supply situation had eased somewhat over the year. The Japanese Foreign Ministry has repeatedly stated that Japanese interests will not be allowed to become involved in the building of the railway unless there is United States involvement as well. In December 1974 Mr Kosygin strongly urged Japan to purchase Soviet crude oil from Tyumen, but Japanese businessmen at that time apparently told their Soviet counterparts that it would be 'difficult' for Japan to participate in the Tyumen project and that prospects for Japanese participation are 'very slim', even if the Russians were to offer more favourable terms. The Soviet side was at pains to point out that the negotiations were not at an end and expressed the hope that progress would be made during the first half of 1975. However, in mid-June of that year a Japanese spokesman for the Japan—Soviet Economic Committee expressed the view that this project had been effectively abandoned.

Turning now to the other major potential Japanese—Soviet energy schemes, on 22 April 1974 Japanese and Soviet officials signed a protocol indicating preliminary agreement on three major *East* Siberian developments — natural gas reserves in northern Yakutia, coking coal reserves in southern Yakutia, and forestry resources in the Soviet Far East. Japan agreed to provide Japanese Export—Import bank credits totalling $1,050m to help in the finance, included in which was a credit of $100m for the exploration stage of the Yakutia natural gas project. This proposed agreement, which is conditional upon US participants extending a similar credit, provides for completion of an exploration project within two years.

Reserves of natural gas have been found in the Yakutia region but they have not yet been proved up. If these reserves prove sufficient, present plans call for Japanese and US partners to extend a credit of more than $3 billion to finance the development of the gas fields and the construction of a pipeline and a gas liquefaction plant. The pipeline would run from Yakutsk to Nakhodka, where the gas would be liquefied and carried by tankers to Japan and the United States. Current projections are that both countries would receive 10 billion cu. metres of gas annually for a period of twenty years. Final agreement in principle on the Yakutia project was reached in late November 1974 between Soviet, Japanese, and US representatives meeting in Paris, and exploration work is now going ahead to confirm the size of the reserves of natural gas in the Yakutia region of eastern Siberia.

This does not yet mean that the whole project will go ahead, since many questions have yet to be answered concerning US trade with the Soviet Union in general and the compatability of the project with US domestic energy policy. It will be necessary to prove up recoverable reserves of around 1,000 billion cu. metres of natural gas but, although Soviet experts estimate the potential at 13,000 billion cu. metres, actual geological exploration of the region to date has been insignificant, principally because there has not so far been the domestic market to justify the very considerable costs involved. Soviet negotiators have, indeed, maintained that the Soviet Union had not intended to raise the output of the Yakutia region in either the 1971--75 five-year plan or the 1976–80 plan, and that the Soviet side could only contemplate proceeding with the project if the Americans and the Japanese were willing to extend the long-term credit to finance the necessary geological, design, research, and construction work and for the purchase of pipe, equipment, construction facilities, and materials. The Paris agreement signed in November 1974 merely indicates that the Japanese and the Americans are *in principle* willing to provide the finance, at least for the initial exploration phase, and the Japanese Export–Import bank agreed to grant the Soviet Union a credit of $100 million provided that a similar credit were to be extended by the United States. The exploration phase of the project will take at least two years, and during this time discussions will continue between all three partners on other equally important aspects of the project including the design and construction of the liquefaction plant at a Soviet port, loading facilities for LNG carriers, and the pipeline to carry the gas from Yakutia to the liquefaction plant. Preliminary indications are that the total non-ruble cost of the project will be around $4·5 billion, and the Soviet Union will require some $2 billion in foreign credits for the purchase of the equipment, pipe, and other supplies and services for that part of the project located within the Soviet Union. The cost of the US LNG tanker fleet, the terminal and a regasification plant in the United States would be approximately $1·5 billion, and a further $1 billion would be needed for the Japanese LNG tanker fleet and regasification plant. It was reported at the end of January 1975 that the talks of Japanese participation in the Yakutia natural gas scheme had run into difficulties because of the Soviet renunciation of the trade agreement with the United States, which automatically put US Export–Import bank finance in danger (see p. 174). However, stage one is now expected to proceed as scheduled.

South Yakutia coking coal

A few days after the April 1974 protocol Japanese and Soviet negotiators signed an additional memorandum indicating that formal agreement on joint development of southern Yakutia coking coal was imminent. The memorandum proposed that Japan, as part of a $1,050 billion loan for eight years at 6·375 per cent interest, should extend a credit of about $450m, to be repaid in the form of 104m tons of coal, delivered between 1979 and 1998. The Japanese loan would be used to buy Japanese railway and other equipment needed to develop and transport the coal.

On 3 June 1974, a general agreement was signed in Moscow concerning the delivery from the Soviet Union to Japan of Yakutia coal, and the delivery by Japan of machinery, materials and other goods for the development of the southern Yakutia coal basin. The carrying out of this agreement would permit the acceleration of the development of the new coal basins in Eastern Siberia for the supplying of coking coal to new enterprises in this region, as well as for export. With the $450m credit extended by Japan, Soviet foreign trade organizations will purchase trucks, trains, loading machinery, earth-moving equipment, machinery and equipment for bridge construction, drilling equipment, and a wide range of other technological goods and materials. The construction of the complex and of the railroad leading to it will be carried out by Soviet organizations, it is believed that the scheme is going ahead normally, and interim deliveries of up to 20m tons of West Siberian (presumably Kuznetsk) coal will be made to Japan.

Sakhalin projects

Soviet and Japanese negotiators have for a long time also been discussing the exploitation of natural gas and oil reserves on and surrounding the island of Sakhalin. Discussions have centred on a formula similar to that of the Tyumen project. In one of the Sakhalin projects Japan would provide credits for the construction of pipelines and the liquefaction plant and would receive some 2—2·4 billion cu. metres of gas annually. Although the exploration and development of Sakhalin oil and gas resources was first tentatively proposed in 1966, little progress was made, primarily because the Soviet negotiators subsequently advised that the on-shore reserves of gas on Sakhalin Island had been overestimated, and it seemed that the Soviet Union was far more interested in the development of the Yakutia gas reserves.

An agreement on the joint development of Sakhalin off-shore mineral resources was, however, signed in Tokyo on 28 January 1975 by Imazato, President of the Sakhalin Oil Development Corporation Company Limited, and Sushkov, a Soviet Deputy Minister of Foreign Trade. Under this agreement Japan is to grant the Soviet Union a $100m credit covering the first five years of development at an annual interest rate of 6 per cent on a 'no success—no repayment basis'. The credit is to cover the lease of a seismic survey vessel, drilling equipment and the supply of exploration materials and services. In addition, Japan is to grant a $22·5m loan to the Soviet Union for the purchase of durable equipment (including computers) to be taken aboard the seismic vessel. A loan for a further $52m was negotiated in July to cover additional purchases of seismic equipment and exploration expenses. The loans are to be extended by a syndicate of Japanese banks at an interest rate of 6·75 per cent. Japan is also to grant a stand-by credit of $30m (in yen) as an operating fund provided by the Japan Development Corporation and the syndicate of Japanese banks at an interest rate of 7·25 per cent. In the event of the discovery of oil or gas in commercial quantities, both sides, subject to mutual consent, are to commence development. In this case Japan would raise up to 50 per cent of the development fund in loans extended by the Japanese Export—Import Bank and by other private banks. The fund would be made available to the Soviet Foreign Trade Bank, the amount and other terms being determined by the inter-bank credit grant agreement. Under the proposed joint development programme the Soviet Union is to supply Japan with 50 per cent of any resulting oil output, while the percentage of natural gas that Japan would receive is to be determined at a later stage. This guarantee of supplies of hydrocarbons to Japan would cover the period of repayment of the credits including interest payments, and extends for ten years after completion of repayment. The credits (including interest) are to be refunded with oil and gas extracted within fifteen years of the start of the exploration venture. In return for the credits granted by Japan on a 'no success—no repayment' basis, the Soviet Union is to apply an 8·4 per cent discount rate on oil and gas delivered to Japan over a ten-year period after the commencement of production. The exploration of the area is expected to be conducted jointly between Japan, the Soviet Union and the United States, but the specific terms of US participation have yet to be announced.

Summary

To summarize the position of the various Japan—Soviet energy schemes as at mid-1975 — the *Tyumen oil* scheme has a very low probability of being successfully negotiated in the near future, at least in its current form, and the Japanese maintain that the ball is in the Soviet court. Although the *Yakutia gas scheme* was temporarily held up pending the clarification of events following the renunciation of the Soviet trade agreement with the United States, the first (exploration) stage is now going ahead. The *Sakhalin off-shore* exploration project is also going ahead, and exploration teams commenced work in June 1975. The $450m Japanese loan scheme to be repaid by deliveries of *Yakutia coking coal* appears to be going ahead normally.

It will have become clearer from the above how closely economic relations between East and West become intertwined with political and strategic considerations. Japan is dependent upon outside sources for almost 100 per cent of its oil, some 80 per cent of which comes from the Middle East, notably from Iran, Saudi Arabia, and Kuwait. Oil consumption has been increasing at over 10 per cent annually in recent years, and even taking into consideration efforts to economise on the use of oil which will probably bring the rate down to nearer 6 per cent annually, a 1974 requirement of some 230m tons is likely to have risen to over 310m tons by 1980 and to nearer 400m tons by 1985. Oil accounts for almost 75 per cent of Japan's energy supply but independent Japanese companies account for less than 10 per cent of the total supply of Japan's crude oil. Well before the October 1973 world oil crisis, the Japanese government had taken steps to gain control of a greater share of the country's supplies, with the objective of bringing 30 per cent of Japan's oil from 'autonomous' Japanese sources by 1980. But the winter 1973 oil crisis served to emphasize the serious oil supply position in which Japan now finds itself, dependent upon one of the less politically stable regions of the world for most of that oil, and having no say in the negotiations between OPEC and the major oil consortia. Japanese policy has been aimed towards developing a diversification of the sources of its supplies and towards a greater control of those supplies by Japanese companies, even though this might well mean that Japan would have to participate with other governments in the development of the diversified supplies.

The attraction of the Tyumen oil development project for the Japanese government becomes clear in the light of the above, although Japan is rather reluctant to participate alone with such a powerful partner, against which it would have little redress should the Soviet Union decide to change the terms of the agreement after Japanese finance and equipment, etc. had been fully committed. Hence the high level of importance which the Japanese negotiators have all along attached to American participation. Japan's almost total lack of natural gas resources explains why the Yakutia natural gas and the Sakhalin off-shore schemes are also very attractive. Both the Soviet Union and Japan have compelling economic motivations for undertaking co-operative ventures in Siberia and the Far East. Siberia

164

represents an alternative source for Japan's huge import needs for raw materials, while Japan is a potential source for capital and technology which the Soviet Union would like to tap in order to assist in the implementation of its ambitious development plans for the eastern part of the country. The vast undeveloped resources of Siberia and the modern Japanese industrial sector offer a striking degree of economic complementarity. Without the additional incentive of a Japanese market, the development of, particularly the most easterly situated, Siberian resources has hitherto proved relatively unattractive to the Soviet Union. The opening up of coal, gas, oil, timber and metal deposits in various parts of Siberia and the Far East were important elements of the 1971–75 Soviet five-year plan and are expected to be highlighted in the 1976–80 plan. Western observers might argue that the Soviet Union has insufficient capital resources and, in some cases, inadequate technology for exploiting its Siberian reserves either quickly or efficiently, but Soviet spokesmen have consistently maintained that the Soviet Union need not be dependent on foreign capital and is quite capable of developing Siberia on its own. Much depends on the criteria by which speed and efficiency in the Soviet context are to be judged.

Such long-term self-financing development projects involving Western co-operation as those which the Soviet Union clearly has in mind for Siberia would mean not only that the Soviet Union would not have to expend hard currency, but also that there would be quite a considerable technological and infrastructural spin-off from any specific scheme. There would inevitably be an improvement in the general infrastructure of the whole region and the facilities for transportation etc., which would be developed in the Soviet Far East could, of course, be used for many other purposes than those connected with a specific project.

The Kurile Islands

If the economic rationale for both Japan and the Soviet Union to co-operate in the development of Siberian and Far Eastern energy resources is fairly straightforward, the political and strategic considerations are considerably more complex. It is only in recent years that Soviet–Japanese relations have become anything like normal. It may be remembered that the Soviet Union broke a neutrality pact with Japan at the very end of World War II, and after capturing half a million Japanese soldiers in Manchuria, kept them in concentration camps for ten years. For this and other reasons the Japanese people basically dislike and mistrust the

165

Russians. Nevertheless, diplomatic relations have been established for the past nineteen years, although no formal peace treaty has yet been signed. The improvement in Soviet—Japanese relations has in fact proceeded at a rather slow rate, and one of the key factors has been the existence of a dispute about the ownership of four small islands to the north of Hokkaido, part of the Kurile group which the Soviet Union took from Japan at the end of World War II. When the Soviet Union has wished to improve its relations with the Japanese, for example when it wanted them to consider favourably the extension of large credits for the development of Siberia, then the Soviet leaders have hinted that the islands might one day be returned. When, however, the Soviet Union has wished to show displeasure at some aspect of Japanese foreign policy, then it has criticized continuing Japanese interest in the return of the islands as a senseless attempt to revive dead issues from Japan's imperialist past. The issue of the disputed islands has given rise to considerable controversy in Japanese business and government circles in relation to the Siberian co-operation deals. Politicians and diplomats have tended to argue that no large-scale Japanese economic co-operation with the Soviet Union should be permitted until the four islands have been returned to Japan, and some have even gone to the point of arguing that if ever Japan should agree to co-operate economically with the Soviet Union on a large scale, it might have to say goodbye forever to any chance of negotiating the return of the islands. The Japanese business community, on the other hand, has tended to argue that the return of the four islands should be kept entirely separate from any economic considerations, and that any attempt to link the two in negotiations with the Soviet Union would most likely produce negative results on both the economic and the diplomatic fronts.

The China factor

It is possible that the Soviet Union has misgauged the overall Japanese desire to participate in the economic development of the Soviet Far East and Siberia, particularly over the question of oil supplies. But it may also be that the Soviet Union was more concerned at the turn of the last decade to establish relations with the United States and Western Europe on a firmer footing, while keeping relations with Japan ticking over on the economic front. More recently, however, the Soviet Union may have felt obliged to pay more attention to tackling the problem of its political relationships with Japan, increasingly complicated as these are, by the rapidly improving relationships between Japan and China. When, for example, in 1971, the United States moved to improve relations with China, the Soviet Union began blowing extremely warm upon Japan, but China pre-empted any major Soviet—Japanese détente by ending its own hostility towards Japan and by opening diplomatic relations with Japan in September 1972, for the first time in a generation. The Soviet Union clearly has a horror of any really solid economic and political co-operation between Japan and China, particularly if reinforced by intensified US relations with China. It is particularly significant therefore that part of the current deadlock between Japan and the Soviet Union on the Tyumen project and the Baikal—Amur railway is a direct result of an expression of Chinese dissatisfaction that Japan should participate in any such scheme since, from the Chinese standpoint, this would strengthen the Soviet military and economic position in the Far East, particularly its ability to supply its Far Eastern fleet.

Japan started importing small quantities of Soviet oil in 1959. Although the volume reached some 4m tons annually at the end of the 1960s, it has fallen in recent years to a level of below 2m tons annually, and the Soviet Union has indicated to Japan that it can expect no increase in this volume unless it takes part in the major industrial co-operation schemes. How disturbing for the Soviet Union it must have been to learn that China, whose oil production has been increasing at an extremely high rate in recent years, began to sell crude oil (1m tons) to Japan in 1973. The volume increased to 4m tons in 1974 and the Chinese offered to supply up to 10m tons to Japan in 1975 and 7·8m tons had already been contracted for by the autumn of that year. It is now being rumoured that China will possibly have as much as 40m tons of oil to export by the end of this decade, and this has clearly encouraged Japan to look twice at the Soviet Union as a preferred alternative source to the Middle East, particularly since China has so far appeared less demanding than the Soviet Union concerning payment terms. China has shown itself apparently content to accept foreign currency and a small element of equipment and technology in payment for its oil exports, and far from requiring potential customers to become deeply involved in economic co-operation ventures on shore or to extend large lines of credit to enable it to import more foreign equipment and technology, China has so far tended to resist approaches involving joint ventures. This is in keeping with China's ideologically based policy of self-reliance. It is not known at this stage whether China has complained diplomatically to the United States concerning the latter's proposed participation in the Tyumen project. It is perhaps of relevance to note that, according to Japanese sources, China is expecting to produce some 150m tons of oil in 1978 compared with some 60m tons in 1974. By

1988, production is tentatively targeted at 450m tons, but although existing reserves, estimated at between 1·2 and 1·8 billion tons, are considered by Japanese experts as adequate for the fulfilment of the production plans, the 1988 target would seem to be extremely optimistic in view of the high annual growth rates which would be required to reach it. It is not considered likely that China will be in a position to use domestically more than, say, two-thirds of its total production, and there is a very real possibility that the availability of Chinese oil in the Far East will render Soviet oil and hence development projects aimed at its export, far less attractive propositions than they seemed a few years previously. This, of course, probably does not apply to Soviet off-shore resources.

Soviet foreign policy towards China is too vast a subject to be covered fully in a study of this nature, and is, in any case, affected mainly by considerations which have little to do with energy. It may be mentioned, however, that the Soviet Union, for historical, ideological, and strategic reasons, appears to regard China as a far more serious and implacable threat to long-term Soviet security than a rational analysis of the existing and envisaged military balance between the two countries would appear to justify. The fact that the Soviet Union is obliged, for logistic reasons, both to seek its future energy supplies further and further eastwards and to create the necessary infrastructure for the development of those resources and for the eastward location of new industries, based on the long-term plans, means that there is an increased security problem vis-à-vis a perceived threat from China. Massive energy and other industrial developments in the eastern part of the Soviet Union would be seen as increasing Soviet vulnerability to a Chinese long-range missile attack, and the cost of creating appropriate defences along such an extended border as that between the Soviet Union and China must present severe problems to the Soviet planners. The Soviet leadership appears to have accepted the fact that, although the level of verbal hostilities now raging between the two countries' propaganda machines can possibly be lowered as a result of the change in the Chinese leadership that must occur on the death of Chairman Mao Tse-tung, the underlying ideological differences between the two countries are so great that no genuine rapprochement can be foreseen, and the best that can be hoped for is a papering-over-the-cracks offensive which will not, however, do anything to change the long-term situation. China's global political activities, which have grown substantially during the past five years, have in most cases manifested themselves as being in opposition to those put forward by the Soviet Union, for example in regard to the EEC, the European Security Conference and the Soviet-sponsored Asian security proposals.

The Soviet Union used to supply China will small volumes of oil products, but to all intents and purposes these ceased in 1965. While there is a shortage of information about China's overall energy situation, it looks as though it will be well able to meet its own oil requirements for the foreseeable future, and will in no way become dependent upon supplies from the Soviet Union. The relevance of China to the theme of this study lies in its potential as an alternative supplier of energy to Japan, as already discussed. To the extent that China is a very powerful communist state, at present in ideological conflict with the Soviet Union, the latter can no longer ignore Chinese interests when negotiating with one or other of its potential capitalist partners, particularly if these in turn have economic or political interests in preserving or developing good relations with China. It would appear improbable, for example, that the United States, and therefore Japan, would participate in the development of any eastern Siberian scheme which would, for one reason or another, run contrary to China's perceived and clearly stated interests, so that some form of appeasement of China by one or other of the intended participants would appear to be necessary. Therefore, so long as Sino–Soviet relations remain strained, this can be expected to reduce the attractiveness of such a scheme.

Unless China can be persuaded to give up its claims to the disputed areas of the Sino–Soviet border, the Japanese will always have China's political support, in theory, for Japanese demands for the return by the Soviet Union of the disputed Kurile Islands. If the Soviet Union were, for example, to return the islands to Japan, thereby tacitly admitting that they were unjustly obtained in the first place and subsequently unjustly retained, China would immediately and vociferously reiterate its demands that the Soviet Union should admit its 'errors' in respect of the disputed border areas, annexed as a result of various, in Chinese eyes, 'unequal treaties' dating back to 1858. China is currently taking pains to point out to the United States, Western Europe, Japan, and, indeed, Eastern Europe, the risks involved in becoming too closely associated with the Soviet Union, and attributing to the latter the most evil of long-term intentions towards the West. In short, the Soviet Union would find it a good deal easier to engage in economic and political negotiations with the West and with Japan, including those concerning energy matters, if China were suddenly to go away. It is only possible to speculate on the extent to which Japan or the United States might wish to use possible Chinese objections to their major involvement in the development of Siberia and the Far East to enable them to back out at a late stage in negotiations.

Great though the advantages might be if the Soviet Union were to reach some form of accommodation with China, it does not at present seem as though the fear of missing out entirely upon Western economic assistance in the development of the Soviet Far East is going to hasten the Soviet leadership in the direction of making such an accommodation. The economic development of eastern Siberia and the Soviet Far East holds a high priority in the Soviet leadership's long-term planning, but the recent decision to go ahead with the frequently postulated mammoth project of the Baikal–Amur railway is another indication that the Soviet Union is both willing and able to develop its own resources at its own pace, if the political price to be paid for outside assistance is too high.

12　The United States

Historical background

The whole question of potential US involvement in the development of Soviet energy resources is of fairly recent origin, dating officially from November 1971, when the then US Secretary of Commerce, Maurice Stans, visited Moscow and the Soviet Deputy Minister of Foreign Trade, Alkhimov, visited the United States. The latter suggested that American companies could undertake numerous joint projects with the Soviet Union, such as copper mining and off-shore oil exploration ventures. American business executives subsequently travelled to Moscow at the end of November to discuss joint ventures and other trade possibilities, although nothing concrete emerged at that time. President Nixon visited Moscow in May 1972, and a joint US—USSR Commercial Commission was established with the job of drawing up an overall trade agreement and making a study of areas of possible co-operation between the two countries. In July 1972, following many months of rumour and speculation, the Occidental Petroleum Corporation signed a preliminary agreement in Moscow whereby it would provide technological assistance in the production of oil and natural gas in the Soviet Union in exchange for raw materials, including oil and gas. In August 1972, the International Harvester Company announced a deal to supply the Soviet Union with tractors which would be used in the construction of natural gas pipelines. In June 1973, Occidental Petroleum Corporation and the El Paso Natural Gas Company reached an agreement in principle with the Soviet Foreign Trade Ministry whereby the American companies would participate in the exploration and development of natural gas fields in the eastern Siberian region of Yakutia, in conjunction with the Japanese. If the project was successful some 20 billion cu. metres of natural gas per year would be shipped to the United States over a twenty-five year period, and the project was estimated at that time to be going to cost about $10 billion. This project has been discussed in more detail above (pp. 160—1), but it is worth repeating that the Soviet Union would initially receive a loan of $150m from the United States and Japan to assist in the exploration phase of the Yakutia project, subject to approval being given by the US government. The US government hoped to be in a position to grant that approval with the passing of the

Trade Reform Bill which would have accorded most-favoured-nation (m.f.n.) status to the Soviet Union, and would have authorized the granting of the necessary credit by the US Export–Import Bank. In October 1973, the US Treasury Secretary held trade talks in Moscow, and he subsequently noted that further trade expansion between the United States and the Soviet Union was indeed being held up by the m.f.n. issue. This issue was in turn being held up by the Jackson–Vanik amendment to the Trade Reform Bill, denying trade benefits to the Soviet Union until such time as it agreed to allow free emigration, particularly the emigration of Jews. In February 1974, the Soviet Foreign Trade Minister on a visit to the United States, warned that if Congressional attempts to halt credits for the Soviet Union were successful, the Soviet leaders would have to turn to other Western countries for the credits, and for co-operation in the large-scale projects, particularly those involved in the development of energy resources.

In March 1974, the Soviet Foreign Trade Minister declared that trade with the United States could not be carried out in the absence of credits, and expressed disappointment at attempts by various American Congressmen to link trade with the Soviet Union to Soviet internal policies. In May 1974, the Soviet Minister of the Oil Industry was reported by American journalists as saying that the Soviet Union had decided against undertaking joint Soviet oil development projects with Western countries, and would undertake the planned projects on its own, although there was considerable uncertainty both as to exactly what the minister had said and as to subsequent contradictory statements by other Soviet officials. These two incidents are, however, quite significant in that they underline the importance which the Soviet authorities attach to the whole question of obtaining Western credits, while at the same time stressing that the Soviet Union is not going to allow itself to become actually dependent upon those credits, particularly in such a strategically important sector of the economy as the oil industry, even though such credits would be very much appreciated. In July 1974, President Nixon visited Moscow again, and a Soviet–American economic agreement was signed, aimed at establishing the broad framework for trade relations over the next ten years. Among the areas of possible co-operation were listed schemes involving the exploration and development of natural gas.

The Urengoy gas project

In addition to the proposed scheme for Yakutia, American companies had been discussing with their Soviet counterparts another scheme, involving the production of gas from the Urengoy fields in north-western Siberia, the construction of a pipeline from Urengoy to Murmansk and of a liquefaction plant at Murmansk, and the development of a fleet of LNG tankers to carry the gas to the US east coast. Negotiations were under way in mid 1973 between the relevant Soviet ministries and a consortium of three American companies — Tenneco, Texas Eastern Transmission Corporation, and a subsidiary of Halliburton. This west Siberian development scheme was expected to cost about $7·6 billion. Of that sum, the Soviet Union would invest about $1·5 billion for drilling, gas gathering and cleaning equipment. The remainder would be invested by the US consortium in the building of twenty LNG tankers (then costing about $2 billion) and for the construction of the 1,500 mile pipeline and associated compressors, the gas liquefaction plant and the loading facilities etc. The contract was scheduled to run for twenty-five years, with gas deliveries to the United States valued at $450m per year beginning in 1980. The American credit was to have been repaid over a twelve-year period, with 75 per cent of the gas deliveries used to pay off the principal and interest on the loan. The remaining 25 per cent was to be used to buy other US capital goods. After the US loan was fully repaid, gas deliveries to the United States would continue for the duration of the contract, with the proceeds convertible into purchases in the United States. The US Export— Import Bank, and a consortium of private US banks were expected to finance the deal, and under the terms being discussed in 1973 the Soviet Union could have expected to receive somewhat better treatment than other US trade partners — for example, no repayments would have been made by the Soviet Union while the project was under construction. Payments were due to begin only after construction was completed and the project in full operation. At that time there were problems facing the Export—Import Bank's participation, in that the rules of the Bank required a degree of disclosure of information and an acceptance of commercial terms by the Soviet side to which the latter was not accustomed, so that the only alternative open to the Bank would have been to grant the Soviet Union preferred status, something which would have been politically difficult to do.

There was pronounced dissatisfaction in American business circles at the projected cost of the Soviet natural gas, which would, when it eventually arrived, be considerably higher than the current price of United States produced gas. It was at that time expected that domestic gas would cost under 100 cents per 1,000 cu. feet in 1985, whereas Soviet gas would be delivered to American east coast ports at $1·25 per 1,000 cu. feet.

Events connected with the quadrupled oil prices at the end of 1973, and the rapid development of inflation and recession in the United States throughout 1974 resulted in a total rethink of the Urengoy–Murmansk gas project, particularly on the US side, and whatever stage negotiations between the American consortium and the Soviet Union may have reached at the time of writing, further serious discussion will inevitably have been held up until such time as the laws governing the granting of Export–Import Bank credits are clarified. In early 1975, the Soviet Union rejected the US–Soviet trade agreement, following the inclusion of the Jackson–Vanik amendment in the US Trade Reform Act, on the grounds that this represented intolerable interference in Soviet internal affairs by the United States. It should be pointed out at this stage, that over 80 per cent of the trade which the United States and the Soviet Union indulge in or are likely to indulge in, is not affected by m.f.n. considerations. The Soviet Union nevertheless regards the whole issue very seriously as one of principle. What is, however, crucially affected by the Trade Reform Act is the ability of the Export–Import Bank to advance loans in excess of $300m to the Soviet Union between now and the middle of 1978. There is also a $40m ceiling on Export–Import Bank assistance for energy research on exploration projects in the Soviet Union, and Congress has to be notified twenty-five days in advance of any Export–Import Bank action on any proposed energy projects in the Soviet Union that will involve $25m or more of Bank assistance. If the United States decides that it wants to approve loans to the Soviet Union in excess of the $300m ceiling, the President would be required to declare that this was necessary and desirable, as a matter of US national interest, and he would have to win Congressional approval to authorize such loans. As things stand, the Export–Import Bank is probably in a position to advance a $40m credit towards the Yakutia natural gas exploration scheme, but all other major potential US–Soviet energy development schemes which all rely upon massive (i.e. $7–10 billion) credits, are temporarily held up, and there is unlikely to be a change in the law before 1976. This can have serious implications for the future of the big energy schemes, in view of the impending publication of the new Soviet 1976–80 five-year plan, since the Soviet Union may feel compelled to go ahead with the development of its Siberian resources without the help of massive Western credits. It may be noted that there is a legal lending limit of US commercial banks, whereby they are prevented from extending more than 10 per cent of their total lendings to any one borrower which, in spite of the numerous different schemes in question, the Soviet State is taken to be. One highly optimistic calculation is that the banks could, in total, probably legally

174

lend up to $2·5 billion, but this would hardly be sufficient to finance one of the very large energy schemes and the actual lending ability is more likely to be much nearer $1 billion. There are, of course, possibilities of borrowing more money on the European market.

Détente and trade

Large-scale credits will not, presumably, be forthcoming from the United States unless US–Soviet economic and political relations are further improved to the point at which US industrial circles are convinced, with the backing of the US government, that any risk of the Soviet Union making difficulties over repayment is no greater than the risk attached to the extension of such large amounts of credit to other energy schemes in other parts of the world. In fact, as mentioned above, US financial institutions regard the Soviet Union very favourably from the point of view of credit rating. However, support from the US Administration for massive US involvement in the big energy schemes will probably not be forthcoming unless talk about détente is translated into concrete political developments which can be seen by all but the most intransigent cold warriors to be improving US–Soviet global relationships. There are those in the United States in positions of power and authority who are bitterly opposed to any extension of credits to the Soviet Union, since, they say, this enables it to sustain a massive military establishment which it would otherwise find it more difficult to do if it was obliged to pay for Western economic and technical assistance with hard cash, or to finance its own development of resources from the national budget.

Clearly, as has already been shown, there was a great deal more behind the Soviet decision to promote détente with the United States than mere doubts about the future of the Soviet energy industries. Not least of the motives may have been a desire on the part of the Soviet leadership to improve the lot of the Soviet consumer, within ideologically acceptable limits, particularly through the provision of more and better foodstuffs, consumer goods generally, automobiles, textiles, etc. However, the dangers inherent in allowing the infection of the Soviet way of life by the excesses of capitalism have clearly seldom been far from the minds of the Soviet leaders, and US traders have by no means been allowed free access to the Soviet consumer.

Energy matters have always attracted much attention from Western commentators simply because, in their very nature, they have often involved what, in the early 1970s at least, were very big sums of money.

Furthermore, if one of the big energy schemes could have been successfully concluded, it would, as has already been suggested, have served as an excellent example of the economic underpinning of détente which both Mr Nixon and Mr Brezhnev considered so important. Both sides would probably have welcomed, on purely political grounds, the creation of a major energy co-operation scheme, particularly if it turned out to be economically mutually beneficial, and it is quite possible that such conditions could have been negotiated if economic and political developments in the West had not taken a sharp turn for the worse.

It has already been mentioned (p. 136) that, as a result of the increase in the world price of oil, the Soviet Union was able to reverse its adverse trade balance with the industrially developed capitalist countries for 1973 into a relative surplus in 1974; however, 1975 will probably have seen a return to a substantial deficit as a result of large purchases of Western grain. So long as the world price of oil remains at its current level, and so long as the Soviet Union has a surplus to export, which it is expected to have for the rest of the decade, it could generate hard currency surpluses if large imports of grain can be avoided. This change in the Soviet balance-of-payments position means, in effect, that it should be temporarily able to purchase from the United States – and elsewhere – more of the technology and equipment which it needs for the development of its energy and other industries without requiring so large an amount of Western credit. It is true that the price of many of the goods which it wishes to import will have risen considerably as a result of inflation and increased energy costs, but not to the extent that would totally eliminate the massive windfall to the Soviet trading position which the rise in world prices has meant. This raises the question of the Soviet ability to absorb, at least into its energy industries, technology and equipment which it could purchase from the United States. It also raises the question of whether and in what way such an injection of improved technology and equipment can significantly improve the production performance of the industries in question. A rapid improvement is rather unlikely, given the diffusion rate of such a widely dispersed and bureaucratically encumbered organization as a Soviet energy industry. It can be argued that the point has been reached in many sectors of the Soviet economy where any additional investment will result in a smaller increase in unit output, mainly because of human factors – lack of incentive, vested interests, and reluctance to accept managerial changes, etc. Unless the Soviet Union will allow US companies complete freedom to enter the country and to operate without let or hindrance – say, in the exploration of new territories in eastern Siberia – it is unlikely that the Soviet industries will be able to obtain anything like the maximum benefit from 'massive US assistance' which is, potentially, available. Since no Western observers are better aware of the implications of all this than the Soviet energy industries themselves, it must be assumed that they, at least, are under no illusions about the possibility or, indeed, the desirability of relying upon foreign assistance to boost output, as opposed to putting their own house in order, with Western assistance if need be, so that they can boost their own production.

US—Soviet trade relations in 1975

The current somewhat strained state of US—Soviet relations, following the Soviet renunciation of the 1972 trade agreement, may be of more apparent than real significance to future co-operation in energy matters. A $300m ceiling on possible Export—Import Bank credits to the Soviet Union is now, in view of the substantial Soviet dollar earnings, not so much a practical hindrance to increased trade as a political insult, and the Soviet Union has shown that it is certainly not prepared to be seen to be making concessions of a political nature, for example on the question of Jewish emigration, simply in order to obtain access to such paltry sums of credit. Some $470m of Export—Import Bank loans were already outstanding at the time of the renunciation of the trade agreement in mid-January 1975, and a similar amount was outstanding as a result of loans extended earlier by US commercial banks or other lenders, for the purchase by the Soviet Union of equipment and machinery, etc. from the United States. These loans have apparently been unaffected by the renunciation of the trade agreement, but the indications are that the Soviet Union had expected to obtain at least $1 billion additional credits, and clearly felt considerable annoyance at the loss of this potential business. It was to be expected that the Soviet authorities would look more to Western Europe for large amounts of credit, such as that for some £1,000m recently extended by the UK, and it certainly will not totally abandon its longer-terms plans for a major modernization of the Soviet economy with the aid of massive imports of technology from the West, particularly from the United States, just because of difficulties on the credit front.

At the time of the Nixon visit to Moscow in 1972 there was a great deal of euphoria in American business circles about the potential 'killing' to be made by those companies which successfully penetrated the Soviet market. Nevertheless, Soviet trade and energy industry officials had done nothing to discourage this favourable reaction by the American businessman, and no opportunity was lost of describing the fabulous hydrocarbon riches of

Siberia in the most glowing terms. For a long time, American businessmen had watched the Soviet Union increasing its trading contacts with other Western countries, while they themselves were unable to compete on an equal basis because of various US export laws restricting the supply of a number of goods and items of technology to the Soviet bloc. When, following President Nixon's visit, many of the restrictions were lifted and the US government began actively to encourage the development of trade with the Soviet Union, there was no lack of enthusiasm in business circles, and by early 1973, a senior official at the Ministry of Foreign Trade in Moscow revealed that his desk was 'piled high' with projects and proposals for co-operation recently received from American companies, particularly in the field of energy resource development. The Soviet Union was getting into an excellent position to play off one US company against another, and various US consortia against West European and Japanese consortia. The deterioration of economic conditions in the West coupled with the global energy crisis which developed in the last quarter of 1973 brought matters to a halt. By that time, however, there were already signs of increasing scepticism in American business circles about the 'big' Soviet energy projects, as a result of visits by US technical teams to see things on the ground for themselves. The Soviet side was beginning to find it difficult to convince the potential US partners that the hydrocarbons in question were actually present in the amounts which geologists had predicted, and that sufficient reserves could be proved up in a particular part of the country to justify putting together the huge schemes which had been talked of.

Following President Nixon's exhortation that the United States should become independent of energy imports by 1980, many US companies already engaged in negotiations with the Soviet Union started to look twice to see whether their resources of manpower, equipment and finance would not be better employed nearer home. By mid-1975, little appeared to have changed in this respect, and the question was increasingly being asked 'Why should the United States participate in the more speedy development of Siberian energy, when the Soviet Union is apparently not prepared to make the necessary investment itself?'. American business circles had been quite ready to back President Nixon in the early heady days of détente but their ardour was somewhat cooled by such events as the highly successful Soviet purchases of US grain in 1972, the looming world energy crisis and its implications for the domestic economy, and Watergate. Dissatisfaction was increasingly being expressed in US business circles at the extremely slow rate of progress of any discussions with the Soviet Union and at the bureaucracy and red tape which is inevitably

178

encountered in all dealings with Soviet trade and industry officials. There was also growing irritation and the constantly changing Soviet position in connection with negotiations on the energy schemes, brought about, no doubt, as a result of the major reappraisal by Soviet planners at that time of the whole future development of the Soviet and Comecon energy industries. The greater the delays in coming to successful agreements, the harder people looked at the Soviet projects, and the more complicated and uncertain became the international energy scene. The Soviet energy projects lost much of their attraction as Western energy companies became less convinced that they would really be getting value for money.

Attention today seems to be focused less on the development of major new Soviet oil and gas deposits with American assistance than on Soviet acquisition of American equipment, technology, and know-how on the extraction of oil from older deposits by secondary recovery methods, and on the exploration and appraisal of hydrocarbon resources in hitherto virtually unexplored regions of the Soviet Union such as eastern Siberia, and off-shore in the North and Far East. The Soviet Union values US technology and equipment in the oil and gas industries extremely highly, and will undoubtedly step up its purchases thereof. For the time being, however, given the setback on the trade agreement, the short-term impact of the world energy crisis upon Western economies coupled with uncertainties over the future price of OPEC oil and the reappraisal by the Soviet Union of its own energy position, the conclusion of any major US–Soviet co-operation scheme involving the development of Soviet energy resources seems much less likely than it did, say, in the middle of 1973. Every year that passes during which the United States and the Soviet Union *do not* come to an agreement upon a major energy scheme, does, of course, postpone the date at which such a scheme could be brought on stream to contribute to the overall Soviet and American energy supply position. In view of the apparent urgency with which the Soviet oil industry now views the need to prove up new reserves of oil if production rates are to be maintained into the 1980s, the longer the delay in reaching agreement with US companies, the greater the pressures must be upon the Soviet energy industries to work out their own salvation with less rather than more assistance from the United States. This line of reasoning is probably less applicable to the Soviet gas industry than to the oil industry, since the problems in the former have less to do with the availability of proven reserves than with the capability of exploiting them both for domestic uses and for export. It appears likely that large-scale co-operation between the two countries over the development of energy resources will occur in the gas rather than the oil industry.

It seems relevant to point out once again that, even if the Urengoy—Murmansk and the Yakutia gas schemes were to come to fruition, they would only make available some 30 billion cu. metres annually for the United States, starting some time in the early 1980s. This would represent less than 3 per cent of US consumption at that date and possibly 5 per cent of Soviet production. Looked at another way, the impact of the combined 'massive' investment of, say, $12 billion applicable to the two schemes upon the development of the Soviet energy industries as a whole would be rather small. This raises once again the whole question of the significance of 'large-scale' American—Soviet co-operation in the energy field in relation to Soviet foreign policy in general. As mentioned earlier, a major reason behind Soviet encouragement of US co-operation in the energy fields, at least before October 1973, must have been the acquisition of very large amounts of credit and dollar loans with which to purchase American technology and equipment in sufficient quantities to be of use not only in the development of a specific project aimed at exporting gas or oil to the United States, but also for improving the technical level and material base of the Soviet energy and related industries throughout the country. Without the credits, the necessary quantity of purchases could not be made, in view of enduring adverse Soviet trade balances with the United States, and requirements for hard currency purchases relating to other sectors of the Soviet economy. Credits from the United States would not be forthcoming unless repayment was secured in guaranteed supplies of energy and raw materials, for which the United States foresees that it would have an increasing and long-term need. The reasoning begins to look a little shaky if doubt is cast upon the extent of the commercially accessible reserves or if projected Soviet and East European domestic requirements are rather higher than originally supposed, and if the time-lag between the US advancement of the credit and technology, etc. and the ultimate repayment by the Soviet Union in oil and gas is extended during a period of high inflation rates in the capitalist world.

Before concluding this section on the development of Soviet relations with the United States as regards the energy industries, it should be stressed that, apart from the major schemes referred to above, concerning Siberian and Yakutian natural gas and Sakhalin off-shore hydrocarbons, there are a great many other smaller energy-related deals between American engineering and equipment supply companies and the relevant Soviet purchasing organizations under the Ministry of Foreign Trade. Gas compressors, giant pipeline valves, drilling equipment and drilling and production technology are all being supplied or are the subject of advanced negotiations between the two sides, and will not be dependent upon Export—

180

Import Bank credits. The Soviet Union is increasingly paying cash for equipment purchased in the United States, and where credit is required it is being provided by private banks up to the latter's legal lending limits. In addition to energy-related trade, an increasing number of agreements on 'scientific and technical co-operation' are being signed under the auspices of the State Committee for Science and Technology in Moscow, between various Soviet ministries and both the larger and the less well known American companies.

There seems little doubt that, although trade relations between the United States and the Soviet Union at the highest official level suffered a sharp setback in early 1975, this may prove to be temporary, and while it will clearly prevent progress on the negotiations for the larger energy schemes for the time being, Soviet purchases of equipment and know-how, and scientific and technological agreements in the energy fields are likely to proliferate. It is even reported that negotiations are taking place on a scheme whereby the United States would make available uranium ores to be enriched by the Soviet Union and supplied to third parties for use in nuclear power stations.

13   Western Europe

Historical background

Soviet energy relations with Western Europe have been of rather a different nature from those between the Soviet Union and the United States and Japan respectively. West European countries have always been substantial purchasers of Soviet crude oil and products, even during the 1960s, when there was a fairly concerted American-led attempt to make things as difficult as possible for the Soviet Union to increase its exports of oil throughout the world. It was to Western Europe that the main increase in Soviet exports of oil occurred towards the end of the 1960s and during the early 1970s, as the Soviet Union began to be more concerned about the volume of hard currency which it could earn from its oil exports and less about the political advantages which it might be able to obtain from the allocation of its oil surpluses to potential allies, less well endowed with hard currency, elsewhere in the world. On the other hand, while Western Europe was clearly a logical place to which to export natural gas and from which to import steel pipeline, it does not, until very recently, appear to have rated very highly among Soviet plans for the really large energy joint ventures with the West. This may possibly have been partly because the Soviet Union was concentrating all its diplomatic and administrative effort in attracting US and Japanese participation, and partly because although, taken as a whole, the West European requirement for Soviet hydrocarbons could have been quite substantial, there has been little indication even to this day that there is likely to emerge anything like a coherent and united West European energy policy, let alone an energy policy specifically having to do with energy relationships with the Comecon countries.

In its dealings with West European customers the Soviet oil trading organization, Sojuznefteexport, has tended to favour State oil companies, particularly in Finland, France, and Italy, and international brokers in preference to the major international oil companies. It is true that brokers were ready to take Soviet oil during the period of the so-called 'Red Oil Menace', and therefore the Soviet Union continues to stand by them now, but it is likely that another reason for making full use of the broker market is the flexibility which it contributes to the supplier—customer relationship, since the Soviet record of delivery of the right quality of oil in the right quantity at the right place and at the right time, has not always been as good as it is now beginning to become.

Italy

The most dynamic relationship between the Soviet Union and a country of Western Europe with regard to energy matters has been that with Italy. During the 1960s, when ENI, the Italian State company, was asserting its independence from the major international oil companies, the Soviet Union entered into a long-term supply contract with ENI, and deliveries rose steadily to reach a peak of about 12m tons per annum during the late 1960s, although this figure has since fallen to nearer 7m tons. The supply of Soviet oil to Italy at this time was very much a part of an even bigger overall industrial and technological co-operation agreement between the Soviet and Italian governments, and should be viewed in this context. The construction of the Fiat plant at Togliattigrad, and of numerous chemical plants elsewhere in the Soviet Union were all part of the deal, and various Italian companies associated with ENI were involved in the supply of equipment, machinery, and steel pipes, etc. This was, for its time, by far the largest co-operation deal between any communist bloc country and a country of the capitalist West. Whether the relative strength of the Italian Communist Party in the government of the time was a major contributory factor to the deal being concluded with Italy, rather than with some other Western country, is a matter for debate, but many other major Western automobile manufacturing companies were either restrained from getting involved with the Soviet Union as a result of their interest in the United States or were unable to tackle a project so enormous as that at Togliattigrad due to sheer physical limitations and full commitments elsewhere.

More recently ENI has been having discussions with the Soviet energy industries concerning the long-term supply of Soviet oil and gas, in exchange for Italian assistance in the development of Soviet resources and the provision of large quantities of large diameter steel pipeline. Other Italian companies have concluded agreements with the Soviet Union for the supply of gas pumping stations, to be paid for in supplies of oil and gas. In 1974, Italy started to receive Soviet natural gas via the Czechoslovakia—Austria pipeline, at a level of 800m cu. metres per annum. This volume is expected to rise to 6 billion cu. metres in 1977, and to continue at this level for twenty years. In September 1974 the

Italian firm Finsider announced the conclusion of a $1·5 billion deal with the Soviet Union concerning the delivery, over the five year period 1975–79, of 500,000 tons per annum of large diameter steel pipes to be used in the construction of oil and gas pipelines, mainly in western Siberia. Payment by the Soviet side will be in coal and iron ore, both needed by Finsider to expand its own domestic production of steel etc. In 1972, Finsider had completed another pipeline deal involving the supply of 1m tons of steel pipe which was in fact used for the construction of the Czechoslovakia–Austria pipeline.

Finland

Finland has been a purchaser of Soviet crude oil and products for a long time, and relies on Soviet supplies for more than 70 per cent of its demand. Volumes supplied increased steadily until the end of 1973, reaching a level of 6·5m tons of crude annually, but the figure remained the same in 1974, and it was reported that only 6m tons of crude were to be supplied in 1975. Between 3m and 3·5m tons of products are also supplied annually. Future supplies may be less a question of availabilities from the Soviet Union than of the Finnish ability to pay, even though payment for oil is largely made in soft currency, since Finland now has a trade deficit with the Soviet Union, and under barter arrangements an increasingly large part of Finnish industrial production is already finding its way to the Soviet Union. Finland took 500m cu. metres of natural gas from the Soviet Union in 1974, 1·1 billion cu. metres were due to be delivered in 1975, and the volume will increase to 1·4 billion cu. metres annually from 1976 through to 1980. Finland could, reportedly, take double that quantity but the Soviet Union has indicated that it will not have any additional volumes available at least for the time being. The world energy crisis has undoubtedly meant that Finland has temporarily been drawn into a position rather closer to economic dependence on the Soviet Union than it has hitherto maintained, although this may be less of a strain than having to find the hard currency to finance more of its oil imports from OPEC. If the development of North Sea oil and gas, particularly in the Norwegian sector, proceeds as planned, it is possible that Finland could take increasing quantities from that source, and the Soviet Union might even find it fairly convenient to be able to reduce its supplies to Finland so as to make more available for export to the hard currency areas.

184

Sweden

Sweden has been importing quite large quantities of Soviet oil: 2·8m tons in 1965, 4·8m tons in 1970, and 3·2m tons in 1973. In 1973 Sweden was having discussions with the Soviet Union about the possibility of importing Soviet natural gas by pipeline across the Baltic Sea, and had originally envisaged the import of 6 billion cu. metres annually. Towards the end of 1974, however, the Soviet Union stated that it would only be able to supply 1 billion cu. metres per annum, and the project is apparently shelved for the time being.

Norway

Although Norway has been a small importer of Soviet oil during the past ten years, relations between that country and the Soviet Union are now attracting considerable interest in connection with the development of the offshore regions bordering both countries in the Arctic part of the Barents Sea. The problem is a complex one, centring on the demarcation of the Barents Sea, either in accordance with the 1958 Continental Shelf Convention — which may generally be interpreted as implying a preference for the drawing of a median line equidistant from the Norwegian and Soviet coasts, as proposed by Norway — or by means of a sectoral extension radiating from the North Pole, along the same principle as in the Antarctic, a course favoured by the Soviet Union since this would give it a substantially larger area of the Barents Sea. The Soviet Union is not only interested in acquiring the right to develop as much as possible of the reportedly considerable mineral riches underlying the Barents Sea, but it is also concerned to maintain the neutrality of the area, with minimum international interference in what they have come to regard as a Soviet strategic right-of-way for the naval fleets based on Murmansk. The issue is further complicated by the status of Spitzbergen, a group of Norwegian islands situated some 600 miles north of the Norwegian mainland and bordering the Barents Sea, subject to the 1920 Spitzbergen Treaty, to which forty-one countries set their signatures, and which gave them the right to work the mineral deposits of Spitzbergen provided they adhered in all respects to existing Norwegian laws. The crux of the matter is whether or not Spitzbergen is deemed to have a continental shelf of its own, in which case off-shore prospecting by companies of treaty signatory countries could extend well into the Barents Sea, or whether (as Norway claims) it is encompassed by an extension of Norway's own continental shelf, in which case off-shore prospecting would be under the control of the Norwegian government.

Even if the Soviet Union were to support the Norwegian view about its extended continental shelf it would not necessarily be expected to agree to the demarcation of the Barents Sea according to the 1958 Continental Shelf Convention, since this would give the Soviet Union some 65,000 square miles less of the Barents Sea in which to operate. If, on the other hand, the Soviet Union supports the view that Spitzbergen has its own continental shelf, and insists upon a sectoral division of the Barents Sea, then it might have to countenance the activities of international 'oil companies from, potentially, forty other countries, with all the adherent risks of surveillance of its own strategic interests, including its nuclear testing grounds on Novaya Zemlaya. Hitherto, mineral development activity on Spitzbergen has been limited to joint Norwegian and Soviet coal production, but the recent global energy developments have greatly increased the interests of other countries in acquiring the right to prospect for hydrocarbons in the area. Discussions between Norway and the Soviet Union on the Barents Sea issue were held in Moscow in November 1974, but nothing concrete was decided at that time, and further discussions took place late in 1975. At the time of writing, the problem remains unresolved, but it is of interest that the Soviet Union is itself anxious to encourage Western oil companies to co-operate with its own oil industry in developing the hydrocarbon deposits which have been discovered in the more southerly and undisputedly Soviet off-shore regions of the Barents Sea.

Iceland

About 7 per cent of Icelandic trade was with the Soviet Union in 1973. Iceland's main export to the Soviet Union is frozen fish and fish products, while the Soviet Union supplies over 70 per cent of Iceland's oil requirements. The Soviet Union made no concessions to Iceland following the rise in world oil prices in the winter of 1973, but the price paid for Iceland's fish exports has only risen slowly in comparison and, as a result, Iceland now has a large trade deficit with the Soviet Union. Iceland's fishing fleet and busy international airlines are the main consumers of oil.

The strategic importance of Iceland greatly exceeds its importance as a trading partner, and the island is, at present, a member of NATO, harbouring the important air base at Keflavik. Should strains develop in the Soviet-Icelandic trading relationship, for example, where the Soviet

Union might find difficulty in continuing to make the ½m–¾m tons of fuel annually available to Iceland, or where Soviet importers would not be prepared to pay Iceland's price for fish, Iceland would, were it not for the presence of oil in the North Sea, find it extremely difficult to finance supplies from the Middle East. Now that Norway has increasing volumes of North Sea oil available, and has, historically, maintained close relations with Iceand, it seems likely that Iceland will, in due course, be able to reduce its dependence upon Soviet oil, provided an acceptable method of payment for Norwegian oil can be found.

West Germany

Soviet energy relationships with the Federal Republic of Germany have developed rapidly, particularly in relation to natural gas supplies, following the Ostpolitik efforts of the Brandt government, which culminated in treaties with Poland and the Soviet Union (May 1972) giving *de facto* recognition of the Oder-Neisse frontier and to the German Democratic Republic. Although, for much of the 1960s, the export of pipeline from West Germany to the Soviet Union was prevented by COCOM (the Co-ordinating Committee of the NATO powers responsible for preventing the sale to the Warsaw Pact countries of what might be considered strategically important goods or technology), an agreement was finally reached in 1970 between the German firm Mannesmann and the Soviet foreign trade organisation Promsyrioimport whereby the former would supply 1·2m tons of large diameter steel pipe for the construction of gas lines in the Soviet Union, for delivery during 1970–72.

85 per cent of the cost of the pipe was covered by a DM1·2 billion credit extended by a consortium of West German banks to the Soviet Foreign Trade Bank for a ten-year period. The remaining 15 per cent was to be paid in cash, and the credit would be repaid in natural gas supplies. In 1972 a further DM1·2 billion credit was organized, covering the supply of additional pipeline from Mannesmann, of which DM270m was to cover the supply of bulldozers, pipelaying equipment etc. from other West German companies. In 1972, a joint West German–Soviet Economic Commission discussed West German participation in the exploration and development of oil and gas deposits in the Soviet Union. In 1974 a third agreement between Mannesmann and the Soviet Union was signed, covering the supply of a further 950,000 tons of large diameter pipeline between 1975 and 1976, for which a further DM1·5 billion credit was advanced.

187

Soviet natural gas supplies started in 1973 via a transit pipeline across Czechoslovakia, the gas being received by the West German concern of Ruhrgas. The present status of the West German–Soviet natural gas supply arrangements is that between 1973 and the year 2000, West Germany will receive over 200 billion cu. metres of Soviet natural gas, with the annual quantities available to Ruhrgas reaching a 9·5 billion cu. metres from some time in the early 1980s. Soviet imports of large diameter gas pipeline from West Germany so far contracted for will total 3·7m tons by the end of 1976, and a further 1m ton deal is reportedly under discussion at present.

In addition to the above direct supplies of Soviet gas to West Germany, negotiations have been proceeding for a number of years upon a three-cornered arrangement between West Germany, Iran, and the Soviet Union whereby Iran would make increased exports of natural gas to the southern part of the Soviet Union, i.e. in addition to the 12 billion cu. metres annually which it already supplies, and the Soviet Union would, in turn, make additional quantities available to West Germany, probably from existing Soviet gas fields in the Ukraine. Some 13 billion cu. metres annually are involved on the proposed new Iran–Soviet stage, and the latest indications are that Ruhrgas has formed an international consortium comprising Gaz de France, SNAM from Italy, and OMV from Austria, with the intention that 50 per cent of the 13 billion cu. metres exported from the Soviet Union should go to West Germany, 20 per cent to France, 20 per cent to Italy and 10 per cent to Austria. The gas would either come by a pipeline of some 6,000 km in length directly from Iran across the Soviet Union to Western Europe, or it will come by a much shorter pipeline from a Soviet gas field as a result of a logistical swap, although this point is not yet clear. The Soviet Union is to retain 3 billion cu. metres as transit fees.

Apart from supplies of natural gas from the Soviet Union, which began in October 1973, West Germany has been taking Soviet crude oil and products for a considerable number of years, with volumes in the region of 5–7m tons annually since the 1970s. Most of the oil has been supplied via brokers, and although West Germany has expressed interest in increasing its imports from the Soviet Union, the latter has indicated that, for the time being, no additional supplies can be made.

On another energy front, agreement has been reached between the West German company of Kraftwerk Union AG and the Soviet Union for the construction of a 1,300 MW nuclear power station at Kaliningrad on the Soviet Baltic coast. Some DM1·5 billion of credit is involved, and it will be built with West German technical and financial aid. The plant will supply electricity to West Germany and to West Berlin by an electricity line which will cross Poland and East Germany. A similar project is under discussion for Vinnitsa in the Ukraine. Nuclear fuel for the plant will be supplied by the Soviet Union which will enrich raw uranium ores supplied by West Germany. The whole project is still some way from getting off the ground in view of the many complex political and commercial angles involved, but there is also some doubt about whether the COCOM committee will permit the West German company to sell to the Soviet Union various items of nuclear technology and equipment if these are considered to be of 'strategic' value. The Soviet Union, although it has an advanced nuclear power station industry of its own, is anxious to acquire certain items of West German technology in the field of fast breeder reactors. West Germany, for its part, attaches considerable importance to the project as a means of securing power for West Berlin, which will outgrow its locally generated supplies by 1980. The electricity will be delivered to West Germany via West Berlin, an arrangement which ensures that any attempt to cut off Berlin's electricity will also affect West Germany, giving rise to more serious political consequences.

France

During the late 1960s, France and the Soviet Union entered into a number of industrial co-operation ventures, involving the electronics, automobile, and energy industries. Initially, attention was concentrated upon the oil refining industry, and sales of French expertise were completed. France was able to import quite large volumes of Soviet crude oil and products, a total which reached 5·4m tons in 1973. It was not until 1972, however, that a contract between France and the Soviet Union concerning the delivery of natural gas was signed, under which France would receive, from 1976 onwards for a period of twenty years, some 50 billion cu. metres of Soviet natural gas at a rate of 2·5 billion cu. metres per annum. In exchange for this, France would supply large diameter pipeline, compressor stations and gas treatment installations, etc. France would also co-operate with the Soviet Union in joint exploration and production studies, particularly concerning drilling and seismic techniques. The supply of Soviet natural gas to France in 1976 will depend upon the construction, by that time, of an integrated central European gas grid. Meanwhile, France has been discussing off-shore co-operation with the Soviet Union, and French companies have already made supplies of gas treatment equipment to the Orenburg gas complex. It is intended that deliveries of Soviet gas to France will rise to 4 billion cu. metres or more per annum in the 1980s, under an agreement concluded in December 1974.

Austria

Austria has been taking around 1m tons of Soviet oil per annum regularly over the past few years, and Soviet deliveries of natural gas started in 1968. The latter are now running at 2·1 billion cu. metres annually, and should rise to 2·4 billion cu. metres between 1975 and 1977. From 1978 onwards, an additional 500m cu. metres are expected to be delivered, raising total Soviet annual deliveries at that time to 2·9 billion cu. metres. Austria is interested in joining the West German triangular deal with the Soviet Union and Iran, and would, in such a case, receive an additional 1·3 billion cu. metres of Soviet gas annually. Austrian companies have been delivering steel pipe to the Soviet Union, and will deliver a further 200,000 tons between 1975 and 1978.

Conclusions

Soviet energy relations with other West European countries have been mainly on a simple supply of crude oil or products basis, the volumes concerned accounting for almost 70 per cent of Iceland's 1973 requirements but less than 0·1 per cent of the UK's requirement. There are Soviet oil products marketing companies in the UK (Nafta GB) and in Belgium (Nafta B) in addition to those in Finland, but the throughput of these companies is small in relation to the rest of the domestic markets. They are an effective instrument for Soviet involvement in the international oil trading industry, but there are no Soviet-owned or constructed refineries operating in Western Europe.

In its energy dealings with Western Europe as a whole over the last ten years, the Soviet Union can be seen to have acted, in the main, from straightforward economic and commercial motives, although it is possible to argue that Soviet motives in supplying Iceland and Finland, for example, may have had strategic or political overtones. Crude oil and product sales have tended to be made at the higher end of the normal international price ranges, and the objectives seem to have been to earn the maximum amount of hard currency except, of course, in the case of Finland. Clear-cut attempts to use oil for political reasons have been few,

Table 13.1

Relative Importance of Soviet Crude Oil and Products Supplies
to Western Europe 1973

	Total domestic consumption	Imports from USSR	% consumption derived from Soviet imports
Austria	12·3	1·25	10
Belgium	32·7	1·67	5
Denmark	19·0	0·63	3
Finland	13·6	10·03	74
France	127·6	5·35	4
Germany (West)	156·6	5·85	4
Greece	10·8	0·80	7
Iceland	0·7	0·47	70
Ireland	6·0	0·18	3
Italy	107·5	8·65	8
Netherlands	42·9	3·22	8
Norway	8·7	0·60	7
Portugal	6·3	—	—
Spain	40·9	0·51	1
Sweden	31·2	3·22	10
Switzerland	15·6	0·66	4
Turkey	12·2	neg.	neg.
UK	115·8	0·83	1
TOTAL	760·4	43·92	5·8

Sources: Vnesh. torg.; UN, *Annual Bulletin of Energy Statistics for Europe;* OECD.

if any, and almost always capable of reasonable commercial interpretation. For example, at the time when the UK embargoed imports of oil of Soviet origin (the embargo was lifted in 1973), the Soviet Ministry of Foreign Trade made considerable efforts to get the UK government to change its mind, and even offered to place orders for ships to be built in British yards, at a time when the British shipbuilding industry was in an extremely difficult situation, on condition that the government would relax its constraints upon Soviet oil imports. This could have been interpreted as an attempt to embarrass the government, but it was clearly

Table 13.2

Relative importance of Soviet coal supplies
to Western Europe 1973
(Million tons)

	Total domestic consumption (hard coal, brown coal and lignite)	Imports from USSR (hard coal and anthracite)		% Consumption derived from Soviet imports
Austria	6·830	0·77		11·3
Belgium	16·333	0·33		2·0
Denmark	3·535	0·40		11·3
Finland	3·143	0·53		16·9
France	45·537	1·07		2·3
Germany	221·526	0·10		0·1
Greece	13·769	0·04		2·9
Iceland	neg.	—		—
Ireland	0·821	—		—
Italy	12·853	1·85		14·3
Luxembourg	0·305	—		—
Netherlands	4·298	—		—
Norway	0·750	—		—
Portugal	0·805	—		—
Spain	16·318	—		—
Sweden	1·112	0·38		34·2
Switzerland	0·258	—		—
Turkey	9·384	—		—
United Kingdom	131·646	—		—
Total	489·223	5·47	=	1·11% of W.Europ consumpt.
		5·47	=	22·33% Soviet coal exports

Source: Vnesh. torg.

also an attempt to enter an additional market for oil at a time when there was, on the whole, a surplus of oil internationally.

Looked at from another angle, it could be argued that there has been very little opportunity for the Soviet Union to use its oil exports for other than straightforward commercial reasons in its dealings with the countries of Western Europe over the past ten to fifteen years, even if it had so wished. Although it would, theoretically, have been possible for the Soviet government to sell at prices lower than those resulting from the normal market forces of the capitalist world, the Soviet requirement for hard currency earnings and the possible reactions of the Arab oil producers was, and will continue to be, of overriding importance, with oil trading occupying such an important place (in excess of 30 per cent) in the total

192

Table 13.3

Relative importance of Polish hard coal
exports to Western Europe 1973
(Million tons)

Italy	3·0
Denmark	2·6
Finland	2·6
France	1·9
West Germany	1·8
Belgium	1·4
Spain	1·2
Austria	1·1
	15·6 = 3·2% of W. European consumption = 43·5% of Polish exports.

Source: Polish statistical yearbook.

hard currency earnings picture. Sojuzñefteexport has evolved into a very effective international oil trader, particularly on the West European scene, and operates either directly or through brokers, governments, and international oil companies as it considers fit; it does not seem to get involved in political questions except in so far as these may concern decisions in principle about whether or not to sell crude oil in additional quantities to an old customer, or, for the first time, to a potential new customer. At a time when the Soviet Union might have been tempted to experiment in the further penetration of the international oil industry, the global energy crisis happened to coincide with a realization in Soviet energy planning circles of the current limited availability of Soviet crude oil for export to the West. This was compounded by the fact that Western nations cut their demand for crude and products by about 10 per cent in 1974. The available evidence so far suggests that Sojuznefteexport has done its best to fulfil its obligations to its established Western European customers, but has made no secret of the fact that it would be unwise to expect any increase in supplies of Soviet oil for the present. In concluding this section on Soviet oil dealings with Western Europe it is relevant to point out that, of the total Soviet oil exports to the non-communist world, over 85 per cent has gone to Western Europe on average over the past ten years, and Soviet dealings with this part of the world can therefore be taken as typical of their oil trading practices generally.

The supply of Soviet natural gas to Western Europe has, as was shown above, been related almost entirely to the acquisition from West European countries of large diameter steel pipe and compressor stations, etc. for the construction of gas pipelines both for export purposes and for the extension of the domestic gas pipeline network. Here again, commercial considerations seem to have been uppermost in the structuring of the deals so far negotiated, the West European countries all having a growing need for natural gas, and the Soviet Union having a similar growing need for supplies of pipe. Western Europe is clearly the obvious destination for pipeline exports of Soviet natural gas, and although some commentators have suspected the Soviet Union of wishing to attach West European countries to itself by 'umbilical cords' so that it might exert a political influence in their internal affairs by employing the threat to 'turn off the tap', the actual percentage of Soviet supplies in the overall natural gas consumption of any one of the West European countries taking it is extremely small (with the exception of Finland which receives all its natural gas from the Soviet Union) and is likely to remain so even when all the schemes now under discussion and construction are actually in operation. Even in the case of West Germany, which might be taking between 10 and 13 billion cu. metres of Soviet natural gas annually in the early 1980s, this will only amount to 16 per cent of total consumption at that time. Indeed, except in the case of a war situation, any 'turning off' of Soviet supplies under an existing contract to supply would imply a state of major diplomatic and commercial disruption between East and West, and a rejection of any further attempts at the promotion of détente and the acquisition of Western technology and equipment.

In a situation where two or more Western countries are unwise enough to compete for what is perceived to be a limited availability of exportable Soviet natural gas it would be natural to expect that the Soviet Union would attempt to use this competition to achieve at least some influence in one or other of the countries. Such is the scale of operations needed to tackle the enormous logistical and financial problems connected with the large-scale import of energy from the Soviet Union into Western Europe, however, that it seems inevitable that in practice consultation and coordination of activities between several West European countries will evolve, rather than a damaging state of competition between them.

While the next two decades could well see a steady and substantial increase in the volume of Soviet *natural gas* to the countries of Western Europe, it is likely that supplies of Soviet *crude oil* will decline. There is scope for a substantial increase in the supply of Soviet coal to Western Europe, but internal logistical considerations may make this unattractive for the Soviet side, unless the West European countries would be prepared to make substantial investments in the development of the Soviet coal industry.

14 The Middle East and developing countries

The Middle East

Active Soviet involvement in the countries of the Middle East began in about 1955 when Khrushchev decided that this part of the world should feature more prominently in his ambitious policy of undermining Western positions and security arrangements wherever possible. This policy incorporated political, economic, technical, financial, and military aid to whichever of those countries would accept it in exchange for a measure of support for the Soviet anti-imperialist viewpoint and, if possible, the provision of military facilities such as ports or airstrips, etc. by means of which the Soviet Union could extend its influence in the region. Before 1955, Soviet activity in the Eastern Mediterranean and the Persian Gulf had been restrained by the still powerful presence in the area of Great Britain and, subsequently, the United States. Extreme Cold War conditions obtained at that time and many of the countries of the Middle East deliberately pursued a policy of non-involvement with the Soviet Union, having historically been more involved with the West. A policy of non-alignment was, indeed, beginning to emerge in many countries round the world, and the Soviet Union clearly felt that it was time to attempt to establish better relations with these nations as the latter strove increasingly successfully to achieve a greater degree of independence from their former colonialist masters. The fact that many of the countries in the Middle East were far from being pro-communist, seemed less important to the Soviet Union at that time than did the fact that they were anti-colonialist. Nevertheless, whenever Soviet encouragement for the establishment of local Communist Parties became too keen, the hostility of governments was aroused, and the fledgeling Communist Parties were subjected to the full repressive powers of the police, whether in Iraq, Iran, or Egypt. Furthermore, hawk-like elements in the United States were aroused, and the US presence in the Middle East was strengthened accordingly. The West, meanwhile, was beginning to fare badly in the Middle East, not only because of its creation and continued support of Israel but also because of its insistence that a Western presence in the Middle East was justified in view of what it tried to impress upon the local governments was the terrible threat of communism and Soviet invasion. The creation of the Baghdad Pact in 1955 probably precipitated a rapprochement between the Soviet Union and some of the Arab countries. since it split the Arab ranks by forcing them to make a clear choice for or against the West, thereby providing Russia with natural allies among those who wished to remain uncommitted. These countries, which included Egypt and Syria, the Soviet Union proceeded to support with propaganda, arms, diplomatic backing, and economic aid.

In the selection of its policy towards the countries of the Middle East since the mid-1950s, the Soviet Union has clearly considered itself to be in danger of a potential military threat from the West, operating throughout the area. Over the last twenty years its policy, as originally outlined by Khrushchev, has been aimed at diminishing Western influence over the activities of the Middle Eastern countries. It has also aimed at creating a general situation in the area such as would reduce or eliminate the need for Western military intervention in strength, — whether by design or by accident — since this would make direct East—West conflict in the area inevitable. At the same time the policy has aimed at increasing Soviet influence by whatever means possible. The Soviet Union has devoted considerable economic, military and political effort in an attempt to aid the accession to power or the maintenance of regimes friendly to it, notably in Iraq, Syria, and Egypt, but in no case has this resulted in the Soviet Union being able to control the actions of the governments in the countries concerned, at least for any length of time. In the case of Egypt, Soviet assistance actually led to such rebuffs as the imprisonment of members of the Communist Party under Colonel Nasser and, more recently, the expulsion of Soviet and military advisers by President Sadat in 1972. Indeed, during both the 1967 and 1973 Arab—Israeli conflicts it became clear that the Soviet Union was unable to prevent its supposedly 'client' states from taking military action at a time when, from the Soviet point of view, such action was considered to be premature, imprudent, and otherwise totally unacceptable.

The Soviet Union has apparently always regarded the area in the Middle East stretching from Turkey right the way across to Afghanistan as the 'soft under-belly' in its strategic relationships with the military forces of capitalism. It would clearly like to see the various countries come under its own influence, or at least behave neutrally in the context of the global struggle between East and West. In the immediate postwar period, the Soviet Union appears to have been taken somewhat unawares by the speed of the British withdrawal from Iran, at a time when the Soviet authorities clearly envisaged the partition of that country into a northern group of provinces, to be controlled by the Soviet Union, joined, hopefully, to some northern and eastern provinces to be acquired from Turkey, while the south of Iran was to have become a British-controlled region. The British withdrawal coincided with the tenure of the office of Prime Minister Qavam, a determined and courageous man, who made it quite clear to the Soviet Union that he would stop at nothing until the last Soviet troops were withdrawn. The subsequent evolution of Iran as a militarily powerful and economically burgeoning country on the Soviet Union's southern borders, and one not likely to be particularly friendly towards its former occupiers, must have seriously upset whatever Soviet master plan there might have been for the creation of a line of buffer states between the Balkans and the Indian subcontinent.

Soviet overtures in Libya, in support of that country's efforts to rid itself of Western economic and military involvement, resulted in a total rejection, by the Libyan leadership under Colonel Qadhafi, of Soviet and East European interference in Libya's internal affairs during the late 1960s, consequent upon a surge of nationalism in that country. Relations appeared to have improved substantially in early 1975, culminating in the May visit of Mr Kosygin and the signature of various large-scale economic agreements between the two countries. The Kosygin visit may indeed have been made with the express purpose of demonstrating to Egypt that important as the Soviet Union clearly regards its relationships with Egypt, it can get along fairly well with other Arab countries, and is perfectly prepared to play off one country against another in order to secure alternative loci of co-operation in the Middle East, should an existing recipient of economic and military aid bite the Soviet hand that has been feeding it. Other, although not perhaps such serious, rebuffs have been experienced by the Soviet Union in its relationships with Morocco, Algeria, and the Sudan. Whereas there was a time in the early 1970s, when the West was seriously concerned that the Mediterranean was fast becoming a 'Soviet lake', in the last few years Soviet influence in the area must be said to have declined somewhat, not so much as a result of a reversal in the declining fortunes of the Western powers but because the countries of the Middle East themselves have started to play a major role in the determination of their own futures and have managed to achieve a remarkable degree of co-operation between themselves in an attempt to reduce at least political interference in their internal affairs, whatever the source of that interference.

Soviet relations with Syria have not always been as good as they are at present in view of rather over-zealous past attempts by Soviet foreign agents to influence the course of political events in that country. However, largely as a result of the continuing Arab—Israeli conflict and Syria's doubts about alternative sources of political and military support, Soviet influence in that country is probably stronger at present than in any other country in the area.

The essentially defensive basis for the evolution of Soviet policy towards the countries of the Middle East, stemming primarily from what the Soviet Union perceived as the development of an increasingly hostile Western presence along the Soviet southern flank, has not necessarily been the sole motivation for what the Soviet Union has actually achieved or attempted to achieve in the area. The diminution of Western military influence in the area has certainly been one major objective, but another has clearly been the reduction of Western economic and financial influence arising from historically massive Western investment in and control of the oil industries of the producer countries. International monopoly capitalism, of which the international oil companies, are in Soviet eyes, probably the most powerful elements, has long been an object of hate and envy in Soviet ideological circles. Anything that the Soviet Union could do to assist in undermining the commercial interests of the West in the area could be seen as beneficial to the Soviet cause. For example, those oil-producing countries which have progressively worked to bring about the nationalization of Western oil company interests have received firm Soviet support. Similar support has been given to the development of the OPEC organization and, indeed, to moves by OPEC to raise the price of Middle East oil, and also to restrict supplies to those Western countries held to be particularly intransigent supporters of the Israeli cause. Not only has the Soviet Union benefited from rises in world prices of oil, in view of its position as a net exporter of oil to the West, but any additional financial burden which the West has to bear and which slows down its rate of economic progress tends to reduce the perceived gap between the East European and Western rates of improvement in the standard of living.

Over and above these comparatively short-term and opportunistic motives behind Soviet policy in the Middle East there could, possibly, lie a rather more fundamental and longer term concept not so much connected with the efforts of the Soviet Union to secure greater influence in the Middle East as with its ability to exert at least a powerful influence upon, if not control over, the distribution of what amounts to over two-thirds of the world's resources of hydrocarbons, especially oil ('Black Gold'), situated in what has been described as the 'Black Crescent' stretching from the Western Mediterranean up through the Middle East, across the Soviet Union and into the Arctic Circle. It is impossible to say whether the

Soviet Union has such a master plan or not, although in view of the manifold different interests involved in the formulation of Soviet foreign policy and the essentially dynamic and flexible way in which it has manifested itself, this seems rather doubtful. Yet, it would probably be as unwise to dismiss such a possibility as 'unthinkable' as it would be to attach too much significance to it and to see it as underlying every Soviet action in the Middle East. Soviet dealings with the Middle East have been complicated by the fact that the southern republics of the Soviet Union are Muslim and the tenets of communism are fundamentally incompatible with the Muslim religion. Any action by the Soviet Union which would lead directly or indirectly to a global resurgence of Pan-Islam would present the Soviet Union with additional problems of nationalism within its own borders which could prove highly inconvenient.

Increasingly rich and powerful as the North African and Middle East countries are becoming as a result – it may be emphasized – of their continuing sales of hydrocarbons to the capitalist world, it is extremely unlikely that they would ever willingly associate themselves with, or allow themselves to be steam-rollered into, Soviet hegemony, especially given the relationship between communism and Islam. It must also be clear that the Western allies, at least so long as they remain militarily powerful and united, would never allow such a venture to succeed without going to war to prevent it. The very livelihood of the peoples of Western Europe, Japan and, to a lesser extent, the United States, depends upon access to the hydrocarbons contained in the southern half of the 'Black crescent', for the next ten years at least, and the Soviet leadership must be left in no doubt about the seriousness of the West's intentions and ability to protect its interest in this connection.

The Soviet leadership is fully aware of the extent of the dependence upon Middle Eastern oil of the economies of those industrialized countries of the capitalist world which it perceives to be its ideological enemies, and it would be unrealistic to suppose that it is not also very well aware of the repercussions which would be likely to result from any interruption of the supply of Middle Eastern crude to the West. These repercussions could be both beneficial and disadvantageous to the Soviet Union, depending upon whether they were looked at from a purely economic or from an ideological point of view. For example, a reduction in energy contribution made by this to the inflation and general economic malaise in the industrially developed West must give some satisfaction to the Soviet hardliners, who would see any Western difficulties as a gain for the forces of communism. However, these difficulties could be seen as extremely disturbing to those Soviet planners who believe that the best hope for improving the lot of the Soviet and East European consumers, and the economic state of Comecon as a whole, lies in economic co-operation with the industrialized West and in the import of technology and equipment from it. The goose, in other words, will not be able to supply so many golden eggs to the Soviet Union if it is suffering from a shortage of energy, and the cost of the eggs which it can provide will be substantially higher. The Soviet leadership must be well aware too that there will come a point at which the United States and its allies can no longer tolerate the degree of hardship inflicted upon them by an interruption of Middle East energy supplies and will be obliged to take some form of action which will almost inevitably result in military confrontation between the United States and the Soviet Union, something which the latter apparently wishes to avoid at all costs.

Until very recently, the Soviet Union and its allies were relatively immune, from an energy supply point of view, to an occasional oil price rise or supply embargo or even a more generalized disruption of supplies of Middle East oil, for whatever reason; even today, when total Comecon imports from the area are in the region of 10–15m tons, Comecon as a whole does not appear to be suffering too much from the effects of the global energy crisis. However, it has already become apparent to Comecon energy planners that by 1980 the bloc may be importing as much as 30m tons, and the volume might well increase to 80–100m tons by 1985. Such a quantity, if the OPEC countries insist on payment in hard currency and if the world oil price remained at its present levels – or, indeed, rose over the next decade – would cause serious economic strains within the Comecon bloc as a whole, and also to individual member countries, particularly Hungary and Czechoslovakia. Clearly, the Soviet leadership appreciates that it would be imprudent to jeopardize the future supply of what, by 1985, could amount to as much as 10 per cent of total Comecon oil requirements as a result of actions taken today for short-term political gain. On the other hand, in the final analysis, the more hawkish Soviet leaders might consider that the Soviet Union and its allies could do without supplies of OPEC oil, and for a very much longer period, than could the countries of Western Europe, Japan, and the United States. This might lead them to conclude that an advantage would accrue to the Soviet long-term position from any perpetuation of supply instability and price escalation of Middle East oil, provided that this type of situation could be generated and maintained through the manipulation of client states in the area rather than by the direct involvement of Soviet military forces.

In the events leading up to the outbreak of Arab–Israeli hostilities in October 1973, and during the course of the conflict itself, the Soviet

Union did not apparently go out of its way to cool the situation, at least until that point during the war when it became clear that Egypt was about to be severely mauled by the Israeli counter-attack and thrust westwards towards the Suez Canal. It is notable that the Soviet Union does not appear to have made great efforts to exacerbate the situation, as might have been expected had its motives been more aggressive. Whether this was because of a genuine fear of direct confrontation with the United States, or whether it merely stemmed from a desire not to become more deeply involved in what was clearly becoming an increasingly costly and politically unprofitable sphere of overseas activities, is a matter for speculation. However, there are two other aspects of the situation which may perhaps shed some light on what is still an extremely confused picture. The first is the growing realization in East European energy planning circles that, as has already been shown (pp. 18–20), Comecon will itself be requiring increasing quantities of Middle East oil, particularly from 1980 onwards. The second is the appreciation of the growing power and influence of Saudi Arabia in the oil affairs of the Middle East and in Arab affairs generally.

Concerning future requirements of oil imports, Comecon governments and particularly the Soviet Union, have been actively promoting co--operation ventures with the countries of the Middle East, aimed at discovering and securing new supplies of oil, a share of which would ultimately accrue to the East European countries involved in its development. The Soviet Union, for example, has invested several hundred million rubles in the development of the North Rumailah oilfields in Iraq, where, as a result of Soviet assistance, annual production is now over 16m tons and is scheduled to rise to nearer 40m tons by the end of the 1970s. The Soviet Union has already begun to receive payment for its investment in terms of deliveries of 2m tons of North Rumailah crude annually, a volume which was originally scheduled to increase to 8m tons annually by the end of this decade. The increase in the world price of oil will presumably mean that Iraq's repayment schedules can be considerably shortened, although it is likely that, since the Soviet Union and its allies will be increasingly concerned to secure larger volumes of oil, some other adjustment of the repayment terms will probably be worked out, perhaps involving even greater Soviet economic or other assistance. The problem facing the Comecon countries is whether they can, by a proliferation of such schemes, ensure the supply of sufficient OPEC oil on a repayment basis to satisfy their import needs in the 1980s so that they do not have to expend their meagre supplies of hard currency. The indications are that, within OPEC, there are several countries like Iraq which are, despite the price increases for their oil, still obtaining a relatively low per capita income from their oil exports; therefore they would be interested in boosting their oil production as much as possible, with outside help if necessary. Oil from these countries could probably be sufficient to satisfy the volume requirements of the Comecon countries in the mid–1980s, provided that the economic assistance given in the first place would be such as to enable the oil-producing country in question to develop additional quantities of oil for export to the hard currency areas. But the negotiation of the prices and payment terms will not be at all easy for the Comecon countries.

The emergence of Iran and Saudi Arabia as independently powerful states in the Middle East, neither of which will be particularly beholden to the Soviet Union, must be bringing home to Soviet strategic planners the point that even the most powerful nations in the world, if they are prevented from using the full extent of their power, can find themselves in considerable difficulties if they attempt to manipulate the affairs of individual countries or groups of countries with a similar background, in a part of the world where superpower involvement has no justification in terms of the real interests of the peoples of the country or countries involved. While Soviet involvement in the Middle East in the period following World War II may have been motivated originally mainly by defensive considerations, its continuing involvement up to the present time has become rather less defensive, as it has sought actively to assist the action of 'progressive' forces in the region, with the aim of accelerating the withdrawal of both military and economic remnants of Western imperialism. The point has now been reached, however, where the Soviet Union, in view of other geopolitical interests, considers it expedient to co-operate with the United States in reducing tension in the area, just when the perpetuation of the Arab–Israeli conflict might seem to present an excellent justification for continuing Soviet involvement in the area. Since the nature of Western involvement in the Middle East has changed over the last ten years, and can no longer be logically perceived by the Soviet Union as a genuine threat to its southern flank, and since the 'progressive' forces in the area seem increasingly to be able to manage their own affairs, while resenting external interference from whatever source, the Soviet Union may now be seriously considering how it can reduce its hitherto costly military and, to a lesser extent, economic commitment in a part of the world which has proved itself rather fickle as regards its support for Soviet aspirations. Some commitment will be necessary in an economic and commercial framework, to ensure that future Comecon needs for oil imports will be forthcoming on mutually acceptable terms, but apart from that, continuing Soviet involvement on any greater scale in the area may give rise to more disadvantages than advantages. A statement by Foreign Minister Gromyko on 23 April 1975 on the occasion of the visit of the Syrian Foreign Minister to Moscow, to the effect that the USSR would be prepared to give Israel strict guarantees of the security of its borders once it agreed to settle its dispute with the Arabs at the Geneva Conference, and once it had yielded all Arab land occupied since 1967 and worked out a settlement of the problem of the Palestinian refugees, is perhaps an indication that the Soviet Union is increasingly concerned that some form of controlled peace should return to an area which is quite clearly no longer an outpost of Western imperialism. At the same time, it is only to be expected that the Soviet Union will continue to take advantage of any opportunities which may arise, or which it can create without danger to itself, to further diminish Western political standing in the Middle East and to enhance its own. For example, it is likely to exploit any Arab restlessness about the apparent tardiness of Western oil-consuming nations in persuading Israel to come to an agreement with the Arabs along the lines of the United Nations Resolution 242 of 1967, and it will seek to improve its relations both with Saudi Arabia, Libya and any other country which cannot secure from the Western powers the industrial, military, and political support that it might, at any given point in time, feel that it required. Ideologically, the Soviet Union has probably abandoned attempts to bring about the installation of a truly communist regime in any of the countries, and has shown itself quite prepared to deal with not only 'progressive' regimes but also those which are pursuing a 'non-capitalist' path of development.

The future success of Soviet policy in the Middle East may depend, to a greater extent than in the past, less upon its own inherent soundness and appropriateness than upon the reaction or over-reaction of the West, according to the latter's perception of the degree of the Soviet threat to the West's own interests. The lack of success of Soviet policy in the past must be attributable not only to the inappropriateness of that policy but to the basic incompatibility between Soviet interests and those of the countries of the Middle East, and the West should perhaps be less concerned to oppose or neutralize apparent Soviet advances in the Middle East than to redouble their efforts to discover just how their own interests and those of the Middle East countries ought to coincide, even to the extent of promoting a triangular co-operation between themselves, the Soviet Union and its allies, and the countries of the Middle East, whatever their apparent allegiances at the time. If the Soviet Union is concerned that the Middle East should become an area of peace, and a peace on neither

Soviet nor Western terms but on terms acceptable to the local countries, inevitably endorsed by the Eastern and Western superpowers, there should be ample opportunity for it to demonstrate the peacefulness of its true intentions in the area. The West should have little to lose by allowing such a demonstration, although it would be fully justified in maintaining a high state of vigilance in respect of its own interest in the region in case the Soviet Union still felt inclined further to threaten these interests.

Developing countries

The share of Soviet oil exports going to the developing countries, which would, in most cases, be paying for it not with hard currency as such, but with supplies of 'hard' (mainly agricultural) commodities such as citrus fruit, coffee, cocoa, and wine, is extremely small. More important, at least from a propaganda point of view, has been the technological aid which the Soviet Union has extended to some countries desirous of developing their own national oil companies and hydrocarbon resources, in direct competition with or, following the nationalization of, the international oil majors. Such a policy has been noticeable in India, Sri Lanka, Egypt, Algeria, Cuba and Brazil, Syria and Iraq, and has often been accompanied by claims that the capitalist-based oil companies were deliberately failing to discover resources of oil and gas so that they could maintain a monopoly supply position with the cheap oil which they were extorting from the countries of the Middle East. Soviet oil exploration teams, it was claimed, would be able to make substantial discoveries in areas where the capitalists had failed, and this would enable the local energy industries to escape from the grip of the international monopolies. Unfortunately, Soviet exploration teams sent to the developing countries have not been conspicuously successful, and Soviet equipment and the level of technology which accompanied it, proved itself to be clearly inferior to that used by Western oil companies, so that it is probably fair to say that such forays into overseas exploration and production ventures may even have proved counter-productive in some cases. More successful, perhaps, has been the Soviet attempt to train nationals of developing countries to become petroleum engineers and technologists. However, the demand for skilled petroleum operatives in the Soviet Union itself is so great today that it can ill afford to send such people abroad in large numbers, unless the political gains forthcoming can be judged as considerable. On the other hand, it is not to be expected that the Soviet Union would let pass an opportunity of extending technological aid in the energy fields, or of

204

squeezing out some extra drops of oil for supply to any developing country which it conceived to be suffering at the hands of the imperialists, neo-colonialists, or international capitalist monopoly oil companies.

15   Conclusions

In attempting to answer the question 'Are there pressures arising from the development of the Soviet and East European energy situation which might encourage the Soviet leadership to attempt to influence the international situation in any way?', a body of data has been collected regarding the energy industries of the Comecon countries, and a review has been made of the major energy interrelationships between Comecon and the rest of the world. But little attention has so far been paid to how Soviet policy is formulated or the part which energy considerations might play in the process.

Given the wide range of interests and affiliations encompassed by the members of the Politburo, it is inevitable that the collective decision-making process of the Soviet leadership is essentially one of compromise. Because of this it is extremely difficult for Western observers to identify correctly what is or is not a 'matter of national interest' for the Soviet Union, and thus to predict with any accuracy what the Soviet course of action in any international circumstances is likely to be. The prime objective of the Soviet leadership is clearly survival and the maintenance of the existing power structure in the Soviet Union which concentrates that power firmly in the hands of the leading members of the Communist Party. Any processes which might erode that power structure have to be firmly resisted and eradicated where possible; hence the suppression of 'dissident' elements and manifestations of nationalism in individual republics. The second basic priority for the Soviet leadership is the development of the country's military and economic might, initially to the point where any chance of a successful military attack either by one hostile country or by a combination of enemies is eliminated, and where a significant degree of economic dependence upon a country or group of countries possessing non-communist, or indeed, anti-communist leanings is unnecessary. Beyond that point, any further development of the Soviet military capability would have to be seen by the rest of the world as pointing to the adoption of expansionist and imperialist policies, and would be likely to provoke counter-measures and a stepping up of the arms race. In this connection, the problem for the Soviet leadership is to decide when the country has reached a position of military strength sufficient to rule out the possibility of an armed attack, without giving rise to anxieties on the part of its less powerful neighbours, particularly in Europe, that it is over-armed from a purely defensive point of view and therefore contemplating using its armed strength for offensive purposes. The economic strength of the Soviet Union is not in question, and its dependence on outside assistance is very small. Its economic potential is enormous, and the main problem facing the Soviet leadership is the rate at which that potential can be realized. The maintenance, or, as some Western observers would argue, the continued build-up of a massive military capability clearly imposes considerable strain on the whole Soviet economy and the country's economic resources could undoubtedly be developed at a faster rate if the 'defence' demands were reduced. Whether the Soviet Union does or does not cherish long-term expansionist notions is a highly debatable point and one outside the scope of this study although there is little evidence to suggest that the Communist Party of the Soviet Union has abandoned its enduring objectives of bringing about a state of global communist hegemony with allegiance being paid to Moscow and not to Peking.

A third basic priority for the Soviet leadership must be to satisfy the requirements of the Soviet people for improvements in their standard of living, with the proviso that the expectations of the people shall not exceed those determined by the Communist Party of the Soviet Union as being compatible with the overall objectives sanctified by the Party within the framework of the tenets of Marxism–Leninism. There is no question that the standard of living of the Soviet people is improving. Although Western observers may feel that there is some way to go before the level in the advanced industrialized countries of the West is reached, the Soviet leadership is determined that the Soviet people shall not be encouraged to pursue what are seen as the excesses of the capitalist way of life but should develop instead a superior – at least from a moral point of view – Soviet way of life with different criteria against which to measure excellence. The current Soviet leadership seems to be successfully controlling the rate at which the expectations of the Soviet citizen are developing and being fulfilled, and particularly at a time when the capitalist world is going through a period of considerable economic difficulty, there would seem to be little prospect of things getting out of control. But the degree to which Western economic and cultural influences may affect the domestic Soviet environment is very carefully watched by the Soviet leadership. Whereas Soviet economic circles recognize the advantages which could be derived from many aspects of Western economic management if applied to the Soviet economy, the ideologists are well aware of the threat to the whole Party-dominated power structure if the economy were to become seriously infected with elements of capitalism based on market forces.

The apparent pursuit by the Soviet leadership of a policy of détente with the West, at least in the economic field, might suggest that, rather than cut down on military expenditure so as to be able to invest more in the development of the economy and the well-being of the Soviet people, it has chosen to attempt to secure, in connection with large-scale Western credits, those elements of Western technology etc. which would enable the economic improvements to be made without the necessity for military cutbacks. The Soviet leadership may consider, therefore, that, over a given time span, the balance of advantages (in relation to the priorities described above) to be achieved through economic détente with the West will exceed the disadvantages implicit in the resulting degree of economic dependence which may result, and conversely, that a policy of autarky might stimulate a hardening of Western attitudes and a rejuvenation of the Western will to oppose the expansion of Soviet global influence.

As Soviet military and economic power has increased during the last thirty years, so has Soviet foreign policy been directed towards the extension of Soviet influence in those areas where the Soviet leadership has perceived that the influence of the Western powers, for whatever reason, has been declining. But while opportunities have frequently been taken to probe what might be called Western soft spots, at no time — with the possible exception of the Cuban missile incident — has that policy been pushed to the point where a direct conflict with the West has seemed probable. It is a tenet of Soviet ideology that, historically, the capitalist world is declining and is ultimately doomed to crumble. It is the responsibility of Soviet communism to assist in that process of decline and to ensure that Soviet influence increases in proportion to that decline, but care must be taken to avoid provoking the ailing capitalist creature into taking retaliatory action which, even though it would surely bring about the final death of capitalism, might also result in unacceptable damage to the Soviet communist cause such as would leave it vulnerable to, for example, a Chinese communist offensive.

At some time in the future the Soviet leadership may consider that the Soviet Union has either derived the maximum possible benefit from East—West economic co-operation, or that long-term communist objectives would be better served by a policy of autarky, as the Soviet Union will have long since reached a state of invulnerability in any circumstance short of an ultimate nuclear conflict with the West. When, if ever, this point will be judged to have arrived is impossible to predict given the fact that the deliberations of the Soviet leadership are affected not only by purely domestic influences but also by the way that other global powers act, or react to Soviet actions. However, until such time as the Soviet leadership is convinced of the country's total military and economic superiority over all its ideological opponents, of whatever colour, there is little likelihood that Soviet foreign policy would permit any overt action which would be interpreted by its opponents as a serious enough threat to their survival to justify concerted reprisals.

Since, for the time being, economic détente with the West seems to be the policy which the Soviet leadership is pursuing, there are one or two outstanding features of the Soviet energy situation which may serve as landmarks to those wishing to adjust their models representing future Soviet behaviour on the international stage.

In the first place, at a time when all major industrialized countries of the capitalist world are experiencing an immediate and extremely traumatic energy supply and price situation such as is capable of radically affecting the whole structure of those international relationships based upon the concept of a market economy, the Soviet Union is faced with no such acute problem, and is at least temporarily able to remain comparatively aloof from the global energy crisis if it so wishes. The capitalist consumer countries are not only becoming increasingly embroiled in controversy over whether and how to treat with the producer countries on purely energy matters, but they are also finding that a degree of co-operation between countries producing commodities other than energy has been stimulated by the energy crisis. While neither the producers nor the consumers appear to know what long-term solution to the various problems would really be to everybody's mutual benefit, there does exist a very serious threat to the whole structure of the capitalist system, and one which could undeniably be exploited by the ideological enemies of capitalism. On the other hand, the Soviet Union, at least temporarily, is not only benefiting from the rise in world energy prices, but is also largely self-sufficient in most of the major internationally traded commodities, with the exception of grain.

In the second place, the Soviet Union has substantial and only partially utilized reserves of all the major sources of energy, on a scale sufficient to permit the Soviet leadership to pursue, if forced, a policy of energy independence for Comecon as a whole, even though a shortage of oil in the early 1980s seems almost inevitable. This position of potential overall energy independence in the long term is in marked contrast to that of the industrialized capitalist countries which, at least for the next ten to twenty years (depending upon individual circumstances), have no alternative but to reach accommodation with the energy-exporting countries, primarily those of the Middle East. The question therefore arises as to

209

whether or not the Soviet Union will be inclined to help or hinder the attainment of that accommodation, or whether it will choose to remain aloof.

In the third place, the development of the energy industries of Comecon would undoubtedly benefit from the incorporation of capitalist know-how and technology and the supply of capitalist pipeline and equipment. Not only would the efficiency of production, distribution, and utilization of Comecon energy be improved, but its costs would be lowered and the time required to bring more of it into use would be substantially shortened. The provision of adequate supplies of the right forms of energy is clearly of vital importance to the growth of the economies of the Comecon countries, but their ability to adapt their overall rate of economic growth to, for example, the available energy supply is considerable, and provided that the economic growth rate of Comecon's ideological competitors is sufficiently depressed, the capacity of Comecon to forego, or postpone improvements in their standards of living, hardships such as might be occasioned by a tightened energy supply situation, is also not insignificant. There are on the other hand aspects of the East—West interrelationship, notably the weakness of Soviet agriculture with its implications for Comecon requirements of grain imports, and the problem of the growing power of China in the context of a possible future ideological struggle, which seem to militate against the pursuit of an independent and autarkic Soviet foreign policy. The present Soviet leadership moreover, does appear to have committed itself to a policy of détente with the West both on strategic and economic levels, although on the ideological level the struggle with capitalism is still actively promoted. There comes a point, however, at which ideological and economic objectives vis-à-vis the capitalist world, become incompatible, and this would clearly be the case if the capitalist countries perceived that the Soviet Union was conspiring to exacerbate their raw material and energy supply problems.

A fourth aspect of the Comecon energy situation is that, large though the Soviet energy reserves undoubtedly are, their current state of development is not such as to allow any substantial increase in Soviet energy exports — at least until the early 1980s — even if substantial Western involvement in their development were possible in the immediate future. Further, any hope of a really significant contribution by the Soviet Union to the global energy supply situation will probably not be realized for a decade or two unless a major change is brought about in the whole Soviet framework within which East—West co-operation could be expected to take place. Such a change at present seems to have many unpalatable political and ideological implications for the Soviet leadership and the

210

likelihood of its taking place is fairly remote. The relevance of this is that potential Western partners in any major East—West development scheme for Soviet energy resources should be both able and prepared to take an extremely long-term view, particularly from the point of view of deriving any worthwhile profit from the venture. This is not to suggest that no such ventures should be entered into by Western organizations. On the contrary, if such a major East—West co-operation venture as an energy scheme could be successfully organized it would be good for détente and world peace in general, but until the Soviet Union is prepared to facilitate the implementation of such a project to a far greater extent than has so far been the case, it is difficult to see how it could prove commercially attractive in its own right to any commercial capitalist organization, at a time when the rest of the global energy supply and demand situation is in such a state of uncertainty.

Up to the present energy matters do not seem to have played a vitally important role in the formulation of Soviet foreign policies, except to the extent that as much surplus oil as possible has been produced and exported since the early 1950s, with the twin objectives of earning hard currency and strengthening the degree of economic dependence of the East European Comecon countries (with the exception of Romania) upon the Soviet Union. Opportunities have arisen, for example in the chequered relationship between the international oil companies and certain of the oil-producing countries, notably Iraq and Libya, when the Soviet Union has been able to use its position as an international energy trader to create a short-lived political advantage, and it has been able to use the prospect of its enormous potential energy reserves as an inducement to both the United States and Japan to adopt a more positive approach to economic co-operation and the large-scale advancement of credit than they might otherwise have been inclined to.

For the future, the Soviet Union is committed to supply increasing volumes of oil and gas to the European Comecon countries, and by 1980 will probably still be supplying some 80 per cent of the latters' oil import requirements. The price of Soviet oil to Eastern Europe will have quad-rupled between 1974 and 1980, and this will bring about changes in intra-Comecon trading relationships which will be mainly to the benefit of the Soviet Union, although it should be borne in mind that the Comecon oil importers would be virtually unable to finance adequate alternative supplies from hard currency sources: There will, no doubt, be increases in the export prices of industrial and agricultural goods supplied by Comecon to the Soviet Union, but the terms of trade between the Soviet Union and its allies, with the possible exception of Poland, will be increasingly

211

less favourable to the less powerful members, who will be obliged to provide a higher proportion of their available resources of goods and services to the Soviet Union so as to ensure future supplies of energy. This can possibly result in stagnation, or even a decline, in the growth of trade between the East European countries and the West, unless the West is more favourably disposed to extend further credit facilities to the East European countries, assuming that such credits could be serviced, which could ease the situation somewhat. From a Soviet standpoint, however, the changes in the intra-Comecon energy relationships brought about by the world oil price rises are not without their complications in view of the increasing strain upon the economies, and the resulting diminished possibilities of raising the standard of living of the peoples of Eastern Europe. The regimes in Eastern Europe may be able to go some way towards softening the shock of increased oil and other raw material prices by resorting to subsidies and other fiscal measures, but there is a limit to what can be done, particularly when lasting changes in the terms of trade are involved. The people in the East European countries must already be aware that an increasing proportion of the fruits of their labours will now find their way to the Soviet Union instead of being available for domestic consumption or for export to the West where they could earn hard currency. There will be even greater necessity for the authorities to ensure that such sums of hard currency as are still available as a result of exports to the West are allocated to those sectors of industry in need of advanced capital equipment, rather than to those oriented towards satisfying the demand for consumer goods. All these developments could spell trouble for the regimes since, although they have been at pains to point out the seriousness of the economic difficulties facing the capitalist countries of the developed West, particularly the United States, Italy, and the United Kingdom, the differences in standards of living between Western and Eastern Europe are still clearly visible as, indeed, are those between the countries of Eastern Europe and the Soviet Union, and the new situation will tend to alter the position. The Soviet Union will also have to be careful not to be seen to be profiting too excessively from the new relationship and will have to co-operate with the other Comecon regimes to soften the blow which has inevitably been dealt to the aspirations of the East European people as a whole.

While intra-Comecon relationships will undoubtedly be somewhat strained as a result of global energy developments, it seems unlikely that any really serious uprisings or anti-Soviet manifestations will occur since, unpleasant though some East European people may feel the prospects of closer, enforced integration with the Soviet Union to be, the alternatives may temporarily seem even bleaker, if, in fact, there are any feasible alternatives as far as energy is concerned. Thus, even if Comecon oil imports from the OPEC countries double between now and 1980 from say, 15,000,000 tons to 30,000,000 tons annually, this will still amount to less than one-third of total Comecon requirements, and, as has been pointed out (see p. 121), Comecon will find it hard enough as it is to finance such imports from OPEC in hard currency. A key factor here, as has also been mentioned, is the extent to which imports of oil into Comecon from OPEC can be increased and paid for in soft currency or through goods and services. This in turn will depend upon how successfully the Eastern bloc can develop its overall trading relationships with the OPEC countries, taking into account the latter's increasing wealth and growing nationalism. The Soviet Union and its allies will clearly be assisted in these endeavours by any mistakes in and clumsy handling of international matters of which the capitalist world may be guilty. Yet although the Soviet Union will have to be equally careful not to offend the sensibilities of the OPEC countries by, for example, interfering in their internal affairs or by adopting anything remotely approaching an imperialist posture with regard to the control of events in the Persian Gulf, Suez Canal area, or the Eastern Mediterranean, it has good prospects of further developing and consolidating its legitimate commercial position vis-à-vis the OPEC countries.

The Soviet Union is endowed not only with rich energy resources but also with plentiful supplies of most other types of raw materials, and would be well placed to champion the cause of the producer countries seeking to secure better terms in their relationships with the major importing countries of the industrialized West. It could put itself forward as a true and disinterested friend, should it be called upon to do so, at least to the point of providing political acumen and moral support. It might well feel that its best interests would be served by doing just this and more, unless a significant element of trans-ideological realism can be introduced into the deliberations on the consumer-producer relationships, such as might present the Soviet Union with a more attractive alternative. Perhaps this could be brought about by working with Comecon to develop a global resources relationship, involving grain and other raw materials, energy, finance, and technological know-how, which would require and enable the Soviet Union to play a role calling for considerable statesmanship. This would, of course, increase Soviet prestige in the eyes of the uncommitted nations, but it would also give it broadened global responsibilities.

It seems fair to say that, in comparison with the pressures arising out of the energy crisis affecting the capitalist world, the pressures arising from the Soviet energy situation are relatively gentle, and not such as to 'force' the Soviet Union and its allies to do anything drastic one way or the other on the international energy scene, although some of the smaller Comecon countries have been fairly hard hit. There is no question that Western technological and financial assistance in the development of Comecon energy resources would be highly welcome, although it could be foregone without too much difficulty.

Finally, it would seem that the present Kremlin leadership is, for the moment, agreed that it is economically attractive and politically tolerable for the Soviet Union and its allies to indulge in a fairly limited degree of East—West technological and financial co-operation, including in the energy field. It would also seem that the leadership has decided against any attempt to further trouble the already highly perturbed international scene in any attributable way, which would be almost certain to result in a rapid deterioration of East—West relations, at least until such time as the vexed questions of Sino—Soviet relations and the need for longterm grain imports have been resolved to the Soviet Union's satisfaction. Changes in the Soviet leadership which are expected during the next few years on health or age grounds (if on no others) are not particularly likely to affect the basic factors generating the current policy of détente, and energy matters do not seem destined to play any greater part in the formulation of Soviet foreign policy than they do at present.

Appendices

A Cost calculations for fuels in the USSR

All costs of 'extraction' in the tables below refer to 'total' production costs, i.e. including geological exploration and amortization allowances.

It is extremely difficult to get an accurate picture of Soviet costs or production for fuels since, in addition to the problem of ascertaining which costs the figures refer to, there are also problems of deciding on the boundaries of the area in question. Different sources may cite areas in different ways, for instance in the case of crude oil sources 'Volga, Urals, Po–Volga, Volga–Urals, Volgograd and Saratov' undoubtedly refer to different parts of the same area, but one cannot be sure that to compare the figures cited for different years will give a true indication of a trend in costs, since the designation is different each time. Similar problems occur when trying to interpret the terms: 'Far East, Central Asia, Siberia', etc.

In order to get an idea of how costs change over time, it is necessary, but difficult to establish exactly which year figures refer to. In the following tables an indication is given for costs in 1970, together with, wherever possible, a more recent estimate.

The same difficulties arise when considering transportation costs. These are usually given in two forms – either costs per thousand km through a certain diameter pipeline or by rail, or in terms of delivered cost of fuel from a given source to a certain centre of consumption. Both methods are presented below; in many cases the data are far from recent, but where possible the costs at extraction area are cited in order to isolate the pure transportation factor in the total delivered cost.

It is important to stress that these figures cannot be regarded as exact; they are designed to indicate a range rather than an actual figure. Thus for the most part care should be taken to interpret the figures merely as rough generalizations, e.g. the cost of transporting Ekibastuz coal to Moscow is roughly four times the extraction cost of the coal, and so forth. All costs include an interest charge of 12–15 per cent.

Table A.1

Soviet crude oil extraction costs
(Production costs plus geological and amortization costs)
(Rubles per ton of standard fuel)

	Cost in 1970	Latest cost estimates
Komi ASSR	10·8	6·8†
Orenburg and Perm	10·3−10·5	
Bashkir ASSR	8·9	10·0
Tatar ASSR	6·1	7·1
Volga−Urals		7·3*
Kuibyshev Oblast	8·0	
Stavropol and Krasnodar Krai	11·4−15·2	
Chechen−Ingush ASSR	14·0	
Tyumen Oblast	6·2	9·0−12·0
Irkutsk Oblast	9·1	
Ukraine	9·3	7·9*
Azerbaidzhan	18·7	20·8†
Turkmenia	15·9	
Kazakhstan (Mangyshlak)	6·6 (6·2)	(4·5)
Belorussia		8·5*

*Estimated 1975 costs.
†Cost of production from newly completed wells (1973).
Sources: Melnikov, p. 179; *Vyshka,* 12 Dec. 1973; *Problemi severa,* 1971, pp. 56−62; *Ek.neft.prom.,* Dec. 1972; *Plan.khoz.,* 2 (1975).

Table A.2

Delivered cost of Soviet crude oil to central areas and Urals
(Rubles/ton of standard fuel)

Crude oil sources	Extraction area*	Leningrad	Moscow	Riga	Voronezh	Gorkii	Sverdlovsk	Magnitogorsk	Donets–Dnepr	Minsk	Ukraine
Tyumen	5·2		8·4				14·7		15·7		17·8
Urals	7·2†		8·0								
North Caucasus	8·8										
Komi	9·7										
Mangyshlak			9·5								
Belorussia	10·4										
Ukraine	10·6										
Fuel oil		9·4	8·1	9·2	11·6	7·7	7·3†	11·9	10·8	9·3	

*i.e. delivered cost of crude to local refinery.
†Volga–Urals.
Sources: A Probst, *Vopr. ekon,* 1971, no. 6, p. 56; Melnikov, p. 183; *Ek.neft. prom.,* Oct 1973.

Table A.3

Cost of crude oil transportation
(Rubles/ton of standard fuel)

Method	Distance (km)		
From Tyumen and Tataria			
Pipeline	1,000	2,000	3,000
520 mm	1·9	3·7	5·6
720 mm	1·1	2·1	3·1
1,020 mm	0·7	1·5	2·2
1,220 mm	0·7	1·3	1·9
Rail	3·0	5·5	7·9
From Tyumen			
Pipeline			
1,420 mm	0·4	0·9	1·3
From Mangyshlak			
Pipeline			
1,420 mm	0·6	1·1	1·6

217

Table A.4

Soviet coal extraction costs
(Production costs plus geological and amortization costs)
(Rubles per ton of standard fuel)

	Costs in 1970	Latest costs estimates*
Donets		
Old mines	14·8	11·2
New mines	16·9	
Kuznetsk		
Old mines	8·8	10·6
Reconstructed opencasts	6·8	4·8
New opencasts	7·7	
Pechora		
Old mines	8·2	19·5†
New mines	7·7	
Old opencasts	4·0	
Kansk–Achinsk		
Coal	1·3	2·0–4·0
Lignite		1·7–1·8
Ekibastuz		2·1†
Old mines	2·2	
New mines	2·8	
Far East		3·9–17·3**
Old mines	14·5	
New mines	13·2	
New opencasts	5·8	
Minusinsk		4·7
Karaganda		9·8
Podmoscow (lignite)		14·3
Kizelov		15·3
Lengerov		23·4
Kirghiz		12·9

*Figures refer to expected production costs 1975–1990 and include a 12·5% simple interest charge on investment.
†Type of mine not specified.
**Estimates for a whole range of mines in the area.
Sources: Melnikov, pp. 179–80; Probst, *Vopr.ekon.*, 6(1971); Dienes, *Energy policy*, June 1973; *Plan.khoz.*, 2 (1975).

Table A.5

Delivered costs of Soviet coal to central regions and Urals
(Rubles per ton of standard fuel)

Source of coal,	Extraction area	Leningrad	Moscow	Riga	Minsk	Voronezh	Gorkii	Donets–Dnepr	Sverdlovsk	Magnitogorsk
Donbass	15·3	20·3	18·4		18·6	17·5	18·8	15·6		
Pechora	13·4	17·6	19·7*							
Moscow (Lignite)	20·9		23·1							
Kuzbas (general)										11·6*
Mine	11·0	18·1	21·5*	19·0	18·0	17·7	16·6		14·6	14·6
Opencast	7·7	16·3	17·6*	17·4	16·3	15·9	14·4		12·2	12·5
Ekibastuz	2·8		14·6*			11·7				8·1*
Kansk–Achinsk										
Dried fines	4·2	14·1	12·5	14·8	13·8	13·0	12·5	14·5	10·0	10·3
Semi coke fines	4·3	11·7	10·5	12·2	11·5	10·7	10·5	12·0	8·7	8·9
Semi coke nuts	4·5	11·9	11·0	12·7	11·3	11·6	10·5	12·5	8·8	9·0
Lignite	1·6		24·8*							
Kazakhstan										
Open pit		17·3	20·8*			15·2	15·0			

*Estimated from recent data.

Table A.6

Cost of coal transportation
(Rubles per ton of standard fuel)

Source	Method	Distance			
		1,000 km	2,000 km	3,000 km	4,000 km
Kuznetsk	Rail	3·2	6·2	9·2	
Ekibastuz	Rail	4·2	8·2	12·1	
Kansk–Achinsk	Rail	5·4	10·4	15·4	
Not Stated	*Rail*				
6000 kcal/kg		1·9	4·0	5·6	7·0
3500 kcal/kg		3·2	6·8	9·6	12·0

Sources: Probst, *Vopr.ekon.,* 6 (1971) and Melnikov, p. 183.

Table A.7

Soviet gas extraction costs
(Production costs plus geological and amortization costs)
(Rubles per ton of standard fuel)

	Costs in 1970	Latest estimates
Ukraine	5·5	7·4*
Stavropol	4·5	
Krasnodar	4·8	8·2*
Azerbaidzhan	13·2	
Volgograd	9·7	9·7*
Tyumen	2·2	3·0–5·0
Turkmenia	4·1	
Uzbekistan	5·5	
Tomsk	6·5	
Yakutsk	5·2	
Central Asia	5·4	5·5–6·0
Orenburg		2·9
Komi		6·1
(Vuktyl)		(3·0)*

*1975 cost estimates.
Sources: Melnikov, pp. 178–9; *Problemi severa,* publ. no. 15, 1971; *Plan.khoz.,* 2 (1975); *Vopr.ekon.* 8 (1973).

Table A.8

Delivered costs of Soviet natural gas
to central regions and Urals
(Rubles per ton of standard fuel)

Source	Extraction area	Leningrad	Moscow	Riga	Minsk	Voronezh	Gorkii	Donets–Dnepr	Sverdlovsk	Magnitogorsk
Tyumen	2·2	10·8	13·4–14·3	10·0	11·4	13·3*	10·0			
Central Asia			10·1–10·9			10·4		12·9		
Komi (Vuktyl)			7·1							
Uzbekistan	5·7		9·9			8·2				8·2
Stavropol	4·6								6·2	
Turkmenistan	4·2		8·5			9·6		9·1		

*Saratov
Sources: Melnikov, p. 183; Probst, *Vopr.ekon.,* 6 (1971); *Geologiya neft i gaza,* Oct 1972.

Table A.9

Cost of gas transportation
(Rubles per ton of standard fuel)

Source	Method	Distance (km)		
	Pipeline	1,000	2,000	3,000
Tyumen	1,420 mm	2·2	4·3	6·5
	2,520 mm*	1·4	2·8	4·2
Central Asia	1,420 mm	2·2	4·3	6·5
Not stated	1,020 mm	2·6	5·3	
	1,220 mm	2·3	4·58	
	1,420 mm	2·2–2·3	4·3–4·9	
	2,020 mm*	1·6–1·9	3·2–4·0	
	2,520 mm*	1·4–1·6	2·8–3·3	

*Estimated

B Terminology used in respect of western reserves

1 The 'expected ultimate recovery' is the total volume of hydrocarbons, gas and/or oil, which may be expected to be recoverable commercially from a given area at current or anticipated prices and costs, under existing or anticipated regulatory practices and with known methods and equipment. This total can be expressed as the sum of the 'ultimate recovery from existing fields' and the 'expectation from future discoveries'.

2 The 'ultimate recovery from existing fields' is the sum of the 'cumulative production' from such fields and the 'reserves from existing fields'.

3 The 'reserves from existing fields' is the sum of 'proven reserves', 'discounted (i.e. 50 per cent of) probable reserves' and 'discounted (i.e. 25 per cent of) possible reserves'.

4 'Proven reserves' represent the quantities of crude oil and/or natural gas and natural gas liquids which geological and engineering data demonstrate with reasonable certainty to be recoverable in the future from known oil and/or gas reservoirs. They represent strictly technical judgements, and are not knowingly influenced by attitudes of conservatism or optimism.

5 'Discounted (i.e. 50 per cent of) probable reserves' are those quantities of crude oil and/or natural gas and natural gas liquids, for which there exists a probability of 50 per cent that they will materialize. Such reserves are usually allocated to some conjectural part of a field or reservoir as yet undrilled or incompletely evaluated where, while characteristics of the productive zone and fluid content are reasonably favourable, other uncertain features may have equal chances of being favourable or unfavourable for commercial production.

6 'Discounted (i.e. 25 per cent of) possible reserves' are those quantities of crude oil and/or natural gas and natural gas liquids thought to be potentially producible but where the chance of their being realised is thought to be of the order of 25 per cent. Reserves in this category are usually allocated to possible extensions of existing fields where, although geological data may be favourable, uncertainties as to the characteristics of the productive zone and/or fluid content are such as to preclude a probability greater than 25 per cent.

It should be noted that the terms 'gas-in-place' and 'oil-in-place' represent estimates of the total hydrocarbons present which, in conjunction with various engineering and economic criteria, provide the basis for the 'reserve' estimates. They should never be confused with 'reserves'; this word implies that physical recovery is possible.

The following represents Soviet reserve classifications.

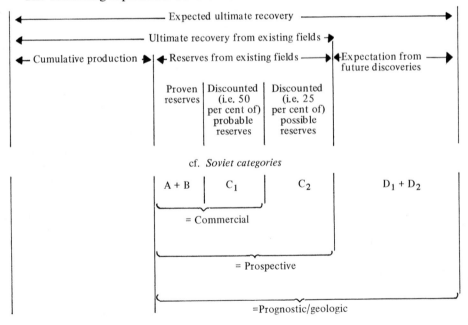

C Management reforms in the Soviet energy industries 1971—75

In an attempt to streamline the apparatus of the energy industries, the 1971—75 five-year plan saw the introduction of a new system of management. The reform involved a reduction in the number of decision-making levels of the industries from five or six to two or three. The three-tier system, ministry—operational division—enterprise. and the two-tier system, whereby only the operational divisions and the ministry are involved in decision-making, have been designed to combat managerial inefficiency and inflexibility which in the past has hampered the performance of the energy industries. The two, three, and sometimes four-tier systems coexist both between different geographical *regions* in an industry and between different *functions* in an industry. Hence in the coal industry most regional organizations operate on the three-tier system, but the Ukraine still operates a four-tier system, although long-term plans envisage a general transfer to the two-tier system. In the gas industry, the gas transport operational division reports directly to the ministry whereas other branches work on the three-tier system.

The reforms essentially comprised a recentralization of the major functions of each industry: production, transport, storage, distribution, construction, repairs, etc. whereby each function is now dealt with by an operational division, as opposed to the old system — under which each enterprise organized its own facilities on a small scale.

An important exception in this reorganization is 'Glavtyumenneftigaz', Chief Administration for Oil and Gas in Western Siberia, where, because of the necessity to co-ordinate decisions throughout a large number of enterprises in this enormous area, it has been considered expedient that this administration should continue in its present form.

The reforms seem to have been introduced at different times for different industries and also to have been phased in over a period within an industry. According to Oil Minister Shashin, the reform was first introduced at the Kuibyshev Oil Association in 1969 as a three-tier system, and it proved so successful in terms of labour productivity that it was possible to transfer more than 18,000 workers to other development administrations. In an early report it was indicated that the bulk of the oil industry would start shifting to the new system at the end of 1970. Yet in October 1974 the minister was still talking of 1973—75 as the changeover period for the industry. Worthy of note are the new oil industry administrations, 'Neftigazodobivayushchie Upravlenie' (NGDU — Oil and Gas Extraction Administrations) and the 'Upravlenie Burvikh Rabot' (UBR — Administrations for Drilling Operations).

In the gas industry the gestation period for the reforms was planned as 1973–75, whereas in the coal industry, the transition period was 1969–72, when 90 trusts and 2 concerns were abolished and the industry moved from a five- and four-tier system to a four and three-tier system, an attempt to further streamline the industry began in early 1975.

According to preliminary estimates these reforms should result in a yearly saving of 100–110m rubles in the gas industry and 120–130m rubles in the coal industry.

A good example of the reforms is provided by the newly reorganized gas industry, a description of which is set out below.

The mangement structure of the gas industry

The following is a condensed version of two articles which appeared in *Gazovaya promyshlennost* in January and October 1974, covering the management structure of the Soviet gas industry which was introduced at the end of 1974.

The main departments of the ministry are linked by operational divisions reflecting the territorial divisions of the country. There are thirty-two such divisions covering regional production, transport, and supply. These units, with the headquarters of each administration given in brackets (unless this is evident by the title) are as follows:

Administrations for gas transport and supply (GTSA). Armenia (Erevan), Azerbaidzhan (Baku), Bashkir (Ufa), Central Asia (Urgench), Georgia (Tbilisi), Gorkii, Kharkov, Kiev, Kuibyshev, Leningrad, Moscow, North Caucasus (Groznyy), Saratov, Tashkent, Tatar (Kazan), Trans-Caspian (Shevchenko), Tyumen (Komsomolsk), Ukhta, Ural (Sverdlovsk), Volgograd, Western (Minsk), Nadym GPA, Norlisk GPA, Yakutsk, Transport and Supply Administration for Liquefied Gas (Moscow).

Gasification* administrations (GA). Kirghiz (Frunze), Mari (Yoshkar-Ola), Siberia (Omsk), Tadzhik (Dushanbe), Tselinograd, Turkmen (Ashkhabad), Tyumen.

Based on the thirty-one regional administrations are the following Federal Industrial Boards for Gas Production (FIBGP): Komi (Ukhta), Kras–nodar, Orenburg, Stravopol, Turkmenia (Ashkhabad), Tyumen, Ukraine (Kiev), Uzbekistan (Bukhara). In addition there are Federal Industrial Boards for underground gas storage (Shchelkova) Soyuzpodzemgaz; for gasification and supply of liquefied gas to the national economy (Moscow)

*Denotes gas utilized in the production of electricity.

Soyuzgazificatsiya; for the manufacture of gas devices (Moscow) Soyuz-gazmashapparat; and for spare part manufacture and overhauling of technological equipment (Moscow) Soyuzgazmashremont.

Each of the thirty-two regional administrations comprise its own enterprises dealing with: drilling, gas production, transport, gas processing plants, engineering and repair organizations, scientific research and planning institutes, supporting and servicing sub-units.

In the *gas producing* branch of the industry, the three-tier system is advantageous owing to the multiple activities within the regions: production, local transport, development and exploratory drilling, etc. In addition to this, the large number of enterprises within a division (in some cases numbering as many as forty-five), and the geographical dispersion of these units (scattered over a radius of 300 km on average) make the centralizing and co-ordinating function of the operational units highly desirable.

In the interregional *gas-transport,* system, the new operational divisions dealing with gas transport and supply report direct to the ministry. Their duties also include servicing pipeline facilities, compressor stations, and communications systems.

The following changes have taken place with respect to other functions of the gas industry:

Gas storage

There is a new division — 'Soyuzpodzemgaz' (Union underground gas storage board) — whose responsibilities include: the search for structures, and also the design, construction, stocking, and servicing of underground storage caverns. It is intended to raise this division to the rank of a Federal Industrial Board.

Machine construction

A unit with the rank of a Federal Industrial Board — 'Soyuzmashapparatura' (Union Gas Industry board for the manufacture of engineering equipment) — has been created.

Gas distribution

Divisions with a certain degree of operational independence based on the old system of 'trusts' are responsible for the construction and repair of the distribution network as well as for underground coal gasification stations. These divisions are linked to the ministry by means of the Federal

Industrial Board – 'Soyuzgazificatsiya' (Federal Board of Gas Distribution) – thus creating a three-tier system of management in this sector.

Repairs and overhauling:

In order to secure the centralization of servicing and repair work, the division 'Soyuzgazmashremont' (Union Board of the Gas Industry for servicing of machinery) has been given the status of Federal Industrial Board. A reduction in the time spent on repairs and an improvement in the reliability of the gas supply should be the two major benefits of this centralization. (This is one area in which the reforms should have a great impact throughout the energy industries.)

A scientific and technical division, 'Soyuzgazavtomatika' (for studies on automation), has been created in order to supervise the introduction of automated management systems (ASU) into the industry. Other new divisions include: the section for standardization of materials, the section for standardization of production quality, and the Federal Board for Foreign Gas (Soyuzzarubezhgaz).

A number of scientific and technical research institutes are being set up within the operational divisions of the gas industry (i.e. Gazkhimya) in order to expedite scientific and technical advances, particularly in the fields of drilling, production, and transport.

D   Manpower and equipment in the Soviet energy industries

Information on manpower and equipment in the energy industries (especially the gas industry) is scanty and incomplete, and is included here in order to give a rough idea of the size of operations in the Soviet Union.

An official source states that in 1973 the labour force engaged in the production of electric and thermal power numbered 659,000 and that dealing with the fuel industry and fuel production from coal, oil, and shale numbered 1,489,000. Thus the total numbers in fuel and power industries amount to 2,148,000, which would appear to be some 6·53 per cent of the total industrial labour force. (This compares with 5·5 per cent in Bulgaria, 9·2 per cent in Hungary, 8·5 per cent in the GDR, 10·6 per cent in Poland, 5·5 per cent in Romania, and 7·6 per cent in Czechoslovakia.) However, these figures would seem to understate the position considerably since data gathered from energy publications suggest that the coal industry alone employs 1·8m workers and that the oil industry accounts for a further three-quarters of a million. (It may be that the former figures taken from the official Comecon yearbook refer only to 'productive' labour.)

The oil industry (i.e. not including refining, petrochemicals, or construction of oil enterprises, nor those parts of the oil industry in the Ministry of Geology, but including research staff of institutes of the oil industry) accounts for about 750,000 workers, of which 77·4 per cent work in oil extraction, 17·3 per cent are engineering and technical personnel, and 4·1 per cent are white-collar workers (the comparable figures for the gas industry are 75·4 per cent, 18·0 per cent, and 3·9 per cent respectively.) The breakdown of workers in the oil industry by function is as follows:

		%
1	Industry (i.e. extraction and fuel)	
	(a) Personnel engaged in industrial production	19·1
	(b) Other organisations	64·0
	including drilling	20·6
2	Geo-exploratory work	4·6
3	Pipelines and storage of oil	7·0
4	Capital construction	5·3

Glavtyumenneftyagas – the chief administration of oil and gas in western Siberia – employs 51,000 workers, engineers, technicians, and white-collar workers.

In 1973 the coal industry employed 1·2m workers in 'productive' jobs and 640,000 in 'non-productive' work; of the former figure, 787,000 workers are engaged in the extraction of hard coal, of which 585,000 are underground workers. The 'non-productive' workers included 87 Doctors of Sciences, 1,317 Candidates of Sciences, and 148,000 graduate technicians.

Machinery and equipment in the Soviet oil industry

The figures taken from a number of different sources suggest that an inventory of machinery and equipment in the Soviet oil industry would be approximately as follows:

Drilling rigs	3,304	Motor vehicles	
Drilling pumps	10,800	including 16,000	
Diesel engines	19,400	tractors	74,000
Electric engines	219,700	Ships	
Metal cutting stands	17,500	including 400 ocean-going	
Presses and hammers	2,500	vessels	780

The value of total fixed assets of the industry in 1972 was stated as 12,542·7m rubles including the following fixed productive assets:

Installations	6,889	Buildings	372
Transmission facilities	1,517	Transportation	81
Machinery and equipment	1,171	Instruments	18

Total = 10,048m rubles

A similar inventory for the coal industry in 1972 would feature:

Cutter loaders	4,107	Chain conveyors	36,119
Cutters	359	Belt conveyors	12,614
Tunnelling machines	1,095	Trolley mine locomotives	13,770
Loading machines	4,513	Excavators	1,356

E The Adria (Yugoslav oil) pipeline

On 12 February 1974, an agreement was signed between Hungary, Yugoslavia, and Czechoslovakia regarding the construction of the Adria pipeline. A contract was signed in Zagreb on 31 July 1975 by the director-general of the specially created Yugoslav Oil Pipeline Company and the director of the Kuwait Foreign Trade Contracting and Investment Company under the terms of which Kuwait is to participate in the construction with a $125m credit. A contract on the delivery of 70,000 tons of pipe was concluded earlier with the firm 'Kuwait Metal Pipes Industry'. Other credit agreements signed include the following: Libya $65–70m; the World Bank $225m; Hungarian National Bank and a Yugoslav oil enterprise of Rijeka have signed an agreement guaranteeing a twelve-year credit of $300m. (The Moscow International Investment Bank is also expected to contribute.) There are as yet no details of financial arrangements with the Yugoslav commercial banks and arrangements with Czechoslovakia which are said to be forthcoming.

The East European agencies involved in the construction are: MINERALIMPEX and the National Petroleum and Gas Industrial Trust of Hungary, Chemapol of Czechoslovakia, and the Yugoslav firms INA of Zagreb, Energoinvest of Sarajevo, and Naftagas of Novi Sad.

According to preliminary estimates, the total cost of the project, including the terminal at Omisalj, should have been on the order of $350m, but latest calculations have increased the figure to $500m. So far, funds amounting to 450m dinars have been agreed by INA, Energoinvest, and Naftagas, towards the cost of the Yugoslav stretch.

The above agreement is to be followed by Hungarian–Yugoslav and

Czechoslovak treaties 'to regulate the State warranties relating to the construction and operation of the pipeline and to the forwarding of the oil'. Each section will be the property of the country where it is laid.

The main line is to start from the Bay of Omisalj (Krk island, near Rijeka) and to run to the Sisak refineries (near Zagreb). From Sisak a branch will go via Gola on the Drava river to Hungary's refining centre of Szazhalombatta near Budapest, where it will link up with the existing Druzhba no. 1 line which will deliver the oil to Bratislava (Czechoslovakia). The other branch will run from Sisak eastwards to feed the refineries of Bosanski Brod, Novi Sad, and Pancevo in northern and north-eastern Yugoslavia.

The total length of the line (including the existing section Szazhalombatta–Bratislava) will be 735 km. The main sections are: Rijeka–Sisak–Gola (Yugoslav section) 300 km; Gola–Szazhalombatta (Hungarian section), 210 km; Szazhalombatta–Bratislava (already existing) 225 km. The Hungarian section, which will be about 340 km, crosses the border at Csurgo.

The main line from the Adriatic to Sisak will have a diameter of 1,000mm and an initial capacity of 22m tons/year in 1978, rising to 34m tons/year in the early 1980s. The diameter of the Hungarian section will be 600mm and its capacity 10m tons/year, one-half of which is scheduled for Czechoslovakia and one half for Hungary. Between Krk island and the mainland, a bridge for the line will be built. Moreover, terminal facilities to accommodate 200,000 ton tankers are foreseen. The 210 km section in Hungary will be constructed jointly by Hungary and Czechoslovakia. There is also a report that these two countries 'have undertaken to participate . . . to the extent of $25m each'. This probably means their contribution to the building of the Yugoslav section and facilities.

The first stage of the line, comprising the Yugoslav sections to Pancevo and to the Hungarian border, and the Hungarian section to Szazhalombatta, should be operational within 36 months from the date of signature, i.e. by early 1977. Full capacity should be attained by 1980–82.

F   The Orenburg natural gas pipeline

In June 1974, at the 28th Comecon congress in Sofia, an agreement was signed between seven of the member-countries: USSR, Bulgaria, Czechoslovakia, Hungary, Poland, Romania, and the GDR, providing for the building of a new gas pipeline to run from the Orenburg natural gas deposits in the Urals to Uzgorod on the Soviet–Czech border (from here it is believed that the line will split into two, one branch will enter Czechoslovakia and link with the 2nd and 3rd strings of the Transit pipeline, while the other will run south to Romania and Bulgaria). The pipeline represents an important step towards further Comecon integration in fuels and energy. Each of the East European countries, except Romania, will build a section of the 2,750 km pipeline, of pipe 1,420mm in diameter, with 22 pumping stations of 25,000 kw units maintaining a pressure of 75 atmospheres. In return for building the sections (each country is responsible for providing and transporting both labour and infrastructure needed to construct its own section with the exception of Hungary) the USSR will provide each country with 2·8 billion cu. metres of gas per year for a period of 20 years.

The project has altered somewhat since its inception with regard to responsibilities for building of the sections, but so far as it is possible to determine the line will be built in the following way:

1st section. Orenburg to Aleksandrov Gay — 58 km and 5 compressor stations. This section was originally to be built by Poland, but it is now believed that the Soviet Union will now build it, with Hungary providing an increased amount of equipment. The official reason given for this change in the organization of the Hungarian contribution was that the training of personnel for specialized work in such arduous conditions would have taken so long (given that the largest diameter pipe used in Hungary is only 800mm) that it was more expedient for the USSR to take over the building and work for Hungary to provide more of the equipment.

2nd section. Alexandrov Gay to Sakhranovka — 562 km and 5 compressor stations. This was originally scheduled to be built by Czechoslovakia and in July 1975 it was announced that work had commenced north of Volgograd. However in August it was reported that Czechoslovakia would now only build the compressor stations, housing facilities, stores and approach roads on this section since the pipelaying work had been taken over by the Soviet Union. Czechoslovakia will therefore send a substantially reduced labour force (about 2,300) to the Urals, and in return will devote more resources to the completion of the 2nd and 3rd strings of the Transit pipeline in Czech territory, completion of which is critical if deliveries of Soviet gas to Western Europe are to be on schedule.

3rd Section. Sakhranovka to Kremenchug — 569 km and 4 compressor stations. This was the original Hungarian section now scheduled to be built by Poland. One of the Polish enterprises involved in building the

230

Polish section is Transbud from Nowa Huta, whose team will include about 1,200 workers with 600 vehicles and a large quantity of equipment. One of the most difficult problems is the transportation of pipe from the way sidings to the site, a distance on average of 40 km (since 10 metres of pipe weigh about 10 tons and about 600 km have to be laid, this will pose a considerable problem). It was reported that Polish workers left for the site on 25 June 1975.

4th section. Kremenchug to Bar — 518 km and 5 compressor stations. This is the East German section, for which the contract was signed on 24 July 1975. About 600 workers have now left the GDR to begin preparatory work on the line.

5th section. Bar to Uzhgorod — 515 km and 3 compressor stations. This was originally planned to be built solely by Bulgaria; but it now will be built jointly by that country and Hungary. The exact responsibilities of the two countries are not clear, but the Hungarians will be building all the compressor stations (at Khust, Bogorodchany, and Gusyatin) and the first group of Hungarian workers have arrived at Ivan—Frankovsk which is to be the centre of the Hungarian building effort. In 1976, 3,000 Hungarian experts are expected to work in the area on the compressor stations and other communal projects. As regards the actual building of the line, the contractors began work this summer and will complete in the third quarter of 1978. Details of the Bulgarian effort have not yet been disclosed, but it was announced on 30 May 1975 that workers from that country had set off for the USSR to work on the line.

The preparatory work already completed will enable 250 km of the line to be built this year; in 1976 it is planned to build a further 1,000 km. The line is due for completion in 1978 and will initially (1980) have a throughput of 15·5 billion cu. metres; eventual annual throughput will be 28 billion cu. metres. About 300 excavators, 500 pipelaying machines, more than 30 automatic pipewelding installations, and several thousand bulldozers and trucks will be in operation simultaneously along the route and the participating members will need to supply 110m tons of freight to the route of the pipeline.

The Romanian contribution to the pipeline (which was always planned to be in terms of equipment) is not yet clear, but it has been announced that the USSR and Romania will jointly construct the gas-processing plant at the wellhead. It is likely however that Romania will be required to perform additional tasks, possibly in the shape of manpower to help on the building of other sections, in order to secure its share of the gas.

G Soviet trade with Middle East, OPEC and industrialized Western countries

Table G.1

Soviet trade with non-OPEC Middle East states 1970, 1973, and 1974

(million rubles)

	Turnover			Imports			Exports			Net deficit (surplus)		
	1970	1973	1974	1970	1973	1974	1970	1973	1974	1970	1973	1974
Cyprus	9·3	12·7	19·8	5·2	5·1	9·0	4·1	7·6	10·8	1·1	(2·5)	(1·8)
Egypt	606·4	541·1	728·1	279·5	263·9	426·8	326·9	277·2	301·3	(47·4)	(13·3)	125·5
Jordan	6·4	2·5	2·4	0	0	0	6·4	2·5	2·4	(6·4)	(2·5)	(2·4)
Lebanon	17·5	19·1	32·9	3·8	7·6	7·4	13·7	11·5	25·5	(9·9)	(3·9)	(18·1)
Morocco	50·1	54·4	87·1	17·6	26·1	33·0	32·5	28·3	54·1	(14·9)	(2·2)	(21·1)
Sudan	77·4	2·5	6·2	44·9	0	2·4	32·5	2·5	3·8	12·4	(2·5)	(1·4)
Syria	59·1	118·8	172·4	17·3	46·7	102·3	41·8	72·1	0·1	(24·5)	(25·4)	32·2
Tunisia	5·7		17·1	3·1	5·4	9·0	2·6	5·8	8·1	0·5	(0·4)	0·9
Turkey	83·3	132·8	129·1	27·1	38·9	56·8	56·2	93·9	72·3	(29·1)	(55·0)	(15·5)
Yemen—Aden	4·5	11·6	15·2	0·2	0·1	0·1	4·3	11·5	15·1	(4·1)	(11·4)	(15·0)
Yemen—Sanaa	11·0	3·6	8·6	1·0	0·2	0·1	10·0	3·4	8·5	(9·0)	(3·2)	(8·4)
Total	930·7	910·3	1,218·9	399·7	394·0	646·9	531·0	516·3	572·0	(131·3)	(122·3)	74·9
Grand total (plus OPEC countries)	1,433·5	1,740·3	2,400·3	568·1	841·1	1,303·7	865·4	899·2	1,096·6	(297·3)	(58·1)	107·1

Table G.2

Soviet trade with the OPEC members, 1970, 1973, and 1974
(million rubles)

	Turnover			Imports			Exports			Net deficit (surplus)		
	1970	1973	1974	1970	1973	1974	1970	1973	1974	1970	1973	1974
Algeria	118·3	116·8	171·7	55·8	52·1	61·4	62·5	64·7	110·3	(6·7)	(12·6)	(48·9)
Ecuador	0·8	0·9	4·9	0·7	0·7	4·4	0·1	0·2	0·5	0·6	0·5	3·9
Gabon	0	0	0	0	0	0	0	0	0	0	0	0
Indonesia	24·5	6·9	27·9	25·0	4·2	19·9	4·5	2·7	8·0	21·5	1·5	11·9
Iran	231·2	276·9	495·7	62·2	139·6	229·9	169·0	137·3	265·8	(106·8)	2·3	(35·9)
Iraq	63·5	332·1	453·1	4·1	190·6	270·8	59·4	141·5	182·3	(55·3)	49·1	88·5
Kuwait	10·0	7·9	4·7	0·3	0	0	9·7	7·9	4·7	(9·4)	(7·9)	(4·7)
Libya	12·9	44·5	28·5	0	30·4	0	12·9	14·1	28·5	(12·9)	16·3	(28·5)
Nigeria	31·2	39·9	91·9	20·3	28·9	70·4	10·9	11·0	21·5	9·4	17·9	48·9
Qatar	0	0	0	0	0	0	0	0	0	0	0	0
Saudi Arabia	5·4	2·9	2·8	0	0	0	5·4	2·9	2·8	(5·4)	(2·9)	(2·8)
United Arab Emirates	0	0	0	0	0	0	0	0	0	0	0	0
Venezuela	0	1·2	0·2	0	0·6	0	0	0·6	0·2	0	–	(0·2)
Total	502·8	830·0	1,281·4	168·4	447·1	656·8	334·4	582·9	624·6	(166·0)	64·2	32·2

Table G.3

Soviet trade with the industrially developed capitalist countries, 1970, 1973, and 1974
(million rubles)

	Turnover			Imports			Exports			Net deficit (surplus)		
	1970	1973	1974	1970	1973	1974	1970	1973	1974	1970	1973	1974
Australia	61·8	198·0	183·9	60·3	194·8	178·5	1·5	3·2	5·4	58·8	191·6	173·1
Austria	154·9	189·3	339·6	88·2	89·7	173·6	66·7	99·6	166·0	21·5	(9·9)	7·6
Belgium	149·0	354·3	603·4	75·0	160·0	305·5	74·0	194·3	297·9	1·0	(34·3)	7·6
Canada	125·3	265·0	111·0	117·8	244·1	82·1	7·5	20·9	28·9	110·3	223·2	53·2
Finland	530·7	777·4	1,539·7	272·4	362·3	602·1	258·3	415·1	937·6	14·1	(52·8)	(335·5)
France	412·8	721·6	941·0	286·8	449·4	543·1	126·0	272·2	397·9	160·8	177·2	145·2
Italy	471·9	613·6	1,137·2	281·4	304·1	539·6	190·5	309·5	597·6	90·9	(5·4)	(58·0)
Japan	652·3	994·4	1,683·2	310·9	372·4	777·5	341·4	622·0	905·7	(30·5)	(249·6)	(128·2)
Netherlands	222·9	356·2	570·7	71·7	95·6	176·4	151·2	260·6	394·3	(79·5)	(165·0)	(217·9)
New Zealand	19·6	38·7	61·8	18·9	37·3	59·4	0·7	1·4	2·4	18·2	35·9	57·0
Sweden	234·9	232·3	435·5	129·5	101·6	149·7	105·4	130·7	285·8	24·1	(29·1)	(136·1)
Switzerland	95·1	166·7	244·6	70·5	99·8	165·1	24·6	67·9	79·5	45·9	31·9	85·6
UK	641·4	715·2	890·1	223·2	174·6	199·6	418·2	540·6	690·5	(195·0)	(366·0)	(490·9)
USA	160·9	1,161·0	742·2	103·2	1,023·2	564·9	57·8	137·8	177·3	45·3	885·4	387·6
West Germany	544·0	1,210·2	2,208·7	320·6	756·4	1,374·2	223·4	453·8	834·5	97·2	302·6	539·7
Others	216·7	345·0	711·2	109·8	123·7	255·2	106·9	220·3	456·0	2·9	(96·6)	(200·8)
Total	4,694·2	8,338·9	12,403·8	2,540·1	4,589·0	6,146·5	2,154·1	3,749·9	6,257·3	386·0	839·1	(110·8)

Select bibliography

Books

Campbell, R.W., *The economics of Soviet oil and gas,* Baltimore, 1968.

Ebel, R.E., *Communist trade in oil and gas,* New York, 1970.

Economist Intelligence Unit, *Soviet oil to 1980,* QER Special no. 14, 1973.

Elliot, I.F., *The Soviet energy balance,* New York, 1974.

Hardt, J.P. and Holiday, G.D. (eds), *Reorientation and commercial relations of the economies of Eastern Europe,* submitted to the Joint Economic Committee of the US Congress, 16 August 1974.

Hardt, J.P. and Holiday, G.D. (eds), *Western investment in communist economies,* prepared for subcommittee on Multinational Corporations of the Committee on Foreign Relations US Senate, 5 August 1974.

Hardt, J.P. and Holiday, G.D. (eds), *US–Soviet commercial relations: The interplay of economics, technology transfer and diplomacy,* prepared for the Subcommittee on National security policy and Scientific developments of the Committee on Foreign Affairs, US House of Representatives. 10 June 1973.

Melnikov, N.V., *Mineralnoe toplivo.* Moscow, 1971.

NATO, Directorate of Economic Affairs, *The exploitation of Siberia's natural resources,* 1974.

USSR, Gosplan, *Gosudarstvennie pyatiletnii plan razvitiva narodnogo Khozyaistva SSR na 1971–75 gody,* Moscow, 1972.

Yearbooks

Soviet
Narodnogo khozyaistvo SSSR

Vneshnaya torgovlya SSSR

East European
Statistical Yearbooks of Bulgaria, Czechoslovakia, the GDR, Hungary, Poland, Romania, and Comecon.

UN

Annual Bulletins of General Energy, Coal, Electrical Energy, and Gas Statistics for Europe.

Economic Survey of Europe.

Periodicals

Among the oil journals consulted, the following articles were particularly useful:

Baibakov, N., 'Razvitiye neftyanoy promyshlennosti strani', *Neftyanik,* 5 (1974).

Shashin, V., 'O generalnoe skeme upravleniye neftanoy promyshlennosti', *Neft. khoz.,* 10 (1974)

Three articles in *Ekonomika neftyanoy promyshlennosti:*

Suchkova, L. and others, 'Effektivnost razvitiya promyshlennosti evropey-skikh rayonov strani v tekyshchem pyatiletiye', October 1973.

Nesterova, N. and others, 'Otraslevaya otsenka ekonomicheskoy effektiv-nosti kapitalnikh vlozhenii v neftedobivayushchuyu promyshlennost' po rayonam', June 1972.

Kuznetsova, O., 'Analiz dinamiki fondootdachi v neftedobivayushchey promyshlennosti', June 1972.

In addition this study has relied heavily on *The Review of Sino—Soviet Oil* published by Petroconsultants S.A. in Geneva.

Among the principal Soviet periodicals, *Voprosy ekonomiki* and *Planovoe khozyaistvo* were of most value, and especially the following articles:

Voprosy ekonomiki

Alexeyev, A. and Savenko, Yu. 'Ekonomicheskaya integratsiya v razvitiye toplivno-energeticheskikh otraslei stran-chlenov SEV', 12 (1971).

Brenner, M., 'Razvitiye toplivnoi industrii', 5 (1975).

Khachaturov, T., 'Prirodnye resursi i planirovani ye narodnogo khozyaistvo', 8 (1973).

Pervukhin, M., 'Sovetskaya energetika v devyatom pyatiletiye', 6 (1971).

Probst, A., 'Puti razvitiya toplivnogo khozyaistvo SSSR', 6 (1971).

Savenko, Yu. 'Problemi toplivno-energeticheskogo balansa v stranakh-chlenov SEV', 7 (1969).

Yakovets, Yu, 'Dvizheniye tsen mineralnogo sirya', 6 (1975).

236

Planovoe khozyaistvo

Brigdorchik, A. and others, 'Metodi optimizatsii dolgosrochnogo razvitiya toplivno-energeticheskogo kompleksa SSSR', 7 (1974).

Melnikov, N. and Shelest V., 'Toplivno-energeticheskii kompleks SSSR', 2 (1975).

Pervukhin, M., 'Energeticheskiye resursi i ikh ratsionalnoe ispolzovaniye', 7 (1974).

Shashin, V. 'Puti povisheniya effektivnosti neftyanoi promyshlennosti', 4 (1973).

Of the many English language sources consulted, the following articles were found to be of considerable value:

Chesshire, J and Huggett, C., 'Primary energy in the Soviet Union', *Energy Policy,* September 1975.

Dienes, L., 'Investment priorities in Soviet regions', *Annals of the Association of US Geographers,* September 1972.

Dienes, L., 'Geographical problems of allocation in the Soviet fuel supply', *Energy Policy,* June 1973.

Ebel, R.E., 'Soviet Arctic gas promise awaits technology', *Petroleum Engineering,* June 1974.

Hardt, J.P., 'West Siberia, the quest for energy', *Problems of Communism,* May/June 1973.

Kaser, M., 'Technology and oil in Comecon's external relations', *Journal of Common Market Studies,* 13 (1975).

Ogawa, K., 'Soviet economy and energy supply and demand', *Chemical Economy and Engineering Review,* November 1973.

Sanders, A. and Murarka, D., 'Tapping Siberia's riches', *Far Eastern Economic Review,* 31 January 1975.

Index

The author

After graduating from Cambridge, Jeremy Russell joined Shell on the International Chemical side in 1959 and worked in the Agricultural Division. In 1962 he moved to the East European division of Shell International Petroleum Co. Ltd to understudy the Area Manager for Czechoslovakia, Yugoslavia and Poland. He became involved with USSR relations in 1965 and was appointed Area Manager for the USSR in 1969.

Other SAXON HOUSE Studies